Thank You, John

A MEMOIR

Michelle Gurule

THE UNNAMED PRESS
LOS ANGELES, CA

AN UNNAMED PRESS BOOK

Copyright © 2025 by Michelle Gurule

Published in North America by the Unnamed Press.

www.unnamedpress.com

Unnamed Press, and the colophon, are registered trademarks of Unnamed Media LLC.

Hardcover ISBN: 978-1-961884-68-7
EBook ISBN: 978-1-961884-69-4
LCCN: 2025940200

Cover Photograph by Joe St.Pierre, Courtesy of Stocksy
Cover Design and Typeset by Jaya Nicely

Manufactured in the United States of America by Sheridan

Distributed by Publishers Group West

First Edition

To my family. Ever loving and ever unruly.

Author's Note

This is a work of nonfiction based on my personal memories and experiences. In order to protect the privacy and dignity of individuals, names and identifying details have been changed. Any resemblance to real people beyond those explicitly acknowledged is purely coincidental. While every effort has been made to honor the emotional truth of events, this memoir reflects my perspective and recollections.

john (*plural* **johns**)

    1.   (*slang*, *US*) A sex worker's client.

Thank You, John

Part One

The Climb

1

Pretty in the Face

I met **John** during my Wednesday night shift at Penthouse. He appeared with the dinner crowd. Mostly middle-aged men who stopped by for the $13.99 rib-eye deal. This group was despised for its bad manners: a general lack of tipping, shooing women off, and complaining that we strippers were like vultures, only after their money. Forgetting, I suppose, that this was our job.

I had been topless on stage when I caught John's eye. Contrary to how that might sound, it was not me at my prime. "The trick," a customer once told me, referencing my natural asymmetry, "is to never face the crowd head-on." It was, I could later admit, sound advice.

John lifted his hand and wiggled his fingers. Friendly, but awkward. I was prepared to give the cold shoulder I reserved for dinner patrons, except John wasn't eating. *Come on over*, I mouthed and gestured toward my stage. He stayed put as my final song began. An electro version of Ellie Goulding's "Anything Could Happen." I stripped down to my underwear, then imitated tucking dollars into my waistband in tandem with the bass. When I caught my reflection in the mirrors, it looked like I was scratching. Not good.

I wasn't much of what the industry called a "stage-money girl." Dancers who'd mastered the art of pussy popping could rake in the Washingtons on weekends, but I was born with my mom's white rhythm gene rather than my dad's suaver Chicano one, so I stuck to weekday evenings when I'd peel a dollar or two from the floor before homing in on my niche market—lonesome men dropping in after work. I prayed I could scramble together $350: about half of what a seasoned dancer could pull on the same shift.

In a last-ditch effort for a buck, I plastered one foot to the ground, hooked my other calf around the pole and spun. Ellie's voice crooned over the sound system. John bobbed his head along. It was, yet again, a profitless set.

I played it cavalier as I collected myself on stage, but it stung to dress without a single dollar to fold away. I was nude aside from a microscopic G-string, and the lack of financial appreciation made it feel as though every customer thought, *Not for me.* To rub salt in the wound, I spotted the shift manager by the bar, arms crossed, looking fussy. I worried these public rejections would cost me the gig.

Dancing wasn't my dream, but it was the only job I'd ever had that sustained my being alive. An absurd fact, considering I was living pretty bottom of the barrel. At twenty-four years old, I was halfway through state college, in $35,000 of student loan debt, freshly dumped by my ex-girlfriend, once again living at my mother's place: a two-bedroom apartment where my older sister and seven-year-old nephew also resided. I lived off bare necessities. No frivolous shopping, no health insurance, not even lattes. I comforted myself by admitting that while I wasn't the best stripper, I was a reliable employee. I showed up to all my sets on time, never missed a shift, and I respected all the Penthouse rules even when I was invited into the VIP lounge the *one* time.

The next dancer, Cindy, a lean pseudo-Australian, strutted on stage, swaying to a Poison song. It was bad stripper etiquette to linger while the next girl performed, but my dress was an impossible-to-get-into bodycon from Forever 21 (on sale). And legally, I couldn't leave the stage until I was *decently* covered. A man stood from his table and moved to the stage. Before Cindy had even taken off her top, he threw four singles. She climbed the pole, wrapped her thighs around the metal, leaned back, twirled down, and landed, miraculously, in a split. I was still there. "Sorry," I whispered and tugged at my dress harder.

When I eventually left the stage, I nodded to my manager as though to say, *Don't count me out yet*, and sauntered over to John. "Hey there," I said. "I'm Lola. Mind if I join you?"

"Please," John said as he booted the roller armchair out from underneath the table. Fairly polite for Penthouse standards. I took a quick inventory of him. Asian American and presumably in his mid-fifties. His head was shaved. An acceptance of the fact that he was balding rather than for style. I looked back at the manager to check if he'd witnessed this exchange, this small yes, but he had disappeared into the club.

"So," I said to John, teasing. "I saw you waving. Why didn't you come say hi?"

"I'm shy," he said, hiding behind his hands, then peeking through his fingers.

There was a sweetness to John's demeanor. Something I'd learned to sniff out at the club after being insulted a few too many times. I relaxed a little and eased into my spiel of asking a handful of basic questions, Where did he work? Was he from Denver? How was his night? etcetera, etcetera, nothing special. A few minutes into it and everything was par for the course, so I moved into phase two of getting a customer to buy a lap dance: breaking the barrier between our bodies with a neck massage.

"My massages make up for my lack of dance skills," I said to John. This line was rehearsed. It was usually a success.

He smiled, revealing two perfectly square front teeth. "What are you talking about? You're a great dancer!"

I paused, slapped his shoulder in a contrived, playful way and said, "Oh, you're just being nice," then thumbed deep into his traps. While I worked, I studied Cindy's set to scavenge a few easy-to-do moves for my own routine. Like rolling her hips with slightly bent knees. The men showered her with dollar bills. When her second song began, she untied her sequined bikini top to reveal flawless, silicone breasts. Embarrassed, I checked John's face to see if he'd regretted not waiting for her. He was undeterred. The colored light streaming from the ceiling melted from purple to blue and then, at last, Cindy shimmered an extraterrestrial green.

"It looks like she's about to be abducted by aliens," I said.

John rotated his head to the side, ear to shoulder for effect, and said, "Huh. I guess it kind of does."

We both laughed.

"Are you a believer?" I asked, lowering my voice. "In aliens?"

"Uh," John stumbled, unsure which answer I wanted to hear. Then he laughed again, nervous and prickly. "Not really. Are you?"

I nodded. "My dad raised me like *The X-Files* was a docuseries. He's convinced Earth is on the cusp of an extraterrestrial takeover."

"Is that so?" John said, very cool about our impending doom. "Does he think we're all screwed?"

"Well, he thinks people like us are screwed," I said, motioning between the two of us.

"*People like us?*" he teased. "What are you trying to say about me?"

I flicked his polo collar. Grabbed his hands and rubbed his smooth, callous-less skin.

John smiled. "Okay. You caught me. What about your dad?"

"He intends to survive," I said, then told John that my dad, who was raised on a ranch and had been a laborer his entire life, had been plotting his post-apocalypse plans for years. The key elements of which included a house, ten guns ranging in size and power, and, until recently, a dragon's hoard of canned Chef Boyardee ravioli. "He called me the other day, and said, 'Did you know canned foods expire? I was checking my supply out, and I saw a goddamn expiration date on the bottom of a can.'"

John looked astonished. "Doesn't everyone know they expire? It's *food*."

I shook my head. "My dad had a good rebuttal. He said, 'In any movie I've seen, they're always eating old-ass canned beans.'"

John's face dropped into concern. "What's he going to do with all those raviolis?"

"He's dedicated himself to eating his whole stockpile before time is up," I said. "He refuses to waste money."

"You're so comical," John said, without so much as a chuckle. The word *comical* stuck with me because it was stiff. It was exactly the word a man like John would use. "You should write a book about your dad."

Funny for John to say that, because I penned stories about my dad all the time. In fact, writing a book about my family's chaotic yet playful antics had been a dream of mine ever since I was a kid. One I didn't take too seriously after hearing the phrase "starving artist" enough times to heed the warnings of financial insecurity. At seventeen, I proudly told my dad that I knew better than to sink myself into student loan debt for the humanities, so passion forlorn, I would treat my writing like a hobby and study something practical in college. I thought he'd be impressed, but my dad shook his head and counseled that college was a money death pit for *little blancas* like me who didn't have parents to pay the bill. He recommended my following in his footsteps to get a Commercial Driver's License. I refused, believing what all my teachers preached: a college degree was the key to financial security. I opted for the careers a women's studies degree would open up.

"Tell me five jobs you could get with that degree," my dad said when I broke the news.

I could only think of one. "Nonprofit work or . . . hmm."

"Flipping burgers," my dad interrupted. "Might as well have stuck with poetry. Pursuing your dream or passions, or even these feminist interests of yours, is for rich people."

"In a parallel universe where I have the time and money to write a book, I'm doing just that," I said to John now. "But in this one, I'm stripping to pay my way through college, and on slow nights, sitting in the dressing room, drafting stories in my Notes app."

Mindful not to dominate the conversation, which could deter the customers, I turned the attention back to John. "So," I said, "who are you in a parallel universe?"

"Hmm." John paused for a long moment and told me that he'd never thought about anything like that before.

It was the first gap I'd feel between us. I wondered how John had gone through his days unbothered by all the what-ifs. The other routes he could've taken. The families he could've reared. The alternate careers. If he had accessed another Universal plane, he might've discovered something better out there. I looked at John. Studied his upright posture. Noted his too-perfect teeth, indubitably the work of a cosmetic dentist. His gold-plated watch. Perhaps John had never needed to think about better things. Which was something I resented and envied in equal measure.

"Well, I have always wished that I wasn't such a nerd," John said. "So, could I just be someone else? Someone cooler?" His voice revealed utmost sincerity, but John caught himself and backpedaled. "That's embarrassing. Now you're going to think, *Wow, this guy is a loser.*"

"No," I said. "I don't think that at all. Did you hear what I just said? I'm a total loser."

John smiled and took a sip of his beer. "You're just being nice."

"I wish I was being nice," I said. "And I only gave you a portion of the story. I'm a real mess."

"Paint me the whole picture then," John said, good-naturedly. "I can take it."

Most Penthouse men wanted the conversation to revolve around them. My job was to pepper in compliments about how smart they were or how cool their career sounded. But John was different. He was interested in an actual back-and-forth. "Okay," I said and gave him the whole lowdown—commuter college student without so much as a laptop, doing all my schoolwork in the computer labs, in debt, living at home— then topped it with a luscious cherry, "I sleep on the couch." I made an *L* with my thumb and forefinger, pressing it to my forehead.

"Oof," John grimaced. "Sounds crowded." Then he smiled and found the only possible way to compliment me. "You must be pretty smart and dedicated to be in school and stripping at the same time."

I beamed and then told John that words of affirmation were my second-favorite love language.

"Love language?" John asked. "What's that?"

I explained that love languages are how we prefer to receive and give love. "There's five of them," I said. "Words of affirmation, physical touch, quality time, gifts, and acts of service."

"I've never even heard of these before." John ran his hand across his chin and asked where I had.

"Alanis Morissette," I said, not missing a beat.

"The singer?" he asked, confused.

"She's so much more than that." Alanis is a songwriter, a poet, a self-work guru, and, though I assume she would frown upon this, my personal deity. "When I was eleven, I wrote 'therapy' at the top of my Christmas list all because Alanis sang about her shrink's leather couch. My parents couldn't afford it, *of course*. Left to scrounge for free resources, I started reading Alanis's blog on the family PC (which went with my dad in the divorce). She wrote about emotional intelligence, Maslow's Hierarchy of Needs, connection to the divine, and, yeah, attachment styles." What I withheld from John was that after my ex-girlfriend left me—a total shell of myself, but still too broke for therapy—I'd begun obsessively listening to Alanis's podcast episodes. With her help, I'd moved beyond naming my love languages and was now able to diagnose myself with all sorts of attachment issues. I was a parentified child with a disorganized attachment style and a core fear that the world was unreliable.

"You're so . . ." John took a moment to find the right word. "Fascinating."

Whenever I told a customer he was fascinating, I'd watch his poised veneer melt away to reveal the wounded man beneath. Which, in the context of simulated intimacy and tip expectation, felt sort of tragic. But when John was awed by the love languages and gazed at the "self-actualization" tip of Maslow's diagram as if it were a mountain peak and told me I was the most interesting person he'd ever met, I swelled with an unfamiliar fondness. For the first time at Penthouse, I wasn't just some half-naked girl there to boost a man's ego or listen to him speak until I was nothing more than a mirror. I felt seen. John was doing my job better than I was. Soon enough, I broke my own club rule and told him my real name, Michelle.

★

I'd gotten so caught up in talking that I forgot to mention my three-for-a-hundred-bucks lap dance deal. I only remembered at 9:00 p.m. when John looked at his watch and said, "I should probably get out of here."

I glanced at my flat empty purse, feeling a surge of anxiety. Not many men would trickle in during the late hours on a Wednesday, and I worried I had blown my only chance of making any cash that night. Giving one customer too much attention was such an amateur stripper move that even I knew it. "Would you be interested in some private time before you leave?" I asked.

"I think I'd rather be surprised," he said. Then, in one swift movement, he whipped his business card and $400—the price of twelve lap dances!!—from his wallet, leaving it all on the table. "Call me if you want to have dinner." He paused, looked at me confidently, and added, "I'll compensate you for your time."

Without further warning he turned and walked away, disappearing under the glowing red exit sign. Never mind the weird comment at the end, I couldn't believe my luck. It was exceptionally rare for me to make my nightly goal in one fell swoop. And this may have been the most organic connection I'd ever had with a customer. It hadn't even felt like work.

With John gone, I turned my attention to the stage and admired the current dancer's ability to look sensual during "Cherry Pie." Had she ever had a nice time with a customer then later had a compensated dinner with him? What precisely did a compensated "dinner" entail? I'd heard of girls having highly profitable drinks with men from the club (even the lesbians like me), but each occasion included a bit of gray area. Hand holding. A lower back graze. A kiss. I could've easily found a girl on shift to talk to about John's invite and whether this was some ruse for sex, but I didn't want to become locker-room fodder. I'd heard rumors of girls sleeping with wealthy VIPs or, more commonly, getting felt up in the lap dance cubicles for an extra charge, but no one ever spoke about this as good business. Just basic catty remarks, "slut" this and "whore" that.

I figured if John would pay me $400 to talk with him at the club, an off-site meal would likely be more lucrative. I started counting the money in my mind. Paying bills with it. Daydreaming that I would charm John so much, he'd want to see me once a week, and I could replace one of my Penthouse shifts with dinner!

Then I remembered John saying, "I think I'd rather be surprised" about, presumably, seeing my vagina later, and since I definitely didn't want him to pull any kind of move on me, I decided that I wouldn't agree to anything sexual in text message, and if John later gunned for something extra in person, I would just dodge his advance and go about my life a couple of hundred bucks richer. No harm done.

Indigo lights cascaded across the room, tarrying for a beat when the color refracted off John's business card. It felt like a sign. No! More than that. It felt like a message from the Universe, passed to me through John's hand. Like *John Linghu, Senior Lead at WebRoom* was code for *Michelle, you are exactly where you're meant to be.* Because, frankly, it had been quite a journey before arriving at that moment at Penthouse.

Just three weeks earlier, I'd been bagging groceries at Whole Foods, standing at the end of a cashier named Inés's register, waiting for the items she scanned to slide my way. Up first, a seventeen-dollar jar of cashew butter.

"Isn't it wild that we live in a world where nut spread can be an example of classism?" I asked Inés, trying to sound philosophical yet relatable. During our last shift, while attempting to flirt, I'd asked Inés if she would read Harper Lee's big-deal sequel, *Go Set a Watchman.* She raised her eyebrows at me like I was an out-of-touch boomer. *Book? It's 2015, bitch. We have YouTube.*

"Michelle," Inés said. My name crawled from her mouth at a perma-stoned pace. "It's Whole Foods. Even the condiments are bougie." She lifted a bottle of Old Style Grain Mustard. "Like, what the fuck are mustard seeds?"

The customer, unmoved, puttered her thumbs against her phone.

"I'm 'bout to blast anyway," Inés said. I was only four years older, but half of Inés's verbs were utterly foreign to me. The third time I'd had to ask *What's HAM again?* ("hard as a motherfucker" apparently), I felt geriatric.

"When are you, uh, blasting?" I asked, nailing it.

"As soon as I can get hired at a strip club," she said. Then, to the woman still locked in on her screen, "That'll be $134.17."

To state it plainly, Inés was hot. Twenty years old, with warm, smooth skin. She had full lips and a delicate nose. Her thick, black hair fell to the belt loops on her high-waisted jeans. She could've been an Instagram influencer.

"You could walk out of here right now and get hired," I said, hoisting the woman's bags into her cart. Gathering this was my potential *in* with Inés, I added, "I actually stripped when I was your age."

Back when I was nineteen, my noncommittal, twenty-eight-year-old "boyfriend" dumped me. The breakup had stolen an extra fifteen pounds I was hauling around, so when a friend mentioned auditioning at a strip club, I tagged along. The gig lasted five months, until my belly had resurrected itself and Penthouse launched its 2011 Weight Restriction campaign. I quit before a manager could escort me to the office where they were weighing dancers on a bathroom scale.

"That's dope," Inés said. I felt instantly cooler. "Which club?"

"Penthouse," I said. The gentlemen's clubs in Denver had rank, and, while Penthouse wasn't the *crème de la fancy*—hiring entertainers with tattoos and C-section scars—it sure as hell wasn't Paper Tiger, where a local magazine reported "strippers went to die."

"Sick," Inés said. "I want to try Diamond Cabaret, but I don't think I'm what they're looking for."

Diamond Cabaret was top tier. Clientele often wore three-piece suits and wedding bands. Glitter was discouraged. The club preferred "classic" entertainers, meaning blonde hair and big boobs. Inés and I had neither.

"Diamond is big money," I said, "but they're picky. What about La Boheme?" This club sat off 16th Street Mall, making it a tourist hub, and opportunely close to a three-story Forever 21, which was a superb spot to shop for stage wear. La Bo favored girls with a unique edge, like brown hair.

"If I don't get hired at Diamond, then I'm going there," Inés said.

"And if that doesn't work, Penthouse will totally take you," I said.

"Okay." She nodded. "That'll be my backup-backup plan."

Inés turned her attention to our latest customer, a middle-aged man who'd heard every word of our discussion. "Dude. Nice selection of bananas. These look super fucking good."

This was a Monday evening, and the dinner rush was in full swing. Checkout lines clogged. I nestled my arches into the floor mat, bagging and chatting with Inés for an hour. She had endless questions. I was full of answers. It was the best conversation we'd ever had.

During my stripping debut, I told Inés, I'd confused audition for interview and wore a business suit to Penthouse. A stripper named Lux begrudgingly loaned me her spare outfit, a fluorescent orange bikini covered in rhinestones, hissing "FYI, this cost more than my rent" as she handed it over.

I unzipped my pencil skirt and, as gingerly as I could, tugged on the panties, which were two sizes too small. I waddled over to the mirror. There I was: a glistening can of Fanta Orange.

Inés scoffed. "Everyone knows it's not an interview. What else you got?"

I'd acquired most of my stripping strategies from Lux that first night. Mostly about aggressive self-marketing. "It's all about the hustle," she explained. "There are thirty girls working any given night, and you need men to want your lap dances. What's going to be special about *you*?"

"I guess my boobs." (At nineteen they were at their peak.)

Lux slammed her locker shut and spun to face me. "A lot of girls have nice tits, Michelle. You need to bring something nobody else can offer."

"Uh, all right," Inés said. "What was your thing?"

I tossed a container of hummus on top of two avocados, then I took everything out and put the hummus in first. "My biggest asset was my personality."

Inés ceased scanning to frame her chin with the back of her hand. "I think my biggest asset will be my face."

When the horde of shoppers died down, I gazed dramatically out the widows behind to the gridlocked parking lot. A real hazard to us baggers. There were carts everywhere.

"I wish I could strip again," I said to Inés.

"What's stopping you?"

"I already tried stripping again when I was twenty-two," I told her. Explaining that, by BMI standards, I'd been overweight. I'd skipped Denver's "classy" clubs and instead trekked to the grimiest dives—the desperate ones that advertised in the back of local magazines with shit like "WE LOVE ALL GIRLS!!! NO HOUSE FEES 4 1-WEEK!"—and four times in a row a manager wearing a cheap suit looked me in the eye and said, "Sorry, baby girl. You're too big." Soon after, I was hired at a sandwich shop, and one month after that, I matched with my future ex-girlfriend, Stevie, on Tinder. We had two years of breakups and reconciliations, during which I'd stress-dropped thirty-four pounds, all without counting a single calorie. So, with my post-breakup bod, the thinnest I'd ever been in my life, Inés looked at me, motioned her hand across my body and said, "I think you should try again."

Skinny as I was, Inés thought I ought to try the nicest club in Denver, Diamond Cabaret. I don't know why I listened.

"The manager on duty is named Chubs," the hostess told me the next afternoon as I handed her my ID. "Let him know when you're ready to go up."

When I eventually thumped on the manager's office door, a corpulent man, presumably Chubs, rose to greet me. His face was puffy, and his cheeks looked wind chapped. He reminded me of a cartoon, and this, on top of his name, made me like him instantly.

When my name was called over the loudspeaker, I was nervous but optimistic. Although I hadn't stripped in years, I knew the drill. Strut on stage, do a passable job, then wow Chubs later by raking in cash through my superior listening skills. Kelly Rowland's "Motivation" boomed through the club and my old routine flooded back to me. I cocked my hip and trailed my hands down my body. By the second verse, I was on the ground thrusting. Just like riding a bike.

A customer tossed a dollar bill onto my stage. I dropped to my knees and seductively crawled toward him. The man tilted forward and shouted in my ear, "I want a dance from you after this!" I flashed a thumbs up. The club pocketed a percentage of every lap dance. A reasonable fee for providing security, they claimed. Meaning that I'd just made Diamond Cabaret ten bucks. In other words, I'd just landed myself the job.

When my set was over, I informed my patron that I needed to ask Chubs if we could sign the hiring paperwork post lap dance. Chubs was behind his oversized desk, shuffling papers, preparing my I-9, I thought, when I appeared in the doorway. At the sight of me, he slapped both of his palms against the veneer tabletop. "Sorry, sweetheart. We're looking for someone prettier in the face."

"Thank you for your time," I managed to whimper before backing out of his office and into the dressing room. I pulled my jeans over my lingerie and counted the bills I'd collected. Twelve dollars for ugly-faced me. En route to the exit, I broke it to my admirer that I hadn't gotten the job.

"I'm not pretty enough for Diamond," I said, insinuating that he should disagree.

"Who said that?" he asked, scanning the room and puffing his chest out like a gorilla. Close enough for me.

I arrived at Penthouse thirty minutes later. After informing the manager that I had worked for the club before and wanted to again, he said, "You wanna dance tonight?" Three weeks later, when I was exactly where the Universe had led me, John offered his card.

It was fate. I had to say yes.

The music lowered, and my stage name, Lola, came over the loud-speaker. I folded the money, tucked it into my clutch, a fuchsia Louis Vuitton knockoff, and headed for the pole.

★

Around 2:00 a.m., I left the club and loaded into my '92 Honda Accord. I bought the car three months earlier for $800. The Honda was dark blue in patches, but most of the paint had rusted away in its twenty-four years on the road. The engine sounded like a dinosaur and leaked oil constantly, an issue I addressed by stashing quarts of Pennzoil in my back seat. The rear doors didn't open and neither did the trunk or the glove compartment come to think of it, but the passenger window still worked. While these may sound like endless headaches, I had gone nose blind to my own life. Things simply were the way they were. And given my past inability to afford a car at all (even one as troublesome as this), the Honda was a great, big, clunking relief.

I pulled out of the parking lot of Penthouse and called my dad just as I usually did after a shift. He worked as an overnight truck driver and appreciated the late-night conversation.

When I was younger, I'd made the mistake of telling my friends I was a stripper, which resulted in endless gossip and "Easy-A" level social demise. I'd learned my lesson, so this time around, I kept quiet and just let my friends think I was still working at Whole Foods. On the contrary, at nineteen, I'd kept my family in the dark about my dancing, claiming I'd been hired at Penthouse as a cocktail waitress. This worked until I made $1,000 off a guy who swore he'd been Britney Spears's bodyguard for a week in 2007. Unable to contain my excitement, I told my family about my good luck. "I'm not an idiot, Shell," my dad said. "I know you're not making that kind of money serving drinks, and I don't care. Just let me know which club you're working at so I don't see you there. Now tell me more about Britney." Unsurprising, really. When I first told my dad that I was gay, he'd nodded then said, "So, is scissoring real?" All that to say, my family knew I worked at Penthouse, and they were the only people that knew.

This night I had serious gossip. I told my dad about John, the $400 for nothing but conversation, and the paid dinner invitation. My dad interrupted me several times to tell me to speak up, "I can't hear what you're saying over the goddamn engine," so I made sure to really belt out the most important part: "I'M GOING TO ACCEPT JOHN'S DINNER OFFER."

My dad was skeptical.

"Nobody pays someone to have dinner with them, Shell," he said, his voice loud but staticky through his Samsung headset. I imagined the road before him. Orion's Belt and the occasional roadkill. "Didn't I raise you smarter than that?"

"Millionaires pay people to have dinner," I said. "Super lonely millionaires." I didn't know if John was super lonely or a millionaire, but saying so made it seem plausible that paying for a nice dinner was NBD to him.

"I know ten thousand things I'd rather spend four hundred bucks on than dinner."

"You have no concept of real money," I said. "To him, $400 is probably like four bucks to us. You wouldn't treat someone to a meal off the dollar menu if you really wanted some company?" Then I remembered my dad had broken up with a woman after she declined a date at McDonald's. *She's too good for the drive-through?* he scoffed. *Who does she think she is?*

"He sounds like a perv," my dad said. "That's all I know."

"Maybe. *Orrr*," I said, drawing it out, "a generous, super nice, lonely gentleman."

"Perv," my dad repeated. "Perv alert!"

When I opened the front door of the apartment, my mom was in the kitchen assembling a ham sandwich. Nothing fancy. Just a few Oscar Mayer honey slices and a layer of Lay's Originals for a little crunch. Junk food was my mom's vice. Harmless enough, except three years prior, my mom's doctor diagnosed her with type 2 diabetes. He advised to exchange processed grains for whole, which my mom claimed was impossible on the spot. Unrefined carbs, she explained, made her gag.

Biting into the ham-and-potato-chip sandwich, she chewed with one side of her mouth and used the other to talk. "You want me to make you one?"

"No," I said. "I'm a vegetarian."

"You won't even eat ham?"

"Especially not ham," I said, pointing to the pig tattooed on my wrist as testament to this.

She shrugged. "You're missing out."

As she crunched another bite, I resisted making any comment. My mom hated when I told her to take better care of her health. But pork? At this hour? "Won't your blood sugar soar eating so late?"

"I always snack this late. It helps me get back to sleep after I pee." (Frequent urination, a symptom of diabetes.)

My parents were the kind of parents children think they want: lawless and loving. The kind who served McDonald's for breakfast, lunch, and dinner and believed that french fries dipped in ketchup counted as two servings of vegetables. Parents who suggested you play hooky for a day because Britney Spears was on *Good Morning America* and who kissed you and hugged you and declared their love so often, you never had to question it. Regrettably for them, I offered constant and unwelcome suggestions for improvement.

Because of this inclination to critique, my mom and I sometimes struggled to connect. Back to sharing nine hundred square feet, I'd been trying to remedy this. I usually tried asking open-ended questions—what my mom thought about while daydreaming or what unfulfilled desires she had lurking inside—but her answers were always vague and a little exasperated. "Oh, Michelle, I don't know. Bunnies?"

"I met a nice guy tonight. He said he wants to take me out to dinner." I paused. "*For cash.*"

My mom furrowed her brow. "That sounds dangerous, Shell." Then her voice deepened in intensity, "Don't be getting yourself killed over a free meal."

I should've known this would be her reaction. My mother and I, true-crime devotees, had watched every *Forensic Files* episode produced. Thrice. Our collective brain was crammed with murder facts, including that just because someone seems friendly and rich doesn't mean they won't axe you. "I would meet him inside the restaurant, Mom. Where there would be a lot of witnesses."

She swallowed a bite of her sandwich, unplacated by my promise. "Are you even allowed to meet customers for dinner? You aren't going to get fired, are you?"

"Yes, I'm allowed," I said, annoyed. As if Penthouse management paid any attention to us beyond our waistlines. We weren't even employees to them. We were easy-to-replace merchandise. If any manager knew I was meeting John for dinner they'd probably demand a cut. "Everybody does it. I'm just having dinner, but some girls meet guys there and get paid to bang them!"

I worried my mom might warn me against the temptation to sleep with someone for cash, but she pivoted the conversation to her day at the physical rehab facility where she'd been tending the front desk for a decade, during which her hourly wage glacially increased by two dollars. Somehow, this did not depress her. "One of our patients bit a nurse today," she said, giggling. "They didn't have their teeth in, thank goodness. The nurse said it felt like a trout attack."

I typed "trout attack" into my Notes app, where I also kept a running list of quotes to write into my stories, and waited for more, but the story was over.

Sitting at our kitchen table, I began organizing my money before stashing it in the safe I'd purchased at Walmart for fourteen bucks. I could deposit petty sums of cash into my bank account without ringing alarm bells, but I relished the ceremony of flattening out crumpled singles and watching the pile grow. Like the rest of our apartment, clear space on the table was in short supply, complicating my task. My elbows stuck to glossy coupons. A picture book sprawled open to an illustration of astronaut otters on Mars. A mountain of bills from Xcel, Discover, and Labcorp, all addressed to my mother, loomed over it all.

I'd made good money. Nearly five hundred dollars. Almost entirely thanks to John. I felt an overwhelming sense of gratitude, believing, perhaps foolishly, that meeting him was my fate. But how could I not? John had arrived in my life in a momentous, overflowing fashion when my cup was completely and utterly empty. This exchange would be more than a one-off meeting at Penthouse. I was sure of it. I would make sure of it.

I shuffled my mom's bills into a neat pile, slid my cash stack beside it, and compared which was taller. My tips won by a hair. Then I collected the bills, flipped them upside down, and fanned them out.

"Pick an envelope, any envelope!" I said to my mom in a fortune-teller voice. "And I will pay it."

"Are you sure?" Her eyes rounded behind her glasses, suddenly wide awake.

"Yeah," I said. "Go on."

She plucked one from the center of the spread. It had been opened and then folded back into its envelope *for later*. A charge for blood work to monitor her sugar levels.

"$141.50," she whispered, like shrinking her voice could shrink the sum.

I snatched the sheet out of her hand and waved my arm like a magician. "Ta-da!" I said. "It disappeared!"

"Thank you." She pulled me in and kissed me on the cheek. I breathed in her signature perfume: muscle rub, baby powder, ham.

2

First Date with Fate

I awoke the next morning to my seven-year-old nephew crushing my feet. Chuy was shirtless, slurping cerulean milk from a bowl of Froot Loops. It was routine for me to wake up alongside a dining member of my family, because, as any waiter would know, *everything tastes better in a booth*.

"Good morning, Auntie," Chuy said.

I yawned, sat up, complimented his dinosaur briefs, and wrapped the Spider-Man comforter around my shoulders. While quarters were tight, life was not depressing. I enjoyed the intimacy that our physical closeness imposed. I could write my stories on one end of the sofa while Chuy could complete a puzzle on the other end. When we both tired of our pastimes, we'd move into the next part of the day together. Like now, as I left sleep and joined him in watching an early-morning cartoon. *Arthur*. Chuy was sucked in, chomping away at his cereal with his eyes glued to the TV. I plucked Chuy's bowl from his hand and stuffed a spoonful of ccreal into my mouth. Crassly, I might add, which would've been fine, except I had a lot of cavities.

I hadn't had dental insurance since I turned eighteen. While placing my sixteenth (and most recent) filling back in '09, the dentist announced that I possessed "deep grooves" and "weak teeth." Hereditary traits. Different areas of my mouth proved weaker than others, however, and cavities disproportionately dotted the upper right bridge. I'd shock trained myself to avoid using these teeth, but in my sleepy daze, this was exactly where the Froot Loops landed.

"Are you okay, Auntie?" Chuy asked over my yelps.

"Mhmm," I said. Although, truthfully, I wasn't so sure. I'd once read an article on WebMD that mentioned plaque's ability to enter the blood system through the gums and cause heart attacks. It was possible my teeth might kill me.

My nephew offered his cup of Kool-Aid to wash away the debris, but I shook my head. "Water. Please."

He sprang off the couch, barely avoiding a fossilized TV dinner, then hopped over the aluminum transition strip into the kitchen.

Chuy returned with a cup of lukewarm tap water, but I'd already cleared the sugar out. I held up a notepad I'd found on his TV tray. On it, handwritten addition problems solved step-by-step. Beside the notepad, a math worksheet Chuy was copying the answers onto during commercial breaks.

"Is Grandma doing your homework for you again?" I asked, annoyed, but not entirely surprised. When I was a child, my mom regularly whisked me and my sister off to the local library where they, together, completed Bianca's homework. To hide her adult penmanship, my mom either clacked away on the library typewriter, or she'd solve math and science questions on a separate sheet of paper for my sister to duplicate. Inevitably, a Saturday arrived when only my mother and I loaded into the car. "Bianca," she'd said, "wants to stay home to watch TV."

"Goldie, how do you expect Bianca to graduate middle school if she can't read?" I said. I had gone through a phase from ages six to eight when I called my mom by her first name. It felt right, since I sometimes found myself chastising her behavior.

"She can read!" my mom snapped back. "And stop calling me Goldie. It sounds like you're adopted."

My mom, I thought at that age, took the role of parent too far. She would've lived every challenge or inconvenience for my sister (or me had I been willing), and I knew Bianca would have allowed her. Their codependence continued throughout the years, only the stakes grew larger and larger, until, at last, Chuy was born. Without so much as a peep from my sister, my mom stepped in the second the umbilical cord was cut. Ready to do it all.

"Yes," my nephew said, undeterred. "Grandma likes to help me."

I took the notepad and marched into the back bedroom.

The apartment furniture had been arranged with one question in mind: *Where will this fit?* In the bedroom, the TV went on top of the dresser, and the ironing board in front of that. Two twin beds appeared to be one gap-toothed double, which is precisely where I found my mother, watching last night's news recap in her bra and full-coverage Hanes, coated chest to toe in baby powder.

"Mom," I said, shaking the paper at her. "What's this?"

"I'm helping Chuy with his homework," she said, dusting her belly off. "What's the big deal?"

"The big deal is that he needs to learn how to do this on his own. How's he supposed to get a job if he doesn't know what," I paused to look at his homework sheet, "two plus five minus one is?"

"He knows how to do it, Shell," she said. "Watch. CHUY! COME IN HERE!"

My nephew's feet padded across the apartment and then he was in the doorframe.

"Yes, Grandma?"

"Auntie wants you to solve this math problem for her."

He counted on his fingers, two then five, then put one back down. "Six."

"Good job, buddy," my mom said, then eyed me.

"If you know how to do it then go finish your homework on your own," I said to Chuy and shooed him out of the room.

My mom pointed to the television, where a news headline, *CLOWN THREATS SPREAD ACROSS THE METRO*, ran across the screen. "Oh, my goodness. Shell, have you heard about this? People across Denver are dressing up and doing freaky stuff like . . . lurking in parks."

"Yes, I'm aware of these clowns. By *reading* the news," I said.

"I don't care how you found out. Just promise me if you see anybody with a red nose or balloons," she said, sternly, "that you'll dial 9-1-1."

That evening while at Penthouse, I found myself watching the front doors, hoping John might drop in. Unfortunately, my current customer, a square-jawed man in his mid-thirties, was blocking my view.

This man, like many other men I had met at Penthouse, insisted on buying me twelve-dollar vodka sodas in lieu of a lap dance. "I'm enjoying us getting to know one another too much to interrupt our conversation," he said. "You're one of the best listeners I've ever met."

Although it was part of the job, at both nineteen and twenty-four, I'd found the hyper-sexualization of my body a vile aspect. I would put on my lingerie and grievously accept that in doing so I would now be reduced to a flank of meat. Men would throw me a dollar and then say they wanted to taste me. They'd grope at my ass and breasts. They'd brag about their dicks and tricks. Men often wanted to know if this type of work turned me on, but they were never asking what I thought about the other dancers, neglecting the possibility that I might, too, be captivated by the naked women swaying around us. They were curious if grinding on *their* laps, smelling *their* sweat and cologne, made me want to go home with them. It didn't. Never once. And because I couldn't dance well, and I couldn't play the part of some seductress wanting to be there, I knew that to survive the club I'd have to be clever and sweet and funny. I'd have to somehow flaunt parts of myself that had nothing to do with my body. Hence my "great listening skills."

Not always that easy to capitalize on.

Many strip club patrons, or at least the ones I came into contact with, arrived with thinly veiled misogynistic views about us dancers. They thought women who took their clothes off for work must be broken, or stupid, or have low self-esteem. They couldn't imagine a *nice* girl would see stripping as work. As though a girl never came to Penthouse after weighing club wages and ten dollars an hour anywhere else.

All that to say, when I showed up before these men fluttering my false lashes, I'd crack a joke, ask them about their life, listen to their responses, ask follow-up questions which sometimes prompted them to reveal something true about themselves, and they'd grow hearts in their eyes. They'd say, "I can't believe I met someone *like you*, *here*," then claim our meeting felt too romantic—it wouldn't be right to pay me, and could they have my phone number instead?

My customer at the moment was no different. He had been talking at me for nearly an hour—which, in the wake of my conversation with John, felt extra annoying. This man hadn't asked me a single question about myself until, "Break it to me easy. Do you have a boyfriend?"

"No," I said flatly. In 2015, most men assumed that strippers were all straight. While I would've gladly corrected him under different circumstances, I'd made the decision to conceal my queerness at Penthouse after outing myself disrupted too many customers' fantasies about our connection existing independent of the club. Any mention of my attraction to women had almost always shattered that illusion. Conversations were abandoned.

These men came to the strip club to feed their boring, heteronormative fantasies: naked, glistening women, horny for men, without any baggage or real-life issues, or even a real first name. I hated playing into it, but declaring straightness was a strategy of self-preservation at Penthouse. I wasn't authentically connecting or sharing my full self, but, then again, I didn't really want to.

"No, I don't have a boyfriend," I told my customer. Then, to thwart him asking me out, I added, "Stripping and relationships are hard to maintain."

I based this statement on one piece of evidence: my ex-girlfriend, Bailey. A girl I'd met at nineteen, after I'd been dancing for several weeks. It was a time in my life when I still believed honesty was the best policy.

Bailey was "totally cool, like, super fucking cool" with my stripping at first. I trusted her with the particulars of the job—how occasionally men whipped their dicks out in the lap dance cubicles. Or how customers would shoo me away from their tables, look me in the eye and declare that I was too ugly or too chubby to sit with them. Sometimes I would cry over feeling reliant on my body to pay the bills. She called me brave.

After three months, Bailey found my job too taxing. It pained her to picture so many hands on me. And, oh god, how awful to greet me after work and whiff cologne in my hair. "You feel dirty," she'd once said. "It isn't cheating, I know, but it feels that way." Eventually, I would catch wind of the nasty things she and other friends had said about my *slutty, lazy* job. It was cutting to say the least.

"I wouldn't care if *my* girlfriend stripped," the customer said. His eyes were glossy from the stage lights. I could sense him working up to asking my real name, which I would say was Melissa.

"You would," I said, sipping my drink.

He opened his mouth to say more just as "Lo-lo-lo-lo-Lola! You're up on stage three, my yummy, sexy lady!" came over the loudspeaker.

"Gotta go," I said, taking my vodka soda with me. "Thanks for the drinks."

After my set, during which this man toasted to me twice, but did not tip, I avoided his gaze and made a beeline for the dressing room. Two dancers, Kimmy and Quinn, were sitting in plastic patio chairs before the ten-foot-long mirror, fixing their faces and considering how much money they'd need to bang a customer. I immediately thought of John.

"Portia made $10,000 in VIP," Kimmy said. She had one falsie stuck to her eyelid and the other pinched between her fingertips. White glue lined the rim.

A lump sum of $10,000 sounded like the kind of exorbitant figure reserved for TV game shows. Too big to be true.

"No way. Off *one* dude?" Quinn asked.

"Yeah, he was a Bronco or something." Kimmy repeated it slowly, "Ten thousand dollars. She had to carry the money out in a shoebox."

I pictured Portia—skinny with fake tits and a pretty face—descending the VIP stairs while balancing a shoebox full of cash. I could've toppled over with envy. Ten thousand dollars was a third of my student loan debt. It was a gently used 2010 four-door sedan, or a dental visit. I wondered if John might proposition me over dinner for an equal amount. It seemed like an impossible number to decline. Part of me prayed that he wouldn't, and part of me hoped that he would.

"I'd sleep with anyone for $10,000," I said, joining the conversation.

"I'd let them film it for that much cash," Kimmy said. Kimmy was tall and brunette. I watched her reflection as she smoothed the second falsie, then blinked repeatedly to check they were secure.

"Bob told me he fucked a girl in VIP twenty years ago," Quinn said. Bob came to the club a minimum of three days a week and had apparently done so for the preceding two decades. Last Wednesday, I'd failed to sell him a lap dance. Bob, white-haired, red-cheeked, and round enough that he could've convinced any child he was Santa Claus, told me he'd "have to pass" because he saw my thighs jiggling on stage.

After the dig, I'd tearfully carried myself into the back. Kimmy, who had been listening to a molecular biology lecture, paused the recording to run her acrylics over my bare shoulders. "Fuck these assholes," Kimmy said. Given the context of the club, I couldn't be too sure whether she was just being nice or if she truly cared about me, which was one reason Penthouse customers could be duped broke. Reminded of the labor it took to pause, to read someone's need, to fulfill that need, to fulfill that need when you don't give a shit, I fought the urge to tip her.

"How much did Bob pay for the sex?" I asked Quinn now.

"He said it was free." Quinn laughed, then swigged from a bottle of vodka, chased it with a bottled Starbucks Frappuccino, then passed them both to me.

"You know how these men are," Kimmy said. "They'll offer a girl a thousand bucks for sex, then convince themselves they gave the money out of the kindness of their hearts and that she fucked him for free out of the kindness of hers."

"Cheers to that," Quinn said.

I felt bright from the vodka and, as a result, overly sentimental about being inside the conspiracy of the strip club. Where we dancers understood the customers better than they understood themselves. We were hardworking, emotionally intelligent girls.

I opened my clutch and counted my tips: $147. If I allocated sixty dollars for my next shift's house fees, a ten-dollar tip share for the bartenders, another ten dollars for the DJ and seven dollars for security, I was left with sixty dollars profit. This was not unheard of with other dancers, but it was uncommon. Most women made at least double what I pulled each shift, if not triple.

"It's so frustrating," I said. "These men can't get enough of my company, but whenever I ask them to buy a lap dance, they say they like me *too much to pay me* and ask me out instead."

"Lola," Kimmy said. "Every woman in here has something that sets her apart from the crowd. For Quinn, it's that she can work the pole. For me, it's that I'm getting my PhD in clinical lab science, and I'll let any man know I'm smarter than him. If your thing is conversing until these men think they've found love, then that is your superpower. Next time someone asks you on a date, tap on the table, draw their attention to the entertainment, and say, *Baby, this is a date. I can keep it going all night for a price.*"

Kimmy was right. I blamed the men, but I was part of the problem too. While I'd long since had the genius plan of capitalizing my personality, I hadn't actually figured out how to. I just kept giving it away for free. But who on earth would be willing to pay for my company?

"John," I said aloud.

Kimmy and Quinn eyed me, confused.

"Thanks, girls," I said, not bothering to explain myself.

I hightailed it to the bathroom, where the stall doors had been removed and replaced with curtains. Allegedly this was a safety protocol in case anyone accidentally overdosed, but it felt sort of indecent. I sat on the toilet, underwear pulled up, and transcribed my conversation with Kimmy and Quinn while it was still fresh. I often jotted down quotes and clips of conversations from the strip club, a dialogue trick an old writing professor taught me—then removed John's business card from my clutch and thumbed his digits into a text message.

Hey there. It's Michelle from Penthouse. I'd love to take you up on that dinner!

As I waited for a text back, I used my last bit of cell data to do a little digging on the web. After my breakup, I'd deactivated all my social media accounts, but my sister had given me her Facebook login so I could occasionally stalk people. I searched John's name with every single trick I had to widen the search (job, city, etc.), but alas, nothing. This John Linghu did not have a Facebook profile. Not surprising, since he was a boomer in his fifties. I then turned to Google, where I tried John's name and his company. Bingo. There was his LinkedIn. The information matched his business card, and he had over six hundred connections. I took it as a good sign.

I could find no other traces of John on the internet, but I felt satisfied with this. It was 2015. I didn't have my own laptop, and I was no tech wizard. I wasn't necessarily curious about John's life—I wasn't some crush-struck girl wanting to know every little thing about him—I just wanted to be sure the guy I met at Penthouse was who he said he was. It seemed so.

When I checked my notifications, John had written back.

Hi! Great to hear from you *What about next Thursday? Have you ever been to Morton's Steakhouse?*

I had not, I told him. And next week sounded great.

★

Before meeting John the following Thursday, I gave my mom instructions for what to do in case of an emergency. "If I'm not home by 10:00 p.m.," I said, "call the police and give them John's business card." I'd placed it in a Ziploc baggie, positive that investigators could collect a full thumb and partial index print if need be. Instinctively, I felt John was a good guy, but true crime TV taught me to always be prepared.

"Shell," my mom said, frowning from the sofa. She was eating a bowl of rainbow sherbet. "Is it safe for you to be doing this?"

"Just as safe as it is for me to go on a Tinder date," I said. "Probably safer, because at least I've met this guy."

She pursed her lips, computing. "I guess you've got a point, but you've only met women off Tinder. Which is statistically safer than meeting a man you've already met."

I had been playing it cool to ease my mom, but my palms had been clammy all day. My body was on edge. I'd been unable to eat. This type of outside-the-club-meeting also felt dangerous with presumptions— did John assume that because I was having dinner with him I'd also be having sex with him tonight? Did he expect it? Feel entitled to my body because he was going to buy me a salad and baked potato? I tried to ease my anxieties by thinking of the public-setting aspect. If John propositioned me for sex, I'd simply decline, and if he became irate and murderous, I'd ask the waiter for help to escape and to please give John the check.

My phone pinged. "John just texted me," I said as I grabbed my purse. "Read it out loud."

Park in the valet when you arrive. I'll give you cash for it inside. :)

My mom put her spoon down, took my phone, and analyzed the text. Her face was studious, but I wasn't sure if that was just because she was trying to see through my screen, which was smashed to smithereens.

"John seems nice," she said, eventually. "I like the smiley face."

I arrived outside Morton's The Steakhouse twenty minutes too early, so I stress-cruised downtown to kill time. It was the week after Thanksgiving and the entirety of Denver was decorated for the holidays. Larimer Square, especially, looked like the set of a Hallmark Christmas movie. I turned down California and passed the coffee shop I sometimes wrote in after class. Until recently my family had been my favorite story fodder. They were characters, and because they were all hams, eager for a laugh or reaction, they wrote the best lines themselves. Lately, the strip club was proving to be good material, but I didn't have a plan for anything I was writing. I'd just let it die in my Notes app.

I turned right down Wazee and pulled to the curb in front of Morton's. The valet was a teenage boy with rosacea. Before I surrendered the keys, I explained how to get the Honda going again post-dinner. "The car won't start on the first few go's," I said. "But don't let it discourage you. Pump the gas and keep turning the key. It'll rev up."

"No problem, miss," he said. "I'm familiar." It was snowing ever so slightly. Our breath hung in the air between us. The teenager did not mean that Morton guests often drove cars that struggled to start, but that he, too, owned a beater. I looked down at my feet. They were blue from the cold. I was wearing a fifteen-dollar pair of black heels that I'd had for years. There was a white scuff mark on either toe. I wanted to tell the valet what I was doing there. That John was inside waiting for me with a wad of cash. I was tempted to ask if he'd walk me in and make sure I left safely. But he was so young. It seemed indecent.

I strolled through the front doors at exactly 6:00 p.m. It felt like I was on autopilot. If I stopped to think about what I was doing, I might turn and run. I counted my steps as the maître d' led me past maroon velvet booths in search of my party. Classical music played. The faint smell of garlic was all around. I spotted John in the back looking inconspicuous. This reminded me.

"Where are the restrooms?" I said. "And do they have windows?" My mom told me to ask.

"Right over there, in the back corner." The host nodded discreetly in their direction. "No windows, I'm afraid."

I smiled and said, "There's my friend. I'm all good from here." As I walked a few more steps to John by my lonesome, I scanned the room, praying I wouldn't recognize anyone. I didn't. A middle-aged couple sitting at a nearby table watched as I closed in on him. My face felt hot.

"Hi," John said, rising from the booth to kiss my cheek. He was dressed almost exactly as he'd been at Penthouse. Khakis and a Sport-Tek polo. "You look very sexy."

I was bundled in my only winter coat. It had once been white, but, especially in this light, it was tinged gray like snowmelt, two sizes too big with a torn zipper—not even remotely sexy. I swiftly removed my jacket to reveal a cotton crop top that accentuated my cleavage and tight jeans. I glanced at the nearby couple to check if they'd clocked the situation. The woman was wearing pearls. The man was in a suit jacket. I felt a rush of shame. Who would be stupid enough to wear this outfit to Morton's?

When I took my seat, John angled his knees toward mine underneath the table. I debated if I should press them together—a move I often used at the club to speed up the flirting process—but with a guaranteed payout, no lap dance to run off to, and no desire to give the impression I was DTF, I wasn't sure what my goal was. Enjoy the dinner?

Hard to do in this new context. What were John and I to look at without the other dancers? What if I wasn't as skilled at conversing as I thought, and we failed to reconnect? Where would I escape to without the dressing room? I was stuck until the check. John did have his Mac-Book Pro on the table, however, which I thought might come in handy if things got desperate. Namely YouTube.

The computer screen had nodded off, but once we settled in, John ran his fingers across the mouse pad and typed in a highly complicated password that he'd written down on a sticky note. "This computer is for you," he told me.

I must have looked taken aback because John quickly added, "I didn't buy it! I got it from my work's dead pile. It still works great, especially for things like Word docs or browsing the web, but it's too outdated for our company's programmers to use. They just sit there in a stack collecting dust."

"Really?" I asked, cautious of what this would entail. What John might expect in return. "Are you sure?"

"Absolutely," John nodded. "I remembered what you said last week about doing your schoolwork at the computer labs." He flashed a big smile. "And, of course, your author dreams."

"That's so kind of you," I said. I was overjoyed. My last computer died over a year ago and I hadn't been in a position to buy a new one. This was nicer than anything I could've bought myself.

"The computer has been reset to its factory settings, so it's ready for you," John said. "But I do want to show you one thing really quick."

I peeked at the screen as John expanded Safari. The Marriott Hotel website was already loaded. Ah, here was the clause of accepting this laptop. I was sure that John's next move was going to be, *Great, now that you've agreed to accept my gift, shall I book us a hotel to have sex after dinner?* I tried to think of a polite way to say no while grazing on table bread.

"Have you ever stayed at a Marriott before?" John asked.

Butter coated my tongue. Salty and rich. I preferred the squeezy kind I grew up on. I shook my head cautiously.

"They just launched a new partnership with Alliance Airlines. You stay at different Marriotts around the globe." He clicked through a slideshow. Every photo was an interior shot, making it impossible to tell which city any given room overlooked. John listed off the countries nonetheless: France, Trinidad, Switzerland, Egypt, Kenya, India, Thailand, China. "I've been trying to find a travel buddy. I haven't had any luck yet. But—" John hesitated. Someone in the back of the restaurant laughed loud enough that we both turned our heads. John was smiling when he returned his gaze to me. "Somebody's having fun."

I exhaled sharply, realizing as I did that I'd been holding my breath. Was this guy about to ask me to leave the country with him? On a first "date"?

"Anyway, we had such a great night last week," John continued. "I was thinking maybe we'd have a lot of fun traveling together."

It was an absurd thing to suggest. That we two—strangers aside from one meeting at a strip club where I had introduced myself as Lola—would travel well together. Something only a man would feel inherently safe enough to say, let alone do. I wanted to ask John if it had ever occurred to him that I was capable of danger. That I might accompany him to a foreign country, weapon of choice packed in my luggage, ready to force him into a beehive of ATMs, where we would move from one to the next, withdrawing the maximum amount at each, only to later kill him, steal his passport, and sell his identity. Crude to think it, maybe, but why would my femininity have protected John from my menace? Why couldn't I ruin his life?

"You don't have any close friends you'd rather go with?" I said amiably.

John frowned. "I don't have many friends." He didn't explain further but I guess he didn't need to. John's alternative life was to be someone cooler. He was paying me to have dinner. He wanted to see the world, but he had no one to go with. John scanned my face for judgment, and in his gaze I saw a deep look of longing. But longing for what? A friend? To feel seen? To be touched? Loved? If I'd felt freaked out by the proposition, now I just felt sorry for him.

"I can't really take off any time from school right now," I said, hoping this would be enough to change the subject.

"There's no rush," John said, earnestly. "Maybe we could do something in the summer. Or in a few years, after you graduate."

In a few years? I wondered. John must've read my mind, because he immediately added, "It was just an idea. I've always wanted to travel the world, and I thought you might want to join because you like to write! Don't all the great authors say travel is inspiring? I had this image of you writing that book about your dad on a balcony in Sintra."

Against myself, I envisioned the scene. Me in front of *my* MacBook Pro, writing about my dad surviving the end of the world via Chef Boyardee. All the while I ate room service and sipped champagne. It had the soft edges of an actual dream.

The waiter arrived with our starter salads. John allowed seven seconds of cheese to be grated onto his plate. I shook my head when offered. "No thanks," I said.

"Not a fan of cheese?" John asked. The waiter was fast. Already halfway across the room, tending to other guests.

"Sometimes," I said. "But I'm trying to eat less dairy."

John told me that dairy upset his stomach. But hard cheese, parmesan or asiago, for example, were usually fine. It was easy to imagine John, fetal in bed, clutching his stomach after a bowl of Rocky Road.

Odd, but John's lactose intolerance humanized him to me. He could be a good human, I told myself. He could mean well.

"I'm sorry," John said, after I'd been quiet for too long. "Maybe talking about my milk belly isn't such good dinner banter."

"Why not discuss diarrhea over a side salad?"

John laughed. "I would bet my life's savings that no one has ever said that before."

I smiled and took a bite of my salad. Crisp lettuce and something unfamiliar (radishes or parsnips) tossed in a champagne vinaigrette. It was a joyful moment. I was not thinking about the money. And then I was thinking about the money. I wanted to know how much John would pay me. I could hardly wait.

"My dad is a little lactose intolerant too," I said. "I have a rule with him: no chocolate milk on road trips." I shook my head. "He never listens to me. Last time we had to make a pit stop at Walmart so he could buy new underwear."

"Your dad is such a character," John said. He dabbed the corners of his lips with a cloth napkin, wiping away a single crumble of bacon. "I'm curious what he looks like. Do you take after him?"

I wavered my palm. "If you look hard enough, yes. But not at a quick glance. I'll show you a picture."

It was a peculiar task. I swiped through my iPhone gallery to search for the right photo of my dad. After asking, I learned John was fifty-five. My father was only fifty-three. I worried that having to look this uncomfortable truth in the face would deter John from wanting to take me out again. So to avoid John solely focusing on my father, I found a picture of my whole family. It was from earlier that year. Chuy had just graduated kindergarten. In the photo I was kneeling, hugging Chuy around the waist, while my parents and my sister stood around us.

I offered John my phone.

"Oh gosh!" John said. "Your screen is a mess. How do you see?"

"I've just gotten used to it," I said with a shrug.

"Why don't you send me that photo?" John said. "We can look at it on my phone."

John opened the message and zoomed in until my dad's face was the size of the whole screen.

"Wow," he said. "This is your dad?"

"That is my dad."

"I didn't expect . . ." John fumbled for a way to put it. My father had tan skin and jet-black hair. A crooked nose. A face people often remarked as handsome. "Where's he from?" John asked. "What's his ethnicity?"

"He's Chicano," I said. "From the San Luis Valley."

John had mentioned growing up in Littleton, a Waspy suburb in Colorado as one of the only Chinese kids in his neighborhood. It seemed possible that we might connect over this. That John might ask how my brown father had found Denver in comparison to the tiny Hispanic town in Southern Colorado. And I could ask John about his Chinese heritage, how that was received by his peers over the years, and how he saw himself in the world now.

To move in this direction, I started telling John that I lived much of my life with two pronunciations of my last name. Goo-tu-lé and Guh-rule. The latter was what my dad referred to as the "white version," which I thought maybe meant *English translation*, but is actually just incorrect.

Back in the '80s my dad enlisted in the army, and once, during basic training, he heard the drill sergeant scream, "GUH-RULE, get down and give me twenty push-ups." My dad didn't respond because he'd never heard his surname pronounced this way before. He wasn't being surly, he told me, he truly didn't associate it with himself. The drill sergeant kept screaming, growing more enraged each time. Eventually he stood before my dad and spit, "GUH-RULE, ARE YOU FUCKING DEAF?" My dad, startled to realize that he was the one being shouted at, explained, "SORRY, SIR. I DIDN'T KNOW YOU WERE TALKING TO ME,

SIR. MY LAST NAME IS GOO-TU-LÉ, SIR." And the drill sergeant said, "I DON'T GIVE A FUCK. YOU'RE GUH-RULE FROM HERE ON OUT." My father was in the military for eight years. So, he was Guh-rule day in and day out for eight years. It became a part of his identity. A way he genuinely introduced himself. He was Guh-rule when he met my mom, and she became a Guh-rule when she married him, and we interchanged both pronunciations in our household growing up. I, too, got stuck in between these two pronunciations. I was Michelle Guh-rule when it was easier for the people around me, even though I knew I was truly Michelle Goo-tu-lé.

Usually John was a studious listener, but he was surprised by this new information and, as a result, preoccupied, zoomed in next on my sister. "She takes after your dad." He turned to face me, eyebrows slanted. "I wouldn't know you were related."

I nodded, a little singed. I'd heard this kind of remark my whole life. The genes I acquired from my Chicano father and my Miracle Whip white mother resulted in thick dark hair, big blue eyes, and high cheekbones, which, according to at least four people, gave me a Mila Kunis vibe. I was frequently asked if I was Russian. My sister was blessed with similar features, just a bit darker in complexion, and was frequently asked if she was Mexican.

I told John this, hoping he might invite me to share more. Again, no dice. As he studied my sister's photo, I wondered if I'd still be sitting there with him if I looked more like her. Even when interacting with men of color in the club (John himself was Chinese American), it was a well-known advantage to be white. We had all been privy to a culture that bombarded us with the message: *Whiteness is desirable*, and the strip club mirrored this with spray-tanned, skinny white girls with blonde hair and big breasts outranking us all. It's so force-fed as to be collectively embarrassing.

Growing up, my sister and I both developed quite early, but we'd absorbed different cultural messages about our bodies and what was acceptable. My sister is recognized as a Chicana woman and, although even within marginalized communities the standards of beauty and desirability are often rooted in European ideals, Latinx women are also sexualized and fetishized for voluptuous curves. (Of the right kind and size, I'll add. Cough, J.Lo, cough.) In the white cultural standards that I felt obliged to, thinness took precedence over everything else. During my adolescence, this ideal was embodied by celebs like Paris Hilton, the Olsen twins, and Lindsay Lohan. (The strip club in 2015 was still on the same bandwagon.) Over the years, it was clear that my and my sister's different understandings of beauty expectations sent us down different paths: I shrank from my body, treating it like an unruly child, something to discipline and correct through restricting diets and exercise before I could even start thinking of myself as desirable, whereas my sister leaned into her sexuality with ease. Tapping into my women's studies lingo, *the male gaze*—both in life and at the strip club—had different rules for women of different ethnicities.

I wanted to ask John about his own experiences. How he saw or did not see himself as a sexual being, how he saw his wealth as a mark of value, how both of those things must've been playing into him paying for my company. And I wanted to know, specifically, why me? Why of all the girls at Penthouse that night did John pick me?

If John was attracted to either my whiteness or my thinness, then my getting paid for my company was a fluke. Instead of taking after my brown dad, I was born fair like my mother, and I was only this thin because heartbreak had ravished my body. God only knew how long the weight would stay off. Meaning, god only knew how long I'd be able to survive off it.

"I know we look different," I said. "But they are my family."

John straightened up, finally coming back to earth, and said, "You have a lovely family." Then he saved the photo and sheepishly added, "I prefer very petite women." A big, stellar smile. "Like *you*."

★

After dinner, John and I waited outside while the valet collected our cars. I was snugly holding my new laptop as he placed his palm on my lower back. A cringe rippled through me, and I ducked beside the portable heater, blaming the cold. At Penthouse I didn't mind this kind of touch, but, here, where we were not limited to a lap dance cubicle, and no bouncers were around to say, *Hey, no groping, buddy,* where there were no rules and therefore anything was possible, I felt apprehensive of what'd come next.

"You know," John said, shyly. "If you keep spending time with me, you wouldn't have to work at the club anymore."

"Spending time?" I asked, not that naive.

"Yes. Have dinner with me again next week?"

"*Just* dinner?" I asked, straightening up.

"Just dinner," he said. "But your cell phone screen is a little cracked, so maybe we could go to a repair shop and have that fixed first. Or we can get you a newer iPhone."

This was a kind characterization of my phone, but I was not fooled by his generosity. What would a phone screen cost me in the fine print? A French kiss? I didn't know if I wanted to kiss John more or less than I wanted glass splinters in my thumbs. Though, when I got over myself, what did a peck even mean to me? Once, during a friend's nineteenth birthday party, I sat in a Hummer limo full of lesbians and made out with eight women. Why be finicky now when so much was at stake?

"I think screen repair would be best," I said. "I'm still paying this iPhone off. I've got like $200 left on it. You really don't mind?"

John shook his head and said, "It's my pleasure."

"Speaking of," John continued and reached into his coat and handed me a bank envelope. "There's $500 in there," he said. "Does that seem fair?"

"Absolutely," I said and pocketed the cash. It would've been difficult to make the same amount at Penthouse. Fifteen lap dances between god knows how many men. I felt a wash of relief.

I expected John to try and kiss me then—and I would've allowed it—but in what could only be divine intervention I heard my Honda approaching from around the block.

"Don't say anything about my car," I said.

John stayed silent until the valet had delivered both of our vehicles to the curb. His Lexus was gold. It sparkled under the lampposts. The tires were easily worth more than my entire Honda.

"Maybe we should think about getting you a new car," John said, as he pulled out his wallet, fishing for cash to tip the valet. "A Lexus like mine. We'd write it into a contract, though, so you don't take the car and leave."

I looked at the boy and felt ashamed. For some reason, I couldn't bear the idea of this kid thinking I would do such a thing. I tried silently to explain: *Perhaps John assumes that someone who would accept his dinner-for-cash invitations wants money for the same flashy reasons he does—but he's mistaken. I'm just a broke girl with half a degree and the ugliest car in the whole world. What I want—what I really, truly want—is to reach the starting line of my own life.*

The valet gave me a small, kind smile. "Thank you, sir," he said to John and hurried off.

★

Driving home, I had a heart-to-heart with myself. John was saying just dinner and just time together, but I knew that was bullshit.

My dad was right. John was leaving breadcrumbs—the MacBook, the palm on my lower back, the *I'd rather be surprised*—and it all led to sex.

John wanted a sugar baby.

Like most women, I lived my whole life subliminally receiving the message: *When all else fails, your body can be used for bread.* All the same,

I knew if I accepted this deal, the world would label me a whore until the day I died, and then it would be engraved on my tombstone. I'd gotten the gist of this as a stripper, and I once had a friend, Lila, with an in-home massage business that included happy endings. Word of Lila's job quickly spread around our circle, and I'd gone to party after party where I overheard people (straight men and lesbians alike) talk about the unfortunate "waste of a beautiful girl." Lila, they all seemed to agree, was now un-dateable—though not to be confused with un-fuckable—and disgusting.

Remembering this, I couldn't stop thinking about that statement: *waste of a beautiful girl*. It was familiar to me because men would sometimes say this when I mentioned being gay.

I was quickly learning how sex work was made even more complex for Lila and me because we identified as femme lesbians. On the one hand, being femme allowed us a privileged position. Straight men found our look conventionally attractive, and we could hide our sexual identities quite easily, which was something the queer community already felt weary of. We lacked the experience of being ostracized from the general public. Something a queer-presenting person couldn't avoid. I noticed the differences in the ways I was treated, of course, when I was by myself inconspicuous in public or with my girlfriends, kissing and holding hands. But I'd also experienced homophobia as a femme person by taking people by surprise when I outed myself. Straight men and women alike. Men could feel rejected, while some women had felt betrayed, or allegedly afraid that I was interested in them simply because I was queer. Experiences I wished were more acknowledged as their own challenges for cis femmes.

Prior to ever being sex workers, Lila and I had related over feeling ostracized by the queer community by failing to be gold stars (a girl who's never had sex with a cis man), as though men specifically had done some damage to our bodies that we could never undo (everyone knows that old loose vagina narrative). In addition to our femininity, people often perceived our having slept with a man as evidence that our queerness was not queer enough or that we weren't actually gay at all—that femmes were just going through a phase—but I knew it would be considered deplorable to sleep with one for money: an additional moral qualm. I'd seen it myself when I stripped my clothes off as a dancer and saw it again as Lila had been made party fodder for her business. To be a sex worker was just another circumstance in which our queerness and our value felt up for debate.

All that outside noise to consider, and it didn't even touch on the way *I* felt about this decision! My stomach churned at the idea of John, a man twice my age whom I wasn't emotionally or sexually attracted to, touching me. His hands on my body, or even his tongue in my mouth. Two years older than my dad.

I cringed, yet I couldn't shake the feeling that John, and this cash-in-exchange-for-*whatever* offer, was my *fate*. I just couldn't ignore the serendipitous road that led to these "dinner" offers: heartbreak, weight loss through depression, Diamond's rejection, Penthouse's "sure," our first $400 meeting. This may not seem star-crossed, but my very existence evolved from what looked, to the uninspired eye, like a series of unfortunate events.

When my dad was twenty-three, he'd been working at the nearest Kmart (thirty miles away from San Luis), sleeping on his sister's couch, and cruising around in a piece-of-shit Pontiac. All this changed after he was arrested for cheating a Pac-Man game with a quarter/superglue/string contraption in the town's one and only gas station/pizza place/small grocery. He was charged with petty theft and premeditation to commit a crime thanks to the officer finding a second rigged quarter in his pocket. In what could only be conceivable in a micro-town in 1985 with a population of under eight hundred people, the judge presented my dad with two options: jail or the army. My dad said he chose the military because it sounded like a one-way ticket to a better life. Within weeks he was on his first-ever flight out to Virginia.

Soon after settling into the barracks, my dad visited Busch Gardens, a local amusement park, where his urethra got pinched while he was riding a roller coaster called the Big Bad Wolf. An injury that required emergency surgery.

Meanwhile, my mother, a home health nurse, was tending to a patient who'd been admitted to the same hospital. During a visit, my mom spotted my dad in the TV room, bingeing daytime soaps. Thinking he looked sexy in his open-back gown, she waltzed right up to him and asked, "Do you live here, handsome?" Five years and two accidental pregnancies later, I was born, with the destiny gene tucked neatly inside my DNA.

I considered telling John this over our next dinner but decided against it. I knew that to a wealthy man—the kind of person who associates fate and good fortune with clear-cut *positive* things: an acceptance to an esteemed university, or to a highly competitive, unpaid internship, or winning the lottery—it'd sound insane.

I was not insane.

★

When I arrived back at the apartment, I was still thinking about John's offer, specifically the unmentioned aspects. While I had a pretty good idea of what sugar babying entailed on a macro level, I knew little about the small intricacies of the job. Was sex *always* part of these deals? How much sex? How gross would the sex be? What was the average amount of money one could make? Where should I keep said money? What about taxes? Particularly, how to avoid them. I had no one in the real world to ask except maybe Portia, but her night with a Bronco was a one-off kind of thing. Once inside, I plopped down next to Chuy on the couch, gave him instructions to lower the TV volume and leave me alone because I was doing "research" for my new job (*Congratulations for your new job, Auntie!*), then I got to googling.

I opened an incognito window on my new laptop in case John or The Government was watching and typed: *What's it like being a sugar baby?* The most useful answers were tucked away in a Reddit thread. *New to the sugar bowl, what do I need to know?*

Gingerbaby94 posted: *Sex is required. The price will be decided by you and your sugar daddy, often abbreviated as SD.*

NewYorkBabe wrote: *The sex could be good or bad, depending on how eager your SD is to please you.*

My stomach soured at the line. I didn't want *good* sex with John. I prayed for sex that felt like nothing. Boring, even. I wanted to fully dissociate during the sex, and then, somehow, I wanted to not hate myself after. If that were all possible, then I could do it. Probably.

Sugarsugar92 knew a lot about finances. *Get a safe and start buying things with cash. Don't put your money in a bank, but if you must, never, ever deposit more than $10,000 at once or the banks report it to the IRS.* And, *Find out how much money your SD makes per year!! This can be salary, stock market, real estate, etc. But make sure he can afford you!!*

The sugar babies of Reddit also maintained that I had no obligation to tell anyone about my arrangement, but because I'd implode if I kept it a secret from the whole world, I would tell my family.

The most obvious reason was that I lived with my mother. Though, even if I had my own apartment I still would've shared. My family had few moral qualms. Weeks earlier, my cousin had gone to prison for dealing narcotics out of a stolen car, armed with an unregistered weapon. "He's just trying to survive," I heard my mom say to her sister over the phone. I gave her the thumbs up. Drugs, addiction, dealing, robbery, prison, were all things I had been raised around. While they were never in our home, there was always a cousin or an uncle in some kind of trouble on both sides of my lineage. Poor-people crimes. Desperate-for-a-better-life crimes. I-didn't-know-what-else-to-do crimes. If I decided to do this—sugar babying to survive while putting myself through college—it would not be an issue.

Mostly, I didn't want anyone outside of my family to find out about John. To maintain a good reputation in the world, sugaring would need to stay off my public résumé, and the only way to guarantee my secret's safety was to never tell a non-Gurule.

I opened a new note in my phone and wrote out my SB laws:

1.) My immediate family are the only ones who will ever know.
2.) I will be responsible, smart, and sly and only spend money on invisible things like student loans.
3.) Anything I ever write about John will be called fiction.

And then, the most important rule, the one that would prove to be the most difficult to hold myself accountable to:

4.) If it ever feels unbearable, or like too much, or like it's ruining my life, I will quit.

Satisfied, I took a plunge and texted:
Thank you again for dinner. Same time next week? ;)

3

I'm Her Daddy

My father refused to splurge on cable TV until I was in high school. "Why pay for extra channels," he would ask, "when all the good shit is free?" This catchphrase disappeared when he was introduced to Comcast's treasure trove in the electronics section of Walmart. It took seven minutes of E!'s *The Girls Next Door* for him to crack, and a week later, the two of us were on our couch watching Hugh Hefner's three Playgirls (Bridget Marquardt, Kendra Wilkinson, and Holly Madison) celebrate his eightieth birthday.

The Girls Next Door granted America insight into the world of *spending time* with older men for *undisclosed perks*. Though it looked pretty good to me—so much wealth and free time—the consensus was that Hugh's girls were idiotic, trashy sexpots. Still, they were the only sugar babies I knew of, so when, four weeks into my weekly paid dinners with John, I explained the situation to my dad, this trio came to mind. "John," I told him, "is like my personal Hugh Hefner."

We were at the Aurora Mall with my sister, Bianca. Posted along the perimeter booth of the Kidz Corral. Chuy was out of earshot, breaking into an imaginary space dimension in a rocket ship.

"Well, I'll be damned, Shell," my dad said. "So, you're a prostitute?"

"She's not a prostitute! She's a *sugar baby*," Bianca snapped, before slurping from the lemonade we were sharing between the four of us.

I smiled, feeling protected, though, technically, our dad wasn't wrong. If my suspicions were correct, John was after sex for hire. Still, I much preferred calling it sugar babying. The words felt softer. As if the perceived immorality of selling one's body could be bargained with. Sex with one man once per week. How bad was that?

My dad wrestled the lemonade from my sister's paw and sucked the straw before asking, "What's the difference between a sugar baby and prostitute?"

"Jesus Christ," my sister said. On a good day Bianca had about as much patience in her body as a fire alarm. With my dad, she had even less.

"Sugaring is much more specific," I said. "Prostitution is more of a broad-brush term. And John will be paying for *my company*," I threw up air quotes. "Not sex."

"But that's a part of it?" my dad asked.

"According to Reddit, yep," I said.

"But," my sister added, "Shell hasn't even kissed him yet."

"I've been on high alert for signs that it's coming," I said, "but John is very prudish." One evening while sweeping shreds of pita through a saucer of hummus, our knuckles accidentally grazed. John jolted his hand back, yelling, "Oops! Sorry!" The following week, John chauffeured me to REI to buy me extravagant snow boots after I kept showing up in impractical winter shoes, and when I asked if he enjoyed hiking, he said, "I don't do much other than work." I studied him at the cash register. John radiated zero sexual energy. Looking back, his remark at the strip club—the one implying he wanted to be surprised (presumably when he saw my vagina?)—felt like something he'd said in a burst of uncharacteristic courage. "Sex has never once been mentioned," I said. "I might've found myself a sugar daddy in dire need of *friendship*."

My dad furrowed his brow and tilted his chin toward his chest. "No way," he said, then made a fart noise with his mouth. "Like I told you before. Not even rich people pay for friendship. John's just easing you in. Showing you he's a nice guy, getting you used to the perks, so when he finally gains the courage to ask you for *you-know-what*, you're too attached to the cash to turn it down."

My sister nodded. "Dad's right."

I frowned. Unwilling to release at least the possibility of a nonsexual exchange. "You don't know this guy," I said. "He's very lonely." I then told them about our latest meeting, two days earlier.

While John and I slurped spaghetti at a joint owned by John Elway, we chatted about the most stressful spring of my life.

"It all began smack dab in the middle of my third-grade year," I'd begun. "When I was eight years old. My dad and I were squished onto the seat of an old riding mower, cutting our backyard grass in Virginia. The pungent stench of starter fluid hung in the air."

"I love the sensory details," John said, a fleck of marinara sauce on his chin.

I loved when John praised me. Any stock compliment and my ego could swell like an air balloon to carry us across the whole meal.

"So, out of the blue, my dad says that he's bored of Virginia and desperate to leave. I stalled the machine, and asked, 'Huh?'

Then he said, 'Shell, we're moving to Colorado.'"

At eight years old, I knew three facts about Colorado: my dad was from there, everyone spoke Spanish, and everyone lived on ranches. The latter two were based on our Gurule family visits.

"So, I asked him, 'What's Goldie think?' And he said, 'Your mom doesn't know yet. You're the first person I'm telling.'"

"Oh my god!" John said, grinning. "You've got to be joking!"

"Nope," I said, slurping a bite of spaghetti. My dad had told me, "I'm going to put the house up for sale in the next month, and then hopefully we'll be in Denver by August so you guys can start school out there."

I explained to John that while I worried about my ability to adjust to farm life, my real concern lay with my mom. Being only a phone call away from scarfing down foot-longs at Gus's Hot Dog King with one of her four sisters or parents—all of whom lived within a five-mile radius of one another—was her idea of the perfect life.

"Your mom's favorite love language must be quality time!" John said, playfully referring to our first conversation at Penthouse.

"Yeah," I said. "But also, food. Specifically, takeout. Which I guess counts as gifts?" I told John that my mother, like my dad, experienced food insecurity as a kid. My mom once told me that when she was young, a few cans of tuna went missing from her family's cabinet—clearly one of the seven children had eaten them, but none would admit guilt. Her parents, my grandparents, were furious. The loss, to them, was significant. They couldn't stand that someone's gluttony would cost everyone else a meal, so my grandparents made the kids line up and drink salt water so they each would vomit, exposing the culprit.

"I think takeout must make my mom feel safe," I said to John, channeling my inner self-work guru. "Even if she's going into debt over it, for her, fast food or takeout exemplifies upward mobility, and it's got to feel good to have enough to eat."

"Huh," he said, pondering all this. "Interesting."

How could I explain this calculation to John? A man who had never gone hungry a day in his life. A guy who was currently slipping me $500 over this four-star dinner with no sweat off his back. The truth is I could've said a lot of things. How for years my mom worked for minimum wage at Pizza Hut during the school year and at a Virginia McDonald's in the summer, because this was the way she was able to keep one toe in Newport News after we moved West. Or the fact that after her shifts, she'd been able to feed our whole family dinner with leftovers from the Pizza Hut lunch buffet or employee comped and discounted meals from McDonald's.

I tried to appeal to pathos. "When I was in elementary school, my mom would throw my class a pizza party every year while she worked at Pizza Hut," I said. "Her manager, this guy named Waldo, really loved my mom, so he'd give her the pizzas for free." I thought about the way my mom would arrive at my classrooms dressed in her Pizza Hut uniform, carrying pies in insulated delivery bags, a glowing smile on her face. My classmates would cheer and run up to hug her. Sometimes they'd even hug or thank me. My mom and I were proud in those moments. Sometimes children are cruel, and sometimes children are the only people who can appreciate what we have to offer.

"Well, that was a very nice thing of her to do with the resources she had," John said, sounding like a textbook. "Carry on with your other story."

"Well anyway," I said, trying to remember where I left off. I went into some cheap joke about how I knew Denver would be too rural for fast-food joints, and my mom would have to establish friendships that weren't based on being blood related. Gauging from my dad's inability to manage this in Virginia, I assumed this was impossible for adults. I darted inside to warn my mother, hoping she could stop the move.

"GOLDIE!"

She was on the couch, watching TV.

"Dad says we're moving to Colorado."

"No, we aren't, Michelle." She reserved my name for occasions of annoyance. I'd interrupted her daily afternoon news recap. "I haven't heard anything about that."

"I know you haven't," I said, pressing a finger to my forehead. "That's why *I'm telling you*."

"Two weeks later," I told John, "my mom was slumped across the Barbie comforter on my bed asking, 'Shell, should I divorce your daddy?'"

John threw his head back, laughing. "Oh, no! But you were so young! What'd you say?"

"I said, 'Yes, leave him!'" I'd worked out the best solution for everyone. Unlike the rest of us, my father had no attachment to Virginia. "I told her, 'Dad can leave, and we can live in Grandma's spare bedrooms. Bianca and I will have to share a bed, and we'll probably only get to visit Dad during summer breaks, but these are inconveniences I can accept.'"

John smiled. "You were so mature."

It mirrored what my mother had said. "It's like I'm talking to a grown-up."

"It's like you're talking to a guidance counselor," I'd corrected, patting her on the leg.

"But," I said to John, "in spite of all my reassurances that life as a single mother was *the* thing to do, my mom backpedaled out of any talk of divorce and kept our family together for as long as she could. Hence her working at Pizza Hut in Denver during school months and McDonald's in Virginia in the summers so my sister and I could still see her family." I felt a little somber, as John laughed, realizing that I'd never fully acknowledged how much McDonald's had played a role in her well- being. But no time to get sentimental now, I was on the clock.

John smiled, looked at me, and said, "Your family is so interesting. I hope this story makes it into your book." I'll admit that it pleased me when John spoke of this book as being both underway and bound for success. Of course, all I really had was my running-quotes log, little piles of notes, a few fleshed out stories, and no clear direction. The only thing I'd had with any substance to it was the writing I'd begun about these evenings with John, but that was a dead-end project. This secret was going to the grave with me.

I sipped from my water. "Maybe."

John paused for a moment, twirling his fork on the plate. "Did your mommy ever make any friends?"

"No," I said. "Not really."

"I can sympathize with that." John sighed. He placed his fork on his dish and looked at me. "Do you consider us friends?" he asked, then giggled, clearly embarrassed by the vulnerability of the question.

At Penthouse I often judged wealthy men for how lonely they were. In moments, it was the only thing that made me feel powerful in our stripper-patron dynamic. Men would arrive in suits after work with freshly shorn hair, stinking of disposable income. For them, money was a nonissue, so they'd buy their ten-dollar wristband and tally up forty-dollar dances like it were nothing, while I would work hard at teasing them, praying my body might get them to stay for another song. I would watch these men close their eyes and lose track of time. What really got them was how softly I touched their shoulders, how close I was willing to put my body to their face, how much I let them believe they had *bought* me. Not just a moment with a dancer, or three songs out of my ten-hour shift, but that they had bought an authentic sexual connection. For me, stripping was so much more than selling nudity; it was selling the narrative that money made these men irresistible. I deeply opposed the idea, but I was flat broke, so I'd hungrily take their one hundred dollars, tuck it away, and watch them disappear into the night, reassured that their wealth really gave them power over other people, over us girls, over me.

But there was something sweet about John. His innocence. Or his desire to know me in a way that, even given our dynamic, did not feel exclusively correlated to wanting to fuck me or wanting me to affirm his clout. And while I'd been blessed with friendships my whole life, a rabbit hole of possibility had opened before me. One that promised betterment in the form of income. But one that sprouted a secret, taller and wider each week, wedging its way between me and everyone else.

Everyone except him.

When I overlooked the sexual obligation I feared was coming, this secret together felt happy. Like whatever this was, *was* friendship. It was weird, but it suited us.

"Yes," I'd said to John, nodding. "I do consider us friends."

★

"Holy smokes," my dad said back at the mall. "You tell John all our business?"

"Yeah," I said. "You're my favorite thing to talk about."

My dad smiled, flattered.

The mall was packed with students on winter break. Mariah Carey's "All I Want for Christmas Is You" played over the loudspeaker. We three sang along. My dad, known for his dramatic flair, howled the chorus.

My nephew recognized the rendition as my dad's, and yelled from afar, "Nice pipes, Grandpa!" Then he begged us to watch him jump off the foam rings of Saturn. Chuy stumbled on the landing, shook his fist at the sky, then made us watch him again. Bianca sighed, said, "I gotta pee," and left.

When she disappeared below the bathroom signs, my dad turned to me and said, "Whether John is lonely or not, whatever you're doing sure sounds like prostitution to me." He burped, then added, "Tomato, tomahto."

I shrugged. "Well, what do you want for Christmas?" I said. "John is footing the bill. He said I can buy you all gifts."

My own list was short but extravagant. When John asked me this same question, I'd considered asking for student loan relief, but that felt too broad, too deep, too gleaming a need. So, I started small—and with a tiny white lie. "Well, I think I have a cavity," I'd said (not a mouthful of them). "It might be nice to visit a dentist."

"Go have it filled. Get a cleaning. X-rays. The whole shebang. I'll cover the costs," John said. "But it's not very Christmasy, so at least get some fun things from the mall too." This was a festive offer, but I didn't want clothes from The Gap. I wanted every penny John was willing to spend put toward the dental bill that had far surpassed my gross underestimation.

I'd gone to the dentist almost as soon as John said the word. Dr. Hans, a middle-aged, bald, lanky man, settled into his chair and fastened my X-rays to the backlit board. "It's not going to be good," I said, confidently. I wanted him to understand that I was not clueless, just poor. "I'm guessing ten cavities. At least."

"You?" Dr. Hans said and laughed like he knew everything about me. I was young and pretty and white and wearing new $500 REI boots. I looked like a girl who'd never gone a day in her life without dental insurance. Someone who probably even flossed regularly, owned a water pick, but the way I looked was deceptive. "I highly doubt that."

I stared up at a fluorescent light cover of a beachy scene. White sand, blue water, and palm trees. It was not at all soothing as Dr. Hans hemmed and hawed and assessed my X-rays for what seemed like a long time. Finally, he heaved a sigh.

"How many?" I said, craning my neck.

"Fourteen." Dr. Hans trailed his pen along the transparencies to show me each cavity. All the molars were fucked. Upper, lower, right, and even my good candy eaters on the left. Two teeth, my right cuspid and the third molar on the lower left, were so far gone that I needed to have them crowned.

Dr. Hans's tone shifted serious as he realized he had miscalculated me. "We'll do what we can, focusing on the worst ones first. The two that need crowns. It'll be pricey," he said, gravely. He was worried I'd decline the procedures, as some other clients likely did because they couldn't afford care. "But if we don't fix them now, you'll have bigger problems down the road."

"How much?" I asked.

"We can sign you up for a Comfort Dental credit card if you need help," he said.

"How much?"

The number was both sharp and round and might as well have been infinite: *$5,800.*

I dragged my tongue along my cratered teeth and wondered how other people survived this life. How was it possible that families had summer homes, paid $8,000 vet bills, had lavish weddings, or could do all of the above without batting an eyelash? Who were the people who had even squirrelled enough away to afford something like this? I cried right there in the dental chair. Great big heaping sobs. An assistant came in and offered me a box of tissues. She blinked her big brown eyes at me and said sometimes life unspools before you and all you have are your own two hands to put it back together.

I wondered if this was a premonition. If everyone—me, Dr. Hans, and the assistant—understood what was coming. That I had asked for this visit as a Christmas gift from a man who, as coy as he played, likely had his own ask of me. It felt as clear-cut as an equation. I could compromise access to my body for the greater good of my body. Tit for tat. I licked my teeth. It could be worth it.

And if I was wrong? If John was truly just my friend, well, whatever his Christmas limit didn't cover I'd put on the Comfort Dental credit line. And then I would tally how many dinners it would take to pay it off.

"Presents for us too?" my dad asked now at the mall. "It's like you've won the lottery."

When I'd asked Bianca what she wanted for Christmas, she said, "A dresser from IKEA." I told her that the rear doors on my car don't open, so I couldn't get a dresser home.

"What's John drive?" she'd asked.

"A Lexus. But he's not coming over to Mom's house. Ever," I said. "I'll get you a gift card."

My dad looked at me quizzically and said, "Why's John buying us presents? We're not all gonna have to kiss him, are we?"

I laughed. "John feels sorry for you guys for being so broke. And he told me that he feels like he knows you from my stories. You're his friends too."

"Sounds like bullshit to me," my dad said. "But you can tell *my friend* to get me a power drill."

Chuy was hogging a slide, so I yelled at him to play nice. He ignored me until he caught sight of my dad shaking the Hot-Dog-on-a-Stick cup. *Uh-oh.* The thought registered on Chuy's face as clear as a slot machine landing on jackpot. Except this was the reverse. The cup was almost empty. He needed a final sip.

My nephew surrendered the slide, ran to us—his black hair slick with sweat—and asked for a drink. "No backwashing," I said. I studied my nephew's face as he gulped and swallowed, gulped and swallowed. Chuy's daddy is from Mexico and the oldest in a series of siblings who look like quintuplets. With genes that strong it was a total wonder that baby Chuy bloomed into a mini replica of my sister. It's like he doesn't even have a father. Like his life came only from the egg.

A frosted-blonde woman plopped down a seat over and smiled knowingly at the three of us. To avoid comment I turned back to my nephew.

"That's enough." I tried to pull the cup away from Chuy, but he sank his teeth into the straw. "Drop it," I growled. He released, frowned at me, then ran off again.

The woman nodded toward Chuy. "He looks just like the two of you," she said, moving her eyes between me and my dad.

People often assume I'm in a romantic relationship with my father. This is grossly amplified when my nephew is present. I imagine the calculation goes as follows: *This brown man and this brown little boy and this white woman. Pretty big age gap between the couple. Probably daddy issues.*

"That's because he's my grandson and her nephew," my dad said, then stiffly patted my shoulder. "This is my daughter."

The woman's face flushed. "I thought . . ."

"Happens all the time," he said.

My dad was not being overzealous with his words. It'd been happening my whole life. In fact, the first time I can remember hearing the words "sugar daddy" was after my dad and I had been misidentified as a pair of lovers in a Lowe's parking lot when I was nine.

I loved running errands with my dad, especially trips to Lowe's, which had a food truck out front that lured its patrons with mounds of grilled onions. We Gurules never left the hardware store without ordering a six-inch Philly cheesesteak. This time, though, the grill chef shot us a nasty look, and asked me in a low voice, like the question was a secret, "Is that your boyfriend?"

To be fair, it wasn't totally his fault. Beyond being pasty, thanks to my fast-food diet and supreme stress levels, even as a fourth grader, I was 5'1" and had full A cups (teetering on Bs). My breasts had come in quick, starting out as two hard little knots on my chubby chest. My parents had even taken me to the doctor, worried they were cancerous tumors. My pediatrician assured them that I was cancer free but definitely overweight—a warning my family disregarded, preferring the term *big-boned*. I couldn't explain all of this, so I snapped, "No!" then snatched our sandwich and secretly flipped the guy off in my head.

Afterward, my dad and I sat in the cab of his truck, passing the cheesesteak between us. Fed up with having to explain our relationship to the world, we discussed ways to make it clear that we weren't dating. "What if I get a shirt with a big arrow that says, 'I'm her daddy?'" he suggested. But as soon as he said it, he saw the obvious flaw. "Oh shit, I couldn't do that. They'll think I mean *sugar daddy*."

He didn't have to explain the meaning of the term, so I must've already been familiar. No surprise there. I was pop cultured. Instead of an easily misconstrued T-shirt, my dad and I came up with a strategy to use the words "father" and "daughter" around each other as much as possible. As in, "Oh daughter, what do you think we should get your white-ass mom for her birthday?" or "Father, can you believe that I'm the tallest and biggest-boned kid in my fourth-grade class?"

At the mall, I reminded my dad of the T-shirt plan from way back when.

"It seems sort of ironic now," I said.

Slurping nothing but melted ice, my dad said, "People always think we're dating because I look so youthful and handsome, Shell. They think I'm in my twenties."

"They really don't," I said. "What about Bianca? You two have never been mistaken for lovers." It was sort of relieving to think about this. As a child, people often mistook me for my father's girlfriend because he was brown and I was white, sure, but also because I was large for my age. I had intuited, even as a child, this misunderstanding as something wrong with *me*. At school, I was surrounded by rail-thin classmates, while my body was overly tall, developed, and had curves that felt way too womanly. I was never anyone's childhood crush, and I couldn't have a play boyfriend or girlfriend in elementary or middle school because it would have felt inappropriate. I was too developed, too mature. I hated my body. Even more so, I hated the way the world interacted with my body.

"Let me ask you something," my dad said now. "Do you feel more embarrassed when people think you're dating John or when people think you're dating me?"

With John there were no misinterpretations. People pegged the situation from a mile away. That transparency was shameful in its own way, but it spoke positively to my nine-year-old self, who never believed she would blossom into someone hot, let alone someone hot enough to be paid for her company. Turns out I was more ashamed of people thinking I was unattractive than people thinking I was a slut.

My dad wasn't asking about all that, however. He wanted to know with whom, on a surface level, it was less humiliating to be romantically linked. "Less embarrassed with you, I guess."

"Exactly," he said. "Because your papa is handsome."

I checked to see if the woman beside me was eavesdropping. The only thing worse than her thinking I was banging my father was her hearing my father ask if he were hotter than my sugar daddy. Her face held a residual pink flush of embarrassment. I wanted to say again, *It's no big deal. It really happens all the time.*

I had, then, an *Aha!* moment like a cartoon piano falling on me from the sky. I understood that all those mortifying experiences as a kid had been the Universe grooming me for meeting John. I'd spent years of my life ignoring glares from misinformed know-it-alls. I'd been answering the same question—*Isn't she a little too young for you, sir?*—for nearly two decades. I'd been branded as a woman dating men twice her age so often that it was embedded into my identity. If I thought of it this way, it made all those terrible feelings as a kid have purpose. It made them helpful to my present situation. If I thought of it this way, I felt sure that I was exactly where I was meant to be.

I became the center of gravity. My sister came back from the restroom, my nephew returned to us from outer space, my father zipped up his jacket and turned to face me.

It was undeniable to me. Sugaring was my destiny!

4

First Base at the Cheesecake Factory

*B**e aggressive.** Be patient. Set your expectations high, but not too high.* I was in the dressing room of Penthouse, scrolling through blogs on seekingarrangements.com. This was the site's advice for how to make one's online profile stand out from the crowd. Learning about the process was exhausting. How many emails did "income-cleared daddies" click through before picking a girl? How many messages did babies send to snag a date? How was any bitch supposed to stand out with a few photos and a tight word limit?

I wasn't on the site to make a profile. I was searching for insider answers to what sex with a sugar daddy might be like. That, or a listicle about how to disassociate during the sex. I had gone to Reddit first and skimmed through vague responses to the question *What's it like to sleep with your SD?* One person wrote, *Your body is his wonderland!* Another said, *You are someone he can explore his fantasies with.* This made me queasy. I prayed that John's fantasies were vanilla—with sprinkles at most.

While I would have never contemplated John's fantasies willingly, they had been heavy on my mind since last night. After my fifth lucrative and sexless meal with him, I arrived home with paper carryout bags dangling from my fingers. Ever since I told John that food was my mom's love language, he suggested that I order to-go meals for my family. Two entrées and two desserts. "As a thank you," he'd said, never clarifying for what.

My family had been dispersed across the apartment's nine hundred square feet, but after they'd heard my keys jingling in the door, they ran to greet me in the kitchen. "What'd you get us?" they yelled over one another. "What'd you get us?"

My mom scooched behind me to shuffle through our utensil drawer, which contained a sea of cellophane-wrapped plasticware. She divvied out forks for the entrées and sporks for dessert. The dishes were packaged in thick-bottomed black plastic and secured with clear lids, which we'd upcycle as Tupperware for the next several years.

"Roast beef and mashed potatoes with gravy," I announced.

A hand tugged it out of my grip. Before it even hit the counter, the lid was off and all three forks ravaged the meat.

"What else, what else?" my sister said with a full mouth.

My hand plunged into the bag and reappeared with another container. I felt like a magician pulling rabbits from a hat. My family's admiring *oohs* and *ahhs* added to the effect.

"Chicken strips and french fries. I had to order this off the kid's menu because they didn't have an adult version," I said. "They didn't include any ketchup."

"That's okay. We have some," my nephew said, skipping to the living room/my bedroom where McDonald's sauce packets were strewn across the coffee table. "Grandma took me after school."

Though I soaked it up as a kid, my mom's love of "gifting" McDonald's had been a big tension between us ever since I watched *Super Size Me* when I was twelve. Early puberty had led me to a fraught relationship with my body, and by the time I watched filmmaker Morgan Spurlock clock his thirty-day weight gain at twenty-four pounds, I had already been "dieting" for two years, by which I mean ordering off Taco Bell's Fresco menu or simply not eating—the only two ways I understood might make my body smaller. I cried when I saw Spurlock shirtless on the scale, sure that my own body was a result of my family's obsession with fast food. Of course, it was dramatic that Spurlock consumed only McDonald's and Coca-Cola products (and a lot of alcohol) for thirty days but, minus the liquor, my family's diet was not far off. Even worse, Spurlock's health had seemed to deteriorate. His cholesterol had increased, and his risk of heart disease ostensibly doubled. My mom already took a handful of prescriptions a day for these exact issues. Terrified, I'd stormed into my mom's room, demanding an explanation for feeding both of us trans fats. "We eat perfectly fine," my mom said. "And believe me, it's better than being hungry." A line I could never really argue with.

Although pricier, I suspected the food I was supplying from my dates was not much healthier than Mickey D's, so I made a small suggestion over the sounds of their feast. "Hey! Let's treat my dinners with John like an indulgence for all of us, once a week! What do you say?"

My sister rolled her eyes. "We don't all wanna be skinny like you, bitch."

My mom snapped her fingers appreciatively, slam-poetry style, then asked, "What'd you bring for dessert?"

"Tiramisu and gingerbread toffee cake."

"Nasty," my sister said.

I scowled. "Maybe you should get your own sugar daddy and have *him* buy us desserts."

"Damn, relax. I'm just saying, there were probably better options."

"How would you know? You've never been to a five-star restaurant in your life."

"I'll have some of both," my nephew said, shoving in. Tirami-what? If sugar was the primary ingredient, it was a yes for him. Chuy licked a dollop of whipped cream from his fingertips. "Yum!"

I raised an eyebrow at my sister.

After they'd finished, I told them to thank John. This was our ritual. I demanded that my family show gratitude, so the Universe knew that we wanted the takeout to continue.

"Thank you, John!" my mom and sister said into the room.

"Extra big thank you, John!" my nephew said, a whipped-cream mustache on his upper lip. "For the best cake I've ever tasted."

I sent John a message. *They're eating dinner now. They love it.* <3

He texted back: *I'm so glad I can make you and your loved ones happy. Thanks for hanging out with me tonight. You're so much fun!*

I slipped back into my mom's room and uncovered my safe, which I hid on her closet shelf in case of intruders. The lock had broken a few weeks earlier, but I still preferred it here over a bank, where the IRS couldn't see it. I unfolded the white envelope John gave me and counted the hundred-dollar bills. *One, two, three, four, five.* I closed the lid, fishing a sugary crumble from between my back molars. It tasted expensive.

I had spent much of the night with my stomach in ropes wondering how to break the news about my dental bill to John. My plan was to tell him over appetizers that the cost was ginormous, but there were credit options to cover whatever my Christmas gift didn't. When I couldn't manage the courage, I tried again during dinner, then dessert, then in the parking lot. All to no avail. I knew the only way I'd manage was via text.

Thank you for hanging out! I had a great time! I wrote back. Then a second message: *I meant to tell you about my dental visit over dinner, but I was too embarrassed. (A series of grimacing faces.) I have fourteen cavities. I need two crowns and twelve regular fillings. I know you probably weren't expecting this . . . I wasn't either,* I lied. *It's super expensive. (Grimacing face, crying face.)*

John replied quickly: *Oh wow! Your poor mouth!! I'm sure those had to have been hurting you for a while. Ouchie!* ☹ *I would like to cover the bill, regardless of the cost. You make my life so much better, I want to make your life better too!*

I was in utter disbelief. How was this spectacular thing happening to me? I had lived the last seven years tolerating toothaches. *Years.* Every semester of college I'd attended, every final I took, every kiss I'd shared since high school. Every single one of Chuy's birthday cakes were experienced through gray dull pain. And soon it would be healed. The receptionist helped me book biweekly appointments for the next four months. Dr. Hans recommended that we do the crowns first, which would take two visits each. They would have to drill, take impressions, and make temporary crowns before they could cement the permanent ones. After that, each section of my mouth would require its own day. I understood the meaning of miraculous then. Or better yet, I understood the way money could make miracles happen.

THANK YOU!!!!!!! THANK YOU!!!! I texted back through blurry eyes. It wasn't generous enough, but I had no other words.

My phone pinged again a few minutes later.

My pleasure, John wrote.

Another ping.

I really, really love spending time with you and taking care of you <3 If you are having a nice time and want to continue hanging out with me (I hope you do) then I would like something in return from you . . .

There was no imaginative way to describe it. My heart sank. I was so blind with relief that I'd forgotten that a dreaded request was to be expected.

It must be said that John asking me for sex was the obvious next step in our arrangement. But after five weeks without so much as a peck, and he asking if we were *friends*, a part of me, microscopic and stupid, believed that this request might never come. In a final bid to prove myself wrong—that John was not this typical, that life itself was not this typical, and my whole existence on earth had not been leading up to this moment of corporal exchange—I wrote, *What would you like from me in return?*

John's next text was written in cringey innuendos. *I would like to get to first base, second*

> *base, and third base, but the more often we do home runs, the more gifts you will get.*

At last. The time had arrived to ask myself, deeply and seriously, did I want to be John's sugar baby?

Want was the wrong word.

Did I *want* to sleep with John? No. But could I *tolerate* sex in exchange for money, which was to say the mundane things that make life remarkably better? Faithfully filling my gas tank, getting stitches if I sliced a finger, fixing my teeth? There was no question about it. And I couldn't ignore the fact that this opportunity had miraculously arrived at my doorstep like it had been delivered by a stork. So, did I want to be John's sugar baby? No. But broke as shit, totally heartbroken, and already feeling unlovable, it wasn't a moment in which there was much left to lose.

In the living room my mom and Bianca had planted themselves on the couch, each swiping a thumb up their cell screens. My mom was sharing motivational memes on Facebook, while my sister was taking a *BuzzFeed* quiz about what kind of pizza she was (cheese—classic). My nephew was belly-down on the floor next to an array of colored pencils, sketching a jaguar.

"Go to the back bedroom," I told Chuy.

"Why?" he asked.

"I need to have an adults-only conversation."

His expression soured, but he collected his loose sheets of "art paper" my mom snatched from her work printer.

"Thank you," I said and patted his head as he tottered by.

When the bedroom door shut, I turned to my mom and sister and said, "John is going to pay for my dental bill" (a collective sigh of relief), "but he won't pay me to eat high-dollar noodles with him anymore" (a collective gasp). "If I want to keep seeing him, I've got to . . ." I paused to pull out my phone and read directly from the screen.

"Gifts is sugar lingo for money," I told my mom. I didn't need to explain the baseball references.

A second message arrived, which I also read aloud.

If you agree you can quit Penthouse altogether. I'd pay you per meeting and I'd be happy to still include nice dinners just as long as we can cap the night off with a pleasure session. I shuddered but persevered. *I can match your weekly average from Penthouse. Just let me know the price.*

"What's your weekly average?" my sister asked.

"It fluctuates." The best shift I'd ever had at Penthouse was with Britney Spears's ex-bodyguard and I'd walked away with $900. The least I ever made was zero—though with house fees that actually meant negative sixty dollars. "A good stripper makes something like $600 a shift," I said. "Even more on a weekend."

"How much do you think John is willing to spend?" my mom asked.

"Maybe you should start high and let him talk you down if it's too much," my sister added.

"Good idea." I didn't want to be too greedy, so I texted John, *Wow, you're so generous! Well, I usually work three shifts a week, and on average, I'd walk with $1,200.*

When I looked up my nephew's forehead was peeking from around the corner.

"Not sneaky," I said.

Chuy sighed and revealed himself, nude except for green briefs. He'd cut the elastic waistband at either hip. His own innovation to address the too-tight fit.

"Can I come out yet?"

"No," I said. "Go back into the bedroom and put your headphones on. We'll come get you when it's clear."

"Why does everybody keep secrets from me?" Chuy asked, slinging his arms around.

"We're not keeping secrets! We're preserving your innocence!" I said.

"I don't understand what that means," Chuy said.

"Exactly!"

He huffed, then spun around on his heels.

Once Chuy was out of earshot, I eyed my mom and sister, saying, "Can you imagine if John says yes to $1,200? Earning money without the risk of a shitty night?"

"Oh, he'll say yes," my sister said. My mom bobbed her head in agreement.

My phone buzzed. I read the message aloud, *$1,200 sounds fair to me. :)*

Even as I felt myself barreling toward an exchange I didn't want—John's body colliding with mine—the text message contract felt like a golden rope being tossed into the pit of my existence. I imagined climbing my way into a new life. Financially secure. Fillings in my teeth. No stripping, more time for school and writing. Everything superior to the life I lived now. I felt relieved, but also nauseous.

John texted once more. *We can start slow for your comfort. Perhaps our next dinner can end with a first kiss? <3*

So here I was. In the Penthouse dressing room on seekingarrangements.com.

I read on. The website claimed that the average sugar baby was twenty-five years old and received $2,800 per month, which was a tad more than I'd pull dancing seven nights. For approximately two seconds I considered continuing to work at Penthouse while with John but, honestly, I hadn't sold a lap dance in weeks. I'd probably do better to endure John's kiss just to keep my life afloat.

The dressing room door flew open with a gust of '80s rock. In the mirror Bronco-banger Portia's reflection bobbed in sync with her high heel clicks until she plopped down a chair away from me, nodded, and lit a Camel. Her exhale brought the scent of cigarette smoke and Victoria's Secret body spray my way. It was intoxicating . . . sort of.

Portia and I were all alone in the dressing room. I wanted to ask her what sleeping with someone for money was like. She was the only real-life person I knew who ever (allegedly) had. My mind was loaded with questions—What was the $10,000 sex like? Did you feel different afterward? Were you sad? If so, how sad? Did you tell anyone about it? Do your friends still like you? Do you think anyone would ever date you again if they knew?—but I decided against asking them, not wanting Portia to know she'd been the subject of locker-room gossip. I resumed scrolling.

"I will make $600 tonight," Portia murmured to herself, as she ashed her cigarette into the glass tray between us. The smoke was still in her lungs. Her eyes were closed. Her eyelids sparkled with glitter. She exhaled a gray cloud, while saying, "I will make $600 tonight."

Portia was manifesting wrong. Back in high school, a friend had introduced me to the law of attraction, after reading a book called *The Secret*. You had to speak it like it was already yours. I believed in the good karma of helping out a pal, so I closed my eyes to tap into Portia's prayer. *Portia made $600 dollars tonight. Portia made $600 dollars tonight.* I was interrupted when the DJ's voice came over the PA system out in the main room. "Did he say Leyla or Lola?" I asked, opening my eyes.

Portia shrugged. "It sounds like he's talking into a mitten. They oughta put a speaker back here."

I stood in case they'd said Lola, but before I left, I looked down at Portia. "You made $600 tonight." And then I told myself that I would never see her again, because I was going to kiss John and change my life. "Goodbye, Portia. This is my last night at Penthouse."

She smiled at me with the left side of her mouth, flattening her fingers in a lazy half wave as she ashed her cigarette onto the floor. "Thanks, Leyla. Goodbye. Good luck."

★

The night of the first kiss I held an emergency meeting with my mom and sister in our living room. I considered looping my dad in on speakerphone, but my mom objected. "What good will your dad be?" she asked. "He's probably a worse kisser than John."

I hadn't called this meeting to discuss kissing techniques, but my mother took digs at my dad whenever she could, which, to be honest, was warranted. Twelve years after I'd first suggested it, my mother finally filed for divorce. It had taken my dad introducing four-year-old Chuy to his mistress at Orange Julius. Afterward, Chuy paraded through the house waving his smoothie in the air, screaming, "Grandma! Grandpa has a girlfriend!"

Usually I could entertain this, but not today. After a full day of brooding, I'd managed to convince myself that John might kill me—albeit accidentally, but still. Anyone willing to spend $1,200 on a smooch had to be starved for affection. I imagined John's desperate aggression like a Saint Bernard hurtling toward its beloved owner back from a years-long vacation. The shift in my mind was immediate. The second John asked me for sex he morphed from a lonely, innocent man into a threat.

"What if," I asked my mom and sister, "John doesn't realize how hard he's pressing into my face and suffocates me?"

"That won't happen," my mom assured me, squeezing my hand, her skin dry from the diabetes.

"You'd faint before you died," my sister added. "He'd notice that."

My mom walked me to the door and said, "When you kiss him, think of the money. And if you do faint, tell him to wave a stack of hundreds in front of your nose." She laughed before she delivered the punch line. "The smell should wake you up."

★

As I drove away from the apartment, I watched the sun I'd known for twenty-four years set on my world just as a new, menacing moon was dawning. If I had any sense, I would have talked to one of those counseling interns who worked on a sliding pay scale. A shrink could've diagnosed my *death by kissing* thoughts as anxiety and given me a safe space to unload, but I didn't trust even a professional secret keeper. Instead, I resolved to buy a few vodka shooters on my way to the Cheesecake Factory.

John requested that our date take place at the downtown location. Though I'd never been to a Cheesecake Factory myself I knew a girl who'd worked in the restaurant's bakery five years before. I prayed the Cheesecake Factory had high employee turnover. Maybe I could avoid the bakery altogether or, better yet, I could scope it out to see if she was on shift. If she was, I'd say hello and tell her I was meeting a business associate, which, technically, was the truth.

When I arrived, I told the host that my party had already been seated and sauntered over to the bakery where I pretended to eye the cheesecakes. "That turtle looks yum!" I said to no one in particular. No one responded. All the employees were strangers.

I retreated to a bathroom stall and dug around in my bag for the shooters. I was on a Deep Eddy kick, grapefruit for the time being, as the peach ones were too sweet and hurt my teeth. I shot one. Then another. I almost left after two, but, considering the carb-heavy meal I was about to consume, opened the third. It wasn't until I left the restroom that I realized my mistake. I became too aware of myself. I was a toddler, barely able to walk straight. My rings felt tight around my puffy-drunk fingers. My lips were numb. I recalled having a tongue, but where had it gone? Ah, there it was, hovering inside my construction zone of a mouth.

"Hi, sweetie." The voice came from behind. I spun around to find John at a table for two. He stood to greet me. My drunk brain whispered, *He is dressed exactly like Bill Gates.*

"Hi, there," I said, then hugged him with full body, locker-room aggression.

John pressed his lips to my cheek, inhaled twice, and coughed. "So. How was your day?" he asked through clenched teeth. His words had the slightest undertone of, *At what point did you decide to get absolutely tanked?*

Unable to tell John that I'd needed liquid padding to soften our first kiss, I begged the Universe for a plausible day-drinking excuse. The plotline of a *Bob's Burgers* episode, "Crawl Space" (where Bob gets stuck in his restaurant wall while repairing a leaky roof), was all that came to mind. "It's been good. My friend, Bob—Bobby, was . . . stuck in his wall for a few days and just got out," I said, taking my seat.

"Wow."

"I know! Unbelievable, right? We had a drink to celebrate. I haven't eaten much today, so it hit me hard."

"Did you drive here?" John asked me.

"Yeah, but I wasn't drunk when I got here."

He raised his eyebrows.

"Because . . ." I stretched the *uhhh* for a few seconds. "I knew we were having dinner here, so I met up with him early to have our drink . . . here." Bobby had already left, I said, so no, I could not introduce them. John stopped a passing waiter and asked her to bring bread, pronto.

John looked like he was solving a Rubik's Cube in his mind, trying to decide which question to ask first. *How does someone get stuck in a wall? Was this man injured?* Instead, he asked, "Is your friend Bobby someone I should be worried about?"

"No," I said, jarred by his question. This was not a real date. We were not exclusive. This was not romance! *Spending time* with John was now officially my job, contracted by text message and sealed with payment. I supposed the work could include insincere reassurance. "Bobby has a wife, Be . . . linda, and three kids. They're all hilarious."

John relaxed a little. He crossed his legs and leaned back. For the first time since we met, I thought, *I do not like you.* It was, in part, my lack of inhibition thanks to the vodka, but mostly it was the certainty of how the dinner would end. That those five weeks of generosity—the phone screen, the boots, the to-go orders for my family, my dental bill—were his ways of saying, *I am a nice guy! I do good things! I don't want anything from you except companionship!* Which was, of course, a ruse.

"You don't mind being friends with people who have kids? Because I, uh," John paused. "I have a couple kiddies."

"That's cool," I said, wondering why John had waited so long to tell me this when I talked about my family all the time. Plus, his delivery was weird. Was he hiding something from me? No, John was just more private than I was, I reasoned. A battery-powered candle flicked between us. From the right angle the flame looked real. I wish I could buy some, I thought, then I remembered the money and perked up. "Do you have any pictures? Tell me more!"

John presented his leather wallet and showed me a professional photo of two boys. They looked like replicas of him. When I told John this, he said, "That's not good news for my kids."

"How old are they?"

"Luke is thirteen, Stephen is sixteen."

I smiled and nodded myself into the spins while he told me about Stephen learning to drive and each child's favorite hobby: golf and ice hockey. I sipped water to give my liver a leg up as John told me that the boys wanted to be a software engineer and a doctor, respectively. "They both like money," he said. "They take after me."

"Money is a good thing to like," I said, spotting an opportunity to pry. Before I kissed John and quit Penthouse, I needed to follow the Reddit advice and confirm that he could afford an arrangement. "Do you make all your money from your job, or do you, like, gamble?"

"No gambling," he said. "I'm too careful with my money for that. The most I do is invest a little in high-risk stocks." This set John off on a ramble about investment strategies, which I couldn't understand a lick of, but I'd gotten the information I needed. Not only did John have an impressive salary, but he also raked in cash from the stock market and a couple of rental properties.

Our waiter arrived with the basket of bread, and I nearly knocked it from her hand reaching for a roll. Had I been more mentally present I would have been cautious of resembling a hot-dog-eating competitor, but as I was trying to avoid blacking out, I stuffed the whole thing into my mouth, careful, I might add, of the temporary tooth I was wearing until my permanent crown could be placed.

The waiter smiled, tightly. "I'll give you another minute to look at the menus."

"Back to your family," I said when she was out of earshot. "What about your sons' mom? Why'd you get divorced?" Though, as soon as I asked, I realized John had never outright said this. "You are divorced, right?"

"Oh, yes!" he said, nodding. "I've been divorced for ten years."

"Do the kids live with you or their mom?"

"We split custody," he explained. His ex-wife, Patricia, lived a three-minute drive from his house. The boys spent more time at John's because it was a more spacious "man pad" and he was more likely to order takeout for dinner, but they saw their mother a few nights each week.

When I asked why they divorced, John said, "I'm embarrassed to say," while plucking at the corner of his cloth napkin. "I don't want you to think I'm an asshole who only cares about one thing."

My stomach dropped with dread. This really was leading to sex, wasn't it? Where had the John who was too scared to touch my hand at

REI disappeared to? He was just gaining the courage, of course. He was, just as my dad had said, getting me used to the money so the offer would be harder to decline. "Sex?"

"Cliché," John said. "I know. It was a major point of tension between us. She never, ever wanted to make love." He looked around to make sure no one was listening, then he whispered, "I think she's asexual. She doesn't even," then he mouthed the word, "masturbate."

"Tough," I said. I wished I found the whole situation (a sexless marriage, and now a paid arrangement) pathetic, but I understood John's pain. My last ex-girlfriend, Stevie, and I hadn't slept together for months before our final breakup. Whenever I'd try to talk to her about it, she'd shut me down. All affection had become fraught between us. Kissing, cuddling in bed, even holding hands had been taken off the table. Stevie would tell me years later that our inability to resolve conflict made her feel lonely in our relationship, but at the time her withdrawal had left me feeling confused and touch starved. Still not down enough to pay $1,200 for a kiss, but clearly down enough that I was open to selling one. I considered sharing this with John—friend to friend—until it dawned on me that my long-awaited return to sex, after such a fraught sabbatical, would be with *him*.

I sized John up, not just as a man across the table from me, totally separate, with long, skinny fingers, and a mouth that he merely ate and spoke with, but as a man whose body was like a train arriving at my station. In this moment, he was not touching me, but in an hour, he would be. Tonight, a kiss, but soon it would be more. Those fingers would graze my skin. His mouth would be a mouth that did other things, lick, taste. I felt sick to my stomach. What if I couldn't do it? What if my body went into shock from reintroducing sex in such a way? I would not be turned on. I knew by the way I felt violated in the imagined, my body would feel violated in reality. I felt foolish being there all of a sudden. I hadn't even slept with a cis man since I was nineteen years old. I worried I would be bad at this kind of sex. I worried that this kind of sex would hurt, and I worried the pain would make this deal ten times worse. I wanted more than anything in that moment to scan the restaurant for a pretty face with a spark, a raised eyebrow, a smirk, to pull someone from their table and beg them to fuck me in the bathroom, just to break this celibacy any other way. But life rarely provides us exactly what we want. Unless of course, I thought while looking at John, you can afford it.

"That was all a long time ago," John said, waving his hand. "My ex-wife and I are great friends and great co-parents now. Whenever my family is out together people comment on how happy we are. We're always laughing. I feel lucky the kids get along so well."

"That's how my family is too," I told John.

He seemed grateful for the subject change. "Are your parents still married?"

"Oh no," I said. Even before my dad's new girlfriend showed up, my parents' marriage had been full of holes. As eight-year-old Michelle had expected, the move to Colorado didn't suit my mom. In Virginia, her life had been filled with family and friends and social events, but in the isolation of Aurora she had only three things: my dad, us children, and comfort foods. That list dwindled even more as my dad skedaddled and my sister and I grew into our angsty teen years. As for the foodstuff, it didn't take long for Sonic, Taco Bell, and Wendy's to drive my mom deeper into debt. For years, she paid only the minimum payments and the interest grew unruly. She managed to hide her spending from my dad by only purchasing edible items, but one day he stumbled upon a pantie drawer full of her Discover card statements. Her credit card debt was one reason my parents claimed irreconcilable differences. Despite this, I told John, my parents were still good friends. Seventy-five percent of the time.

"And the other twenty-five?" he asked.

"Their fighting is like the emotional equivalent of WWE wrestling. Stupid, but entertaining."

★

Halfway through a plate of fettuccine Alfredo I was able to make eye contact with John without seeing double. He took a bite of his herb-crusted salmon. I pronged a piece of steamed broccoli. It was still crisp.

"Growing up, we only ever ate canned vegetables," I told John. "Our cabinets looked apocalypse ready." I went on, describing how, aside from the endless Green Giant tins, we had canned raviolis and beans. The freezer was especially lively, as my family's concept of cooking started with one-inch slits in plastic film covers and ended with pushing start on the microwave. "I didn't even know what asparagus was until I was twenty."

"Does your family eat healthy now?"

"They're, um, still figuring it out."

In the summer of 2014, when I turned twenty-three, I converted to vegetarian and then forced my family to watch every health documentary on Netflix. During inspiring scenes of personal transformation—thirty-day vegans comparing their before-and-after cholesterol levels then vowing to exchange prescription meds for fruits and nuts—I asked if anyone was interested in swapping chicken tenders for tofu. The answer was a unanimous no. I tried another angle. "What if I told you we'd save literally thousands of dollars a year cooking at home?"

My sister spoke for the group. "We don't tell you how to spend your money. Don't try and tell us how to spend ours."

She was right, so last week, I'd spent an unprecedented $200 at Sprouts buying groceries for the lot of us. I unbagged a bundle of carrots with the green tops still attached—the first our household had ever seen—and added "nutritionist" to the mental list of roles I played in my family. When my mom and nephew arrived home later, I told them I had a surprise. I covered my nephew's eyes with my hands and guided him into the kitchen.

My mom opened the fridge before I could create suspense with a countdown.

"Ta-da!" I said.

"What are these?" my nephew asked, holding up a bag of brussels sprouts.

"They're brussels sprouts."

"Ew," my mom said. They laughed and laughed like vegetables were a big, stupid joke.

"I find your story inspiring," John said. He told me this often. Usually when telling me how impressive it was that I worked full-time in college. Something he never had to do because his father paid for his degree and living expenses. Now, however, it was inspiring that I ate broccoli.

"Thank you," I said, slowly. "Sometimes I can't believe that my seventeen-year-old self, a kid who'd never tasted a fresh vegetable, had the wherewithal to figure out a FAFSA."

"You must have always been really smart," John said.

"More like desperate," I said. Everything I knew about *responsible spending* I'd learned from an elementary lesson on balancing checkbooks and the many pages of "loan counseling" that FAFSA required me to click through before accepting the maximum offer of subsidized and unsubsidized awards. My student loan debt was currently near $35,000. "Of my whole family, mom's and dad's sides, with thirteen aunts and uncles and about one hundred cousins, only two ever made it to college," I told John. "Both through the G.I. Bill. So, my whole family tree is clueless about this kind of stuff."

"Sounds like you've never really felt taken care of." John rubbed my arm with his forefinger, ignoring, or perhaps misunderstanding, my use of the term "clueless." It wasn't like my family *wanted* to be poor, but it felt like upward mobility required a lot of resources we never had, and knowledge only some people get access to. "I'm so glad I can help you."

While I'd grown accustomed to the men at Penthouse treating me like a charity case, this condescension felt weird and worse from John. I was no longer Lola, the dancer who could take men's cash and disappear into the night, shaking off their savior complexes. Here, I was Michelle, who had to sit across from John and thank him over and over again for his generosity. I mean, he *was* helping me. But wasn't I helping him too? Weren't we striking a deal? Clearly, I needed cash, just as John needed someone to connect to, to touch, to see him. Enough so that he was willing to pay me a $60,000 salary.

You're getting paid to be agreeable, I told myself and smiled, a big shiny white smile, but I felt the truth graze my heart like a dagger. I refused to gaslight myself, so I finished John's sentence in my head. "I'm so glad I can help you, Michelle, now that you've agreed to fuck me."

I put down my last bite of food, excused myself to the restroom, opened my Notes app, wrote down as many details and lines that I could remember from the night.

★

After dinner, John and I walked to a parking garage two blocks up. The air was frigid. I exhaled to see my hot breath. A car honked, then honked again, unclear what they were tooting at. I watched my footsteps to discern whether I could walk in a straight line and determined that I could definitely pass a road test. John linked my fingers with his. We were each carrying brown paper bags for my family in our free hands.

"Thanks for tonight," I said when we arrived at my car. Paint flaked off the trunk. I picked at what I thought was a small chip, but which turned into a long strip that peeled off like snake shed.

"You should think about the upgrade I offered," John said. "A car like mine."

I'd googled the price last week. John's Lexus cost $35,000. Equal to my student loan debt. This led me to calculate the options at hand. At

Whole Foods I survived on a $14,000 salary. To have a similar budget, book myself some kind of writerly weekend away, pay my remaining university fees, and crawl out of student loan debt, I would need $75,000. Meaning, if I could just get through the sex, then I could change the trajectory of my life in exchange for sixty two nights. Not even full nights, but hours. With the interest rates what they were, it would take me decades to pay off my debt working a degree-required career. But if I accepted John's Lexus and then sold it, I could cut even this number in half. "Really?" I asked.

"Really," he said. "We can discuss what would be a fair contract. See me for at least two years, and the car is yours."

I frowned at John, deflated. Two years? What kind of person would try to indenture someone into sex with him for a set number of *years*. I mean, we hadn't even had the kiss yet. What if *he* didn't like it?

"No, thanks," I said, inevitably. "I'm attached to my car."

"When it breaks down, we'll revisit this conversation," John said.

Motors roared through the garage. Tires squealed on pavement. Someone was showing off their speakers, but all I heard was bass. I thought of Penthouse, but didn't miss it.

"I really enjoyed our romantic evening," John said. I tensed at the sentiment. It was too suggestive that there wasn't compensation involved. Which felt like an odd thing to do within the walls of our arrangement. I had sputtered plenty of white lies to keep John a secret as it was (why I was missing shifts at Penthouse, or where I'd gotten a new jacket from, etc.). It seemed like overkill to skirt around the truth with one another. Our liaison was based on *transparency*. I reasoned that a part of sugaring was maintaining a fantasy that John understood was fraudulent. I forced another smile, then John asked, "Can I kiss you?"

Alas, I'd arrived.

I had the feeling of fastening into a roller coaster. That sensation of dread as the cart inches up and up and up and up, until there is nothing but air below, the view beyond, and the thought, *I've got to get off this ride. I do not want to do it.*

It wasn't necessarily John that was the problem, but what this job meant for my relationship with myself. I lived in a world that saw my body, sex with my body specifically, as bartering gold. As much as I complained about patriarchal ideals, I sure did oblige when they benefitted me. I thought of Roxane Gay's book *Bad Feminist* and tried to liken myself to her. We sometimes contradicted ourselves, but how could we not? We were flawed creatures that lived in a flawed world.

John moved closer. I had to either back away now and return to the world I'd come from or fall forward and hope that at the other side of this small self-betrayal I would land on greener pastures. I closed my eyes, leaned in, and puckered up. Three tense pecks. The stubble of his shaven face pricked my skin. I had forgotten that feeling.

I waited for John to slip his tongue into my mouth, but it did not come. He released me from his arms and smiled. "That was so nice. You have such soft lips."

The kisses were so noninvasive that for the first time that night I felt hopeful, like I could do it. Like it'd be easy. Then John's hand sank into his coat and reemerged with a bank envelope that contained $1,200. When he offered it to me, I tucked it into my own pocket, then draped my arms around John's neck and kissed him again. Still not with tongue but with less rigidity. There were no fireworks. No butterflies. It felt like planting my foot on the first rung of a ladder.

★

By the time I arrived home John had texted me. *The kiss was so wonderful!! Thank you. Maybe next time we could have a home run? I can't help it. I'm not a horn dog, you're just so sexy <3*

This wasn't sex I was saying yes to but an opportunity to pay off my student loan debt. Enough cash to take care of my car. A night off. A moment to breathe. The mental space to write my stories. It wasn't sex that awaited me in the future but a mouthful of fillings. A better life is on the other side. That's all I could think. I replied, *Sure*.

John responded immediately. He would rent a room at the Marriott after Christmas shopping. *You can buy anything you'd like*, he wrote. *I'm feeling generous.*

I dragged myself up the apartment building steps to the second floor, trying to process what I'd just agreed to. It was lost on me.

When I opened the front door, my family clamored around me, grabbing the bags of takeout, fighting over the Chicken Bellagio and Red Velvet Cheesecake. My mom and Bianca wanted to know about the kiss, but they would ask later. During the slow lull of digestion.

It was fine, I would tell them. *Everything is fine (fine, fine).*

5

Home Run at the Marriott

*T*he first time I patroned a strip club I was twenty-two years old. I'd arrived with forty dollars in my pocket and after I paid my cover and purchased a vodka soda, I was left with twenty-three bucks to spend. Being strapped for cash wasn't a deterrent because I was there to tuck copies of my DIY feminist zine (which had a special segment on my recent strip club audition rejections) around the club. It was my hope that some of the dancers might stumble upon it, give it a read, and like my Facebook "Author" page. Everything had gone according to plan until, on the way out, I passed by Ophelia, a woman with '50s pinup style and *covered* in tattoos, swaying topless on stage.

I had been watching a lot of *Orange Is the New Black* at the time and felt as though I were staring at Alex Vause (who just happened to be my favorite character). I took a seat at the stage, placed two dollars down, and soon Alex—I mean, Ophelia—kneeled before me, kissing my cheek. She smelled of cigarettes and amber musk. I was a total goner.

Sticking out my hand, I introduced myself and asked how long she'd been working at the club. I tipped her another two dollars.

"Three years." Ophelia smiled but didn't say more.

"I used to dance," I offered, hoping this would intrigue her. I placed another three dollars on stage.

"Really?" She sparkled. "I bet you were great. You're very pretty."

That's all it took for me, a former dancer, who knew a working woman's flirting meant nothing, to lose all common sense. I pictured the rest of our night. Pancakes at IHOP across the street. She would cover our tab because I'd have already given her all my money. We would bond over the stack of crumbled bills she'd pull out of her purse. "Waiters always know my tits are paying the tab," she might say. I'd laugh, knowingly.

I asked Ophelia question after question while placing dollar after dollar on her stage. She stayed in front of me, answering only as much as I asked, occasionally touching my arm or smiling. It seemed sincere. But soon enough I had nothing left to tip. "That's it," I said, ready to give her a copy of my zine.

"Thanks so much for coming in!" she said, then swiftly moved to the guy beside me.

Now, it was 8:00 p.m. in the middle of December two years later and I was thinking of Ophelia because I was trying to conjure up empathy for John. How much money would I have given Ophelia if she had stayed beside me, or, better yet, if she had kissed me? What if I had a bank account as fat as John's? It was possible I would have given her $1,200. Possible, but unlikely.

I was sitting in John's Lexus outside of the Marriott while he checked us into a room. A room for us to have sex. I was a mess of nerves and uncertainty. Thinking of Ophelia did help, a little. I could understand how much John wanted to be wanted. I knew how easy it was to be swayed by a pretty face and a gentle graze. I too had been swept up in the fantasy of romance inside the simulation of desire. But things ended with Ophelia after twenty-three dollars and a single stage set. This part of the story was new for me. The night was black. Shop lights twinkled across the way. It occurred to me that nearly every episode of *Forensic*

Files started in a parking lot. Maybe dying at a hotel in South Denver was my destiny.

I know we fight a lot, I texted my sister. *But if I die tonight, I love you.* I then quickly followed the message with the address, John's full name, and his license plate number.

I love U 2, she responded. *U get my IKEA gift card?*

I had. Earlier that evening John and I braved the Christmas horde at a bougie mall. I picked that location because it sat on the outskirts of Denver where I could stay anonymous. John didn't complain about the forty-minute drive nor charging my family's shopping list to his credit card. "I'm so excited to touch you," he'd said. "Spend away."

Since our first kiss, John wanted to be repaid in pecks for every generosity, opening the car door, picking up my fallen glove, and, worst of all, at each cash register. He would swipe his card, and I would feel the weight of his gaze on my mouth like a boulder. His expectation for a kiss so obvious that each cashier awaited my compliance before asking, "Receipt in the bag okay?" It happened only once that evening, but as we left the Disney Store, two cashiers (obviously high schoolers), snickered as John and I walked off. "Gold digger," I heard one cough before they burst into a fit of giggles. My cheeks burned with embarrassment. I looked at John expecting to see the same flush in his face, but he just smiled and kissed me again.

I tried to be a good sport about it. Tonight was the Christmas gift exchange and John was set to pay me $1,200 plus the $5,800 for my dental tab. For every kiss, I'd secretly lick my teeth. My appreciation would swell but quickly dilute with grief. If I hadn't agreed to sleep with him, I would have carried on into the vast future with this pain. When would I have ever had a spare $6,000 to pay the dentist? Probably never.

Alone in John's Lexus, I pictured his naked body, and my heart skittered around like a rabbit. I dragged my finger down the fog on my window as proof of my being alive and wondered how I could possibly make myself go through with this.

My uncle Johnny was serving life in a Virginia federal prison. He had been repeatedly arrested for robberies before—pharmacies, gas stations, ice cream shop, etc. Crimes he committed to escape the oppressive poverty my mother's family faced. "This was back in the '70s. Things were less secure," my mom always told me, when she explained how Johnny managed to Houdini out of every jail the cops dragged him to. His last escape was in 1980.

Uncle Johnny tried to get straight. For two years, he worked at a shipyard in Norfolk, Virginia. He fell in love and had a kid. One day, the shipyard started fingerprinting their employees, forcing Johnny to quit. Without the shipyard, the outside world grew harder. How does one live their life with a warrant out for their arrest? How does one eat with no job? Johnny eventually returned to the tricks he knew best, only to be caught with no way out. The prison system had changed. That was it. He would spend his natural life behind bars.

Prodding my back tooth, I thought of my own crime, selling my body to take care of my body. As ironic as my uncle ruining his life to better his life. We two were snakes eating our own tails. I had the terrible thought that sugaring was the only way I would ever have this much financial stability, so I would make myself do this.

John materialized in the rearview mirror, waving the key card at me. He looked happy. He looked as though he believed I was happy too. Like we were both looking forward to this. I eyed the time (8:01 p.m.) and opened the Notes app on my phone: *I am shaking so hard, I feel like I'm vibrating. I don't want to do this at all.*

I stepped out onto the icy asphalt and John clenched my hand as we walked across the parking lot, through the lobby, into the elevator up, up, up, then down the long, muted hallway. The green argyle pattern on the carpet was disorienting and felt too soft under my shoes. I had to watch my feet to make sure I kept moving and couldn't raise my eyes until the room door beeped open. Inside, everything felt hotel crisp. Bleached and starched and stiff and cold. We were high, on the sixteenth floor. Our view overlooked the shopping center, and I stared at the glimmering Christmas lights while John removed his coat. I laid my palm against the frigid window, which made me shiver, and John came behind me to massage my shoulders, which made me shiver again. John began closing the blinds. I did not want him to remove my clothes, so I lied and said, "I need to use the restroom." Inside the bathroom I locked the door behind me. Heart racing, I pressed my fingerprints firmly and carefully into the corners of the mirror, the porcelain toilet lid, the glass pane of the framed painting hanging on the wall. I pulled out hairs from my head and hid them in places John wouldn't look. Which seemed ridiculous, but *what if?* I thought. Just, *what if?* I undressed, folded my clothes, and stacked them neatly. I hugged my arms to my chest. Felt the goose bumps, grazed the freckles on my breast, kissed the back of my hands. My body felt sacred in a way it never had before. I heard its whimpers to please pull my clothes back on, please leave, please don't do this. Please, please, please.

But I was already there.

The gifts had been purchased.

A permanent crown had been placed.

The room had been rented.

I had already said yes.

I opened the bathroom door and went to John, who was sprawled in the middle of the king bed with the comforter pulled up to his shoulders. I noticed a purple birthmark, the size of a golf ball on his left pec. John fanned open the sheets and revealed himself: soft and surprising in his near hairlessness. Fear flapped its wings violently inside me. All I could do was crawl in beside him and pray that my body obeyed his commands. I questioned whether I could go through with this, *this thing* that felt irreversible, but John didn't sense my hesitation, or if he did, he ignored it. He kissed me. When I felt his tongue inside my mouth, the thought came again, *Can I go through with it?* And again as he touched me and again as he unwrapped the condom and again as he thrust himself inside me.

But I could.

I did.

When it was over, John told me, "You're the first white woman I've ever fucked," before passing me a thick bank envelope. It felt like a deck of cards. To him this exchange must've felt like power. I wanted to ask how good of a conquest I was, considering the cost. More importantly I wanted to correct him and say, "I'm only half white, remember?" So much of my identity felt invisible, not only in this arrangement, but to the world. My queerness and ethnicity always something I have to prove. *Here is my girlfriend, here is my father. Can you see it yet? Do you believe me?* But, because there is nothing comparable to being flat broke then suddenly having money, I did just like I would at the strip club. I took the cash and let him buy whatever story he wanted.

<hr />

Driving home, I obsessed over what terrible things selling my body had done to me. Of course, there were the physical anxieties, ones that held no water, but thoughts I could not ignore. Had my vagina been stretched out of shape forever? John did not have a penis of any remarkable size, but sex for hire felt so antithetical to sex for pleasure or love that I feared my body knew I had been tainted by a for-profit penis. Even if my anatomy looked the same, how would a future partner feel knowing I'd been sold? Or was the correct term "bought"? "Used." Wouldn't it be gross to touch me? Wasn't my body simply now disgusting?

I understood that these words and their connotations were condemning—and I even knew that they were inaccurate—but still, I deeply feared that if anyone ever found out what I'd done, it would be impossible to cleanse myself from the stigma of sex work. In 2015, there was plenty of sex positivity out there. *BuzzFeed* was publishing listicles about the best sex toys for solo play. Lena Dunham's hit show *Girls* pushed the boundaries with an anilingus scene. Consent was getting talked about as something cool. Women wanted sex! They wanted to have sex when they wanted it—casual and hot or with their long-term partners. But there weren't endless sex-positive messages around sex *work*. Being an empowered person (a cis woman specifically) who had and enjoyed sex was not culturally synonymous with a person who sold access to their body. In my Women and Gender Studies program, we talked a lot about the double standards women faced. Even if I could understand that it was all patriarchal bullshit, those messages were still lodged in me. I had done a deed that I knew would brand me. I had made my bed, and if word ever spread, I would have to lie in it.

Merging onto the highway, I kept to the left where the icy spots seemed less frequent. A car shot past me going over eighty. I imagined them crashing into the median then my car smashing into their wreck because my brakes were no good and my tires were bald. I worried about what the paramedics might think if they found $7,000 in my coat pocket. In shock, I wouldn't know how to explain the cash away. I might even admit I'd earned it by having sex with John. Would they have me arrested? Would they give me fair medical care? Or would they not want to touch me either?

My eyes welled at the thought. And I wondered if anyone could ever understand how knotty tonight's decision had been. I did not want to sleep with John. But I did it because I needed to. And while the $7,000 was enough to make a difference in my life, it would not change my life completely. I'll admit it. I knew if I could just make myself go through with it this once, then I would be a person who had slept with someone for money, and there was no going back from that. If there was no going back, then I might as well sleep with him as many times as I could to make real money—enough to change my life. Not for a moment, or a month, but forever. If I was going to risk this much, shouldn't I make destroying myself worth it?

As I drove, I found myself wondering if John was questioning if the world might find him repulsive for what he's done. Not likely. When we departed the elevator in the hotel lobby, John seized my hand and nodded at the interested crowd waiting to go up. Clearly, he didn't feel dirty for paying to fuck me. But what was shameful about being able to *afford* sex? That was pure power. Meanwhile, my gaze had instinctively fallen to the floor because there was something shameful about *selling* it.

Eventually, I exited the highway and approached a stoplight. Snow fell in fat, heavy flakes, swirling golden in the yellow glow of the streetlight. My wipers dashed across the windshield leaving behind icy streaks. There was a discarded sleeping bag and wet cardboard sign near the underpass but no one around. It was 10:10 p.m., and my attention, finally, fell to the silence. I hadn't turned the radio on.

At home, my mom and nephew were, mercifully, fast asleep. This was a relief. Around the two of them, I wanted to appear imbued with the joyous, elusive magic of Santa Claus, loaded with gifts and mystery. *We're not precisely sure how you're doing it*, I wanted them to think, *but we sure love you for it!* Bianca, ensconced in her room, didn't notice my arrival. I'd talk to her, but after I cleansed any trace of John off me.

I caught a whiff of John's cologne as I took off my jacket. I pressed my face into my coat and my scarf to find the source—not there—then lifted my hair to my nose. Bingo. The further I undressed myself the more I could smell John on my skin. Sometimes I'd leave the strip club smelling of cigar smoke and a cocktail of body sprays. I'd find traces of

someone else's glitter in unexpected places. Inside my socks. My armpits. My underwear. But I'd never felt contaminated the way I did right
then. It was so singular. I knew exactly where the smell originated and
knew exactly when it had transferred onto me. I began to cry. Because I
had left my house a woman who had done many things with her body for
money but never something so extreme. Never sex. And I had returned
reeking of a woman who had.

In the shower I scrubbed until my skin was flushed. I filled my palm
with body wash over and over and circled the loofah in between my legs.
The anxiety was back. *I shouldn't have done this*, I thought. *I have ruined
my life. I have ruined my chance of ever finding love. No one will ever know
the full me again. I can't get the stench off. I feel sick. What if the stress of
this secret kills me? I hope no one saw me at the mall. Please, god, tell me no
one saw me.*

I cupped the back of my head with my damp palms. My thoughts
were all over the place: how I had been ostracized as a teenage dancer, my
ex-girlfriend from that era talking bad about me behind my back, how
my friend's massage business had all but become her perceived identity.
I thought about my dad's whole life of physical labor. My mom so often
working two jobs. How much their bodies suffered for financial need.
I wanted to weep. My body felt used. Soiled. I felt pathetic. I liked to
believe this was fated, but why, of all the destinies available, was mine
sugaring? My mind turned the wheel of the kaleidoscope. I thought of
the cash, I thought of no debt, the fact that I wouldn't have to return to
Penthouse. I wrote the first line of a story in my head, "I met John during
my Wednesday night shift at Penthouse."

★

After my shower, I cracked Bianca's door and was assaulted by her
stench. Corn chips and hair oil. This smell was familiar. This was home.
"Are you awake?"

With Bianca's permission, I tiptoed to her bed, mindful not to step on all the discarded clothes and snack wrappers. I shoved a pile of (clean?) laundry out of the way and made a spot for myself on her bed.

"Drumroll, please!" I said. As my sister pattered her prickly knees, I slung the IKEA gift card at her. "Two hundred and fifty bucks!"

"New dresser, I'm coming for you!"

Bianca already had a six-drawer dresser packed full of too-tight clothes. It also served as her TV stand and a place to hold all her dishes. "What are you going to do with this old one?" I asked.

"Move it over to that wall," she said pointing to the left.

"You won't have any floor space." I meant this literally. Her room was small. If she had two dressers and a queen-size bed in there all the furniture would touch. "You won't even be able to open the bottom drawers. They'll be blocked by the bed."

"I'll just use the top ones," she said, like this was obvious.

I shook my head and considered telling her that she needed to downsize. Adopt a minimalist mindset. That was something rich people did. *One in, one out.* But I had more important things to talk about. If there was anyone I could share the explicit details of my night with, it was my sister.

Boys flocked to her. She was always confident in her body and sense of self, so she explored her sexuality freely and began calling herself a "slut." Bianca used the word proudly, in response to classmates using the word to put her down. A self-declared victory in a prudish world that treated any real fun like a sin. My sister and I didn't grow up with any religion in our home, but the culture all around us communicated the same notion that sexuality was shameful. She didn't buy into it. The mainstream never represented her anyway, so she didn't feel as constricted as I did by it.

Just recently, I'd written a flash story about a memory of Bianca, who, at thirteen, ushered three boys into her bedroom while wearing, unironically, a Winnie the Pooh nightgown:

Though the dress appeared innocent her accessories told a different story. From wrist to elbow her arm was a full ROY G. BIV rainbow of jelly bracelets.

It was 2002. Jelly sex bracelets were all the rage. Teens swapped the bands for sexual favors and each color and variety (solid, glow-in-the-dark, glitter) had a secret meaning. As far as I knew Bianca had collected one in each shade aside from solid black, which was the dirtiest of them all—intercourse. This, she was sure, made her the sluttiest possible virgin.

As Bianca prepared to triple-up on lime green (finger fun) and purple (kissing), I stood in the hallway with my hands on my hips glaring at her.

"You better not tell Mom," Bianca warned me.

"Or what, ya big slut?"

"I'll tell everyone we know you still play with Barbies and that you're a prude, closeted lesbian."

"I remember that day," she said now, fondly. "But I don't remember the nightgown."

I laughed but was quickly brought back to reality when my sister ran her finger up the bridge of my nose. "Goddamn," she said. "John didn't tell you that you need to pluck your unibrow?"

"No," I said, aghast. "He didn't."

We set up for our usual system. The aesthetician wore a camping headlamp and sat pretzel-style with a pillow in her lap. Because the treatment was free, the customer forfeited her right to complain. Once arranged, my sister plucked my eyebrows and asked, "So, tell me, what was it like to bang a dude again?"

I was happy to answer her question. I hadn't slept with a cis man in five years, so of course this was on her mind. I, too, had been thinking about it, worried the sex would hurt, or I'd be terrible (I probably was).

But, as I undressed in the hotel bathroom, I found myself most terrified of the possibility of John murdering me. I braced myself throughout the entire experience, but after surviving the night relatively unscathed, I realized that John's anatomy had nothing to do with how violating the sex felt; it was the idea itself that felt violating. I had arrived at the agonizing moment in which selling someone access to my body was the best way forward. But if the person I was sleeping with was safe, then what did it matter if they had a dick in the face of what I was doing?

"I don't think it's a big deal," my sister said, trying to soothe me. "I've fucked so many dudes that I didn't even like. I wish I'd been paid for it."

Bianca had a point. I'd slept with people I borderline despised. And for what? The experience? Aside from cash, John was no worse than the first boy I'd ever given a blow job.

"Remember José?" I asked.

"Yeah," Bianca said, laughing. "Yuck."

In the summer of 2005, when I was thirteen years old, I had been dangerously close to entering high school without experiencing even a closed-mouth peck. My relationship with my body was still fraught, but after two years of eating nothing but Lean Cuisines and low-fat Yoplaits, I was—for the first time in my life—considered thin. While this had greatly helped in my ability to make "cool" and "pretty" friends, I knew that to establish concrete social cred with them, I needed a few sexual experiences under my belt. My favorite Alanis Morissette song mentioned *going down on someone in a theater*, and to feel closer to my idol, while upping my social status, I pinky swore with myself that before freshman year I would receive my first kiss and go down on someone. Preferably in a theater.

That summer I was consumed with studying the art of oral sex. I turned to a few sexperts for help, but my sister and her friends were lazy teachers and would say things like, "It can't be taught with words, you'll figure it out by doing it." Left to my own devices, I would stroll to the corner gas station and flip through magazines advertising sex tips on the covers. I read articles like "The 14 Best Blow Job Secrets No One Ever Told You" and "Oral Sex Guide: What Women Really Want!" over and over while between magazine racks. My weekly allowance was three lousy dollars but, in pursuit of my goal, I spent that money on two-packs of flavored condoms and oranges, avoiding eye contact with the store clerk. At home I'd practice what drove men wild on my hairbrush and strengthen my tongue on a split orange.

As summer passed, I abandoned the idea of meeting someone organically and asked my sister, a girl with men lined up around the block, to scout a person who would *please* let me give them head. While I would've preferred a girl, I told her, I was desperate and open to anyone. A pimply boy named José was the only person who agreed to do the favor. He was a fifteen-year-old sophomore who'd actually been interested in my sister, but he was also desperate and open to anyone. For further Alanis effect, I asked my sister to drop us off at the closest movie theater, Century 16, where we each bought a matinee ticket to *Charlie and the Chocolate Factory*. As soon as the lights dimmed, José asked me to make out. I shook my head no. I didn't want to waste my first kiss on a stranger. "I'm just here to go down on you," I told him.

"That asshole told everyone at school my blow job was 'whack,'" I said to Bianca.

"Well, look at you now," my sister said, beaming. "A professional."

★

As I lay on the couch that night, I thought about José. Specifically, about the fact that our "date" had taken place at Century 16. A movie theater that had since become the site of the 2012 Batman Dark Knight shooting. I had not been at Century 16 the night of the attack; I was, however, familiar with the location—as were many people I knew—and in the days following the shooting I would scroll through GoFundMe links for my old classmates, my sister's coworkers, my friend's boyfriend.

Each of whom had been badly wounded. Each having received emergency surgeries and were (what came as no shock to many of us from Aurora) uninsured and unable to afford their hospital bills.

The shooter's trial took place three years later in the Spring of 2015 when I was twenty-three. Six months before I met John. For three months I did not look away from the trial coverage: "Jurors Hear Audio of Screams During 9-1-1 Call." "5 Chilling Pages from the Aurora Mass Shooter's Diary." "Shooter Describes What He Saw and Felt as He Entered the Aurora Theater, Began Firing."

I felt like I knew too much, yet I couldn't stop myself from clicking another link, watching another news story, reading another article. I soon knew every move the shooter made the night of the attack. How he had stood outside the theater, peeking through the cracked, emergency exit door, thinking, *Am I really going to do this?* How he had called a crisis hotline as a last attempt to stop himself. How the call had been disconnected, so he walked in, guns blazing. I saw diagrams of where he threw his tear gas grenades. And then I saw diagrams of where every bullet made contact. I began dreaming about the shooting over and over, and the more I knew, the more gruesome, more precise the dreams became.

This would eventually blur into my waking life. I could be sitting in class, someone would reach for their backpack a little too quickly, and I'd picture the shooter standing at the doorway, aiming an AR-15. I would pace the halls to shake the image away, confused as to why I felt so distressed. I had been safe at home when the shooting happened, so why such a visceral response? I stopped feeling safe in public places. Images began to override my own thoughts.

I had no money to see a therapist or any health insurance. I found a place where interns saw clients on a sliding scale, but the waitlist was hopeless. I turned to Google with questions like, *How to stop intrusive thoughts?* and *How to stop thinking about a traumatic event?* I read through articles citing exposure therapy and decided to conduct my own experiment. My plan was to be somewhere very safe, somewhere I could be *sure* of this safety, and then I would confront my fear in a banal way. For me it was looking at the scariest photos of the shooter I could find. I chose my mother's couch (mostly that was my only option), turned on all the lights in the living room and kitchen, wrapped myself in a blanket, loaded the CBS article "Powerful Photos Released from Aurora Theater Shooting," and, like the exposure therapy articles had cautioned, prepared myself for my body's reaction to the perceived threat (accelerated heart rate, tremors, sweaty palms). When it began, I repeated reassurances that I was okay. "It is September of 2015. The shooting was three years ago. I am safe. He is in prison. He cannot hurt anyone again."

Eventually, after repeating this exercise for weeks, it worked. I stopped seeing the shooter everywhere I looked. I stopped dreaming about that night.

Now, as I stared at the living room ceiling, thinking about that theater and José, I thought, too, about John. How my mind had been running in circles all night after seeing him. If I wasn't diligent with navigating the anxiety, my brain might get stuck. I knew that sex work (and John) could haunt me, regardless of whether I kept it a secret from everyone else. "I am safe," I whispered to myself. "I am at home in my mother's apartment. I did not get hurt at the Marriott. My body is safe. My body did not change tonight. My value is not gone.

6

Massages with Mommy

*J*ohn, I was soon happy to discover, was a deep-sea creature of
habit. After that first night at the Marriott, our arrangement sank
quickly into a routine. We were months into the arrangement and there
had only been two wrenches thrown into our relationship. The first by
John when, during our third pleasure session, he could no longer hold
erections while wearing condoms. This, blessedly, resulted in "home
runs" being taken off the table.

I was making $1,200 for this exact routine: Once a week John and I
would undress ourselves separately on opposite sides of our hotel room
and meet at the foot of the bed where I'd come down on my knees and
give John a few minutes of what he called "a blow jobby." John often
spoke in a baby voice during sex and would say absurd things like, "Not
that I'm counting, but you just set my world record for weeks-in-a-row
getting a blow job" (three), "I've never had my balls sucked. You're
popping my cherry," and "Thank you so much, sweetie. I know this is
icky."

I had been taken aback by John's use of the word *icky*. It was apt, of
course. It was icky. It was the ickiest sex I'd ever had. And emotionally,
these were some of the ickiest moments I'd ever lived through. But I was

still surprised by John's recognition. It was the most honest thing he'd ever said to me. A tenderness bloomed inside my heart, but then promptly died when John added, "Now, suck my dick on the bed." This was always the next part of our routine.

From there, we would have a long, wet, sloppy kiss. During which I often thought of two Labradors slurping water from a bowl. When John was ready, he would pull out a bottle of K-Y jelly, signifying that it was time to use our hands. This was (one of) the worst part(s), because it included John's wrinkled fingers touching my body.

Whenever I'd researched the question *What is the sex like with your sugar daddy*, I never found the answers I was looking for. Even responses on my tried-and-true Reddit thread were nondescript. *Sex with older men is great!* the babies always seemed to write. *They know what they're doing. They know where to find the clitoris. They know what a clitoris is.*

I found it far-fetched that none of these girls loathed the sex with their sugar daddies. No one even claimed to feel neutral about it. There was no fear on the threads. No disgust. No moral juggling with themselves. I wondered if this was some attempt at claiming empowerment. That there was some cultural agreement made that for sex work to not be gross or victimizing, it had to be the total opposite. The sex had to be *so good*. Or sex workers themselves had to love having sex enough that they couldn't believe the luck of monetizing off doing it. *If you love your job, you never work a day in your life*, kind of thing.

If someone had ever asked me, *What is the sex like with your sugar daddy?* I would've said it was hard, gross, painful, embarrassing. That each week I'd lain in those sheets pretending I'd been dunked into Novocain. How I had been grateful for my mind's iron resolve but felt terrified of the damage this might be doing to my mind-body connection. I worried these pleasure sessions would taint my ability to be present in sex ever again. That being touched from here on out would sit in my body as a violation. To combat this, I'd write out conversations between my brain (*we need this to thrive*) and body (*I still hate being compromised in this exchange*) and refused to ever have a real orgasm with John. I would simply time how long he had been touching me, and when a believable number of minutes passed, I'd fake a moan and shiver, and move us quickly into the next, and final, part of our routine—the hand job.

After each meeting was over, I'd sit in my car in the parking lot, and I'd count the money John paid me bill by bill. I'd smell the cash, press my finger into their bank-pressed stiffness, making the experience of getting paid as visceral as possible, so my body understood why we had done it.

The second wrench was thrown by me. That spring, I'd requested that John and I start skipping dinners and instead "just meet up for some fun." I'd blamed this change on being swamped with schoolwork, but the reason was more complex.

One afternoon, a lecture in my Crime and Poverty class just so happened to be discussing the criminalization of prostitution. "Why do you think these women risk their lives for this kind of work?" the professor had asked, before pausing for us students to consider. If I hadn't thought my classmates would shame me, I might've shared that, for me, the consistent income of sex work was incredible. With sugaring I could now chew my food with all my teeth, pay my university fees out of pocket, fill my gas tank, and all the while, still have the capacity to see life beyond it. I was not living in survival mode anymore. I could not imagine going back.

A student raised his hand and cautiously said, "Is it because these people have drug dependencies?" I felt a twinge. The professor frowned. "Incorrect. And *that* is an example of stereotyping." The student shrank into his desk. "Don't be too embarrassed," the professor said. "I guarantee you're not the only one who thought that." She overtly scanned the room. "Stereotypes are one reason that we as a society defer to the narrative that prostitutes are criminals. They're addicts. They deserve to go to jail."

Another student interrupted her. "Sorry, but regardless of anything else, like drugs or whatnot, isn't prostitution a crime in and of itself?"

"Are any of these people *criminals*?" The professor asked the class. "Or are the people who work in any form of prostitution *victims*?"

"Well, not all prostitutes," a girl interrupted. "Think about sugar babies or porn stars and whatever."

My heart plummeted at the mere mention. Clearly no one in this discussion had considered the possibility that a sex worker could be among us, which brought about an embarrassing, isolating feeling.

"Those people aren't victims!" a guy called out, playfully. "They're making bank."

"I'd definitely say those people are victims who have fooled themselves into thinking they're not," another person chimed in. "They're reinforcing patriarchy while claiming it's empowering."

"Some people are empowered by enjoying their sexuality," someone else added.

I imagined saying something smart, like pitting sex workers as either empowered people or victims totally overshadows the nuance and complexity that I, as a sex worker, am finally making a livable wage. But even in my head, I could hear the rebuttals.

The conversation would never go beyond the stance that, good money or not, sex work was always exploitative anyway. As if all work weren't exploitative. I'd seen Chuy's dad come home from construction jobs looking wrecked, his body breaking down long before he was even nearing retirement age. A friend of mine had to quit P.F. Chang's because cooking noodles in hot water every day had started to desensitize his hands. Even when I worked at Whole Foods, I watched executives and shareholders make obscene profits while we employees barely scraped by. My dad always told me that work, in all forms, takes something from you. The difference is, some kinds of labor are accepted as just another shitty reality of capitalism, while others are moralized and criminalized.

As the discussion dragged on, my stomach soured at the thought of meeting John in four hours. Ever since I'd started sugaring, I felt anxious before I saw John, because opening my body to him was taxing and I already had an unnecessary stress around getting in legal trouble—whether it be with taxes or for selling sex itself—but after this lecture my anxiety latched even harder onto the idea of arrest.

John had become a sort of succubus. He would hold my hand and kiss me at every opportunity, regardless of how inappropriate the timing. Once, while I was ordering dinner, John sucked, literally sucked, on my earlobe. The waiter glued his eyes to his pad, but he understood the situation. John was in his mid-fifties. He looked tailored and neat. Soft hands and filed nails. John glowed in the way that wealthy people glow. Like he could afford laser treatments and to buy the name-brand creams. I bought my jeans at Ross. The toes on my shoes were still scuffed. I was half his age and wore the truth like a scarlet brooch. I was his sugar baby. Or, if you wanted to be derogatory, I was his whore. I imagined my impending arrest in Maggiano's. The waiter on the phone, an officer's grip jerking me from a velvet booth. Standing, ashamed and on display, as they handcuffed my wrists, I could see twirling forks come to a halt. A sea of patron paparazzi flashing pictures of me, yelling. Eventually, my mug shot would be made public on the internet. My winged liner two dark smudges, and my *crime*, PROSTITUTION, branded below my face. I imagined all the ways this word could haunt me. How it would appear on background checks and steal away decent job offers. How a curious lover might google my name, only to be spooked off by my mug shot. If the world ever found out what I had done, I knew I would be punished for it.

Without word to my professor, I ran out of class to the nearest toilet and vomited. *Oh, get over yourself,* I thought. My professor was originally discussing street prostitution, which was drastically more dangerous and actually prosecuted. Sugar babying was an advantageous type of sex work. There were no streets. No pimps. No undercover cops. And the whole trick was that these arrangements remained just barely *legal*. These daddies were "law-abiding" men who simply wanted to give women "gifts." All the sex that took place inside an arrangement was, allegedly, free and consensual.

This rationale didn't help much, because this anxiety was not earnestly a fear of being arrested. At the core of everything, I was being eaten alive by the burdens of living a double life. I felt consumed by the guilt of constantly deceiving everyone around me. How could I possibly explain myself?

Socializing with anyone outside of my family made my life feel like a game of Jenga. Every question or observation like pulling another block from my shaky, towering lie. For example: Sammy, who, while building our burritos at Chipotle said, "I went to Whole Foods last week and my cashier didn't know who you were," because it had been six entire months since I left my bagging gig, and I was still keeping up this facade. Or Nate, who suggested I was glowing like someone who'd just been fucked. A comment I shot down, but which left me questioning how my body could possibly be responding positively to the sex. Eventually, I figured I was glowing like someone who just got *paid*.

What would people think of me if they knew that the sex work itself had begun to feel less deplorable than the white lies I'd been telling to keep the job private? It was, I was quickly discovering, a catch-22.

All of this (I suspected) resulted in my developing a new condition: chronic migraines with auras. Little spinners in my right mind's eye. Sometimes they were sparkling kaleidoscopes, but other days they were mean and jagged, like evil TV static. I imagined filleting my brain open to find a clenched nerve in the folds. Just another unexpected toll of a double life. How could I reduce the stress? I asked myself, wiping vomit off my lips. I couldn't stop seeing John altogether, but I could see him less publicly and further isolate myself from the world.

John happily accepted the amendment to skip dinners or shopping with only two requests. We stop meeting at fancy hotels and start meeting at La Quinta Inns with "five minutes of conversation before, um, *everything else*."

★

So there we were. John and I at an Aurora La Quinta Inn. In the midst of our five-minute pre-sex chatter. I usually chose the topic. That day, I picked my fifty-seven-year-old mom's finances. While none of us Gurules was thriving, I found my mom's finances the biggest cause for concern. There were a lot of questions that sometimes kept me up at night, like— if my mom already struggled to survive, how would she afford to live once she could no longer work? How would she pay rent and feed herself and have access to her many prescriptions? Sure, there were government assistance programs, but those would only do so much. What plan did my mom have other than flailing into old age?

I figured that eventually the responsibility would fall to the next generation. My sister was making fourteen dollars an hour as a certified nursing assistant. Without a degree, the top of her head was already touching the ceiling positionally and financially. She wouldn't be able to afford taking care of our mother. My mom assumed I was headed for success because I was a college student, but, so far, all higher education had done was mar me. My arrangement was the most hopeful thing I had. Which made it feel like the most hopeful thing any of us had.

I gave John a condensed version of this.

"Oh no!" he said. We were sitting beside one another on the bed. He was unwrapping a package of Grandma's Cookies. A staple treat inside La Quinta's hospitality bag. "Your mommy has no retirement fund?"

I shook my head. "Not a penny."

A few days earlier, my mom had told me that her retirement plan was to "die at work" and then donate her body to science so she could be cremated for free. She also assured me that she had a $30,000 life insurance policy, so my sister, nephew, and I would be okay. After funeral costs and the remainder split three ways, it wouldn't leave us with much. Maybe a couple thousand each. It felt unlike me to think this way about any sum of money, but now that I'd been working with John, making salary-level cash, I saw how quickly money evaporated. I could feel myself growing more and more attached to our arrangement. Good news for John, but a scary position for me. I didn't want to lose my senses and start feeling like no amount of money would ever be enough.

"What's the likelihood of my mom retiring if she starts saving right now, a maximum of a hundred dollars a month, and definitely not consistently?" I asked. Hearing myself say it aloud, it didn't sound good.

"Hmm," John said. "Let me think." Then he handed me one of the cookies. Today, oatmeal raisin, one of my favorites.

I took a big bite and chewed. The sugar touched every ridge in my teeth. It didn't hurt anymore. I'd recently had my very last dental appointment. My dentist, Dr. Hans, said I had been an excellent patient and handled everything like a champ. He patted me approvingly on the shoulder while I was still wearing my bib, dirty with flecks of blood and drilled teeth.

"Than you so mutche," I said with a numb lisp, wishing I had bought him a bouquet of flowers. A bundle of balloons. A cake. I wished I had thrown him a party.

"Floss," Dr. Hans said. "Promise me you'll floss."

John raised his hand to his chin and tapped. "Well, it's a little late for your mom to start saving now. But she should still open a Roth IRA and stash whatever she can every month. Even if it's twenty dollars. Every bit counts."

He then launched into a jargon-bombed speech about after-tax dollars being matched or unmatched, 401(k) limits, rollovers, conversions, and extracting money without penalty.

"I don't know what any of that means," I said.

"Oh sweetie," he said. "You know what? I'll find some easy-to-read articles—a wikiHow or something—and I'll email them to you. Just text me your email address."

All my old social media accounts were deactivated, but I did run a blog in my early twenties that I hadn't yet figured out how to delete. I had a premonition of John typing my Gmail address into a Yahoo! search bar and reading through what was essentially a public diary. An entire year's worth of posts had been about an *almost* girlfriend. I couldn't risk John catching on to my being queer, for that would surely result in him leaving me. "Could you just text me the links?" I asked.

"Yeah, sure." The pace of John's words sped up. "I can do that." He leaned toward my mouth, hovering a centimeter away, and whispered, "If you don't want to give me your email address yet, that's okay." Then he puckered up and kissed me.

"I also have a reading comprehension level above wikiHow," I said, when he was done.

"Of course you do, sweetie. You're very smart." Baby John took over the conversation. "Bery, bery smart. Sexy and smart." He lifted my hand and placed it on his crotch.

★

I keep thinking about your mommy, John texted the next morning. *Maybe you two can go have a nice relaxing spa day on me this weekend. Get lunch and massages at The Brown Palace :) Just keep track of how much you spend and let me know the total. I'll give you cash next week.*

The message was sent alongside links to articles about Roth IRAs and savings accounts and the Fortune 500 and Vanguard. None of which were from wikiHow. They required a financial literacy I didn't have. I would need undivided attention to read through them.

My mom and I were sitting on the couch, folding laundry and watching *Forensic Files*. I leaned over to show my mom the texts. "So," I said, in a scheming voice. "Do you want to get massages? Or do you want to pretend we did and keep the money for something more practical, say, your last lab bill?"

"Hmm, let me think," my mom said. Taking some time with her answer to not hurt my feelings. "I think paying the bill might be best, if that's okay?"

"It's the smarter decision."

On *Forensic Files*, a police officer was recounting an abduction that took place in a Target parking lot. "My advice to all girls is to be vigilant," he said. "Danger is everywhere." It startled me. I wondered what John might do if he found out I'd lied and used his massage money to pay bills. Would he kill me in our motel room? No. Not John, I thought. He was kind. He might even understand.

I wouldn't tell John the total until "after," but I needed to come up with a practical number. I loaded the hotel's menu online and saw a sixteen-dollar club sandwich and a nineteen-dollar cheesesteak. "Mom," I said. "What would you order?"

"The gourmet beef burger," she said. "With waffle fries." (Seventeen dollars.) We scrolled on. "And a caramel apple bourbon pecan pie with vanilla ice cream." She smacked her lips. It was a good price, considering. Only ten dollars.

I tallied everything we would've ordered. Appetizers, entrées, desserts, and four cocktails. The meal, tax, tip, and the spa package added up to $468. The number seemed preposterous for one afternoon. Five hundred dollars was half of our rent. Why hadn't John just offered that? *I'm sorry about your mommy's life, how about I pay her rent this month?* He predominantly gifted me things we didn't need, but Reddit said this was common for sugar daddies. They wanted the feel of *spoiling* their babies, not of keeping their head above water. Still, I found myself wishing I could just be straightforward with him.

Our arrangement existed in a paradoxical state of transparency and fantasy. A fine line that I hadn't a clue on how to navigate. We never spoke about needs or boundaries or safe words or rules or anything at all beyond John's home-run metaphor and my weekly payments. Which seemed absurd, *amateur*, but I was twenty-four years old. I was unskilled with communication in and of itself, and I had no experience communicating inside this context. There was no sugaring HR. No company handbook. I had only Reddit to scour for guidance, but none of the anonymous screen names acknowledged that revealing too much of yourself risked shattering the illusion that these men were buying.

It would've been too confronting for John to admit that I was in this arrangement with him to survive, rather than doing so to get my nails manicured every week. Because only there, in that gluttony, could John convince himself that he was not just the rock across from a hard place for me. That he was not merely taking advantage of a tough situation. His generosity was just generosity.

The TV show cut to a Bank of America commercial. A financially responsible couple had just bought a new house. Hardwood floors, vast windows, and marble counter tops. I wondered if this was what John's house looked like. He had described his home as a four-bed, four-bath, two-story, which he kept up to date, because he did have an affinity for nice things. "I worked hard for it, after all."

Perhaps the reason John wouldn't share extra cash wasn't merely about *wants* vs. *needs*. Maybe it was about who had money and who didn't and who John thought deserved it.

These daddies were *sharing* their money with babies who simply hadn't worked hard enough to have the same wealth. And, regardless of the labor we did with our bodies for these men, they still believed that we were not deserving of handouts. (*Sex isn't real work!* I could imagine these men telling themselves.) Even yet, there was nothing wrong with a little spoiling to tantalize their baby. To remind her who was who. Because these women may be hot. They may be young. But those things are fleeting. Wealth, on the other hand, would never lose value. Wealth was value itself. And regardless of said wealth being inherited, generational, or sprouted from a privileged existence that made affluence more easily attainable—it was still power. What we women needed to understand was that while *everyone* wanted a key to the upper-class world, not everyone deserved one.

Whatever the case, I felt grateful that John was keeping his hands off this gift delivery so we could use his generosity for more practical things.

★

When the alleged spa day arrived, John asked for pictures of me and my mom at the spa. *I want you to see me now, before all my makeup comes off*, I texted, and sent along three photos of my mom and I sitting in her car. My mom wore an orange Broncos T-shirt and Kmart jeans. She was allowed to dress casual for work on the weekends, but this was not classy enough for the hotel we were "having lunch at." I had on red lipstick and faux pearl earrings.

"Here," I said, handing her her jacket. "It's cold out and this looks expensive." I'd bought us discount Columbia jackets from Burlington Coat Factory a few months back. Neither of us had decent winter gear before this even though we lived in a state where it could snow seven months of the year. It didn't make any sense except that we never spent any meaningful time outdoors.

I'm sure you are just as sexy without makeup, John texted back right away. *Very nice pics. Thank you for sharing them. Have fun.* ☺

A few hours later, I sent John our $500 tab and a text that read, *My mom says thank you!! The day was so relaxing it added five years to her life. I told her, uh-oh, she definitely can't afford that! (Crying face, laughing face.)*

John ignored my joke, but wrote, *I love making you and your loved ones happy. I'll bring the money to our next pleasure session <3*

"How much will I get?" my mom asked.

"Two hundred and thirty-four dollars."

My mother's face lit up like I had opened the fridge door on it. "Oh, thank you, Lord," she said, breathy, like an actual prayer.

I felt self-congratulatory for my small generosity, which made me think of John. How my face must've looked exactly like his each time he paid me. This brought about a sort of shoddy feeling about myself and begrudging compassion for John. "It feels good to help people," he once told me.

"I think I'll pay that bill from the lab for doing blood work a few months ago," my mom said. "And take Chuy to the movies with the left-over."

By then $230 already felt like a small amount to me, but the way my mom kept repeating *thank you, thank you, thank you* reminded me of how monstrous it could be. A few years earlier, I'd been short $213 three months in a row and Sallie Mae sent my account to collections. Another time, the starter on my car died and I didn't have $198 to replace it. I'd had to park near other cars, keep my jumper cables on hand, and accept being late to everything for five miserable weeks.

"Mom," I said. "I can give you a couple hundred bucks every month if you need it." Though as the words left my mouth, I had a clairvoyant vision of where the money would go, so I added, "but you've got to spend it wisely, like on bills."

She nodded, her eyes pooling with relieved tears.

I felt hopeful then that life could change. Perhaps this time she would be smart, chipping away at her debt or only buying things she needed. Maybe she'd squirrel it away so that when life threw her a cur-veball she could say, for the first time ever, "No problem. I have some money saved."

★

Later that evening, I read the financial articles John sent. Articles that I quickly discovered were all about making money from money. They had nothing to do with arriving at retirement without savings. I knew what wealthy people thought. That being stupid enough to land at the winter of your life without a robust retirement was your own fault. Who cared that my mom worked nearly every day of her life? Who cared that she just never made enough to substantially save? I understood what John was trying to suggest. That my mom had made her own bed and now she would lie in it. And he was trying to tell me that it was my responsibility to not do the same.

I wanted to tell John that these articles failed to acknowledge that my mom's bed, like so many others, had been made before she was born. She would have needed a miraculous intervention or a secret guide to escape her predetermined path. There was not one mention of college before my generation in our lineage. There was no wealth being passed down through our bloodline. No wisdom on how to turn money into more money. No parent or grandparent or trust fund to pay the rent. Nowhere to even turn and ask for help when help was needed.

I felt the whole weight of my arrangement on my shoulders then. If I wanted a different life for myself, if I wanted financial security, or if I ever wanted to own a home, or retire, or even easily afford my existence in the world, then I would need a miracle. John, and the opportunity he presented to sell my body to him, was that miracle.

In a moment of delusion, I thought of that famous bit of advice, *Worry about what you can change*, and cooked up a quick scheme: If I could make it to my originally planned end date, sixty-two weeks of sugaring, I would be okay in the immediate short term. But if I could push past that end date, and sugar for another year or another five years, or simply as long as I could manage, then I could potentially trickle money into my mother's (future) Roth IRA. Or I could open a college fund for my nephew. And, depending on how much my body could endure, I might even be able to pay my sister's way through trade school. My sugaring could be the secret passageway to a better life for us all.

It sounded easy enough, but when I did the math, I snapped out of it. To pull my whole family aboard my lifeboat, I would have to sell my body to John for the rest of my life.

Part Two
The Descent

7

Parental Advisory

"I haven't heard from John all week," I told my dad. "Which is out of character for him. I'm worried my arrangement is in trouble."

It was the end of summer. August 2016. It was the last weekend before school started up again for Chuy and me. Donald Trump and Hillary Clinton were the presidential candidates of a depressingly close race. Brexit was underway. The world felt nasty.

Chuy and I had joined my dad on his old speedboat in Pueblo, a small city south of Colorado Springs, where a man-made reservoir sat on the town outskirts. The speedboat was an antique with sun-bleached decals and a blistered Bimini top. The single new addition was a leaky crack along the hull. An issue my dad declared only "a slight inconvenience," as long as a passenger was willing to scoop water from the boat and empty it overboard. Before we left the dock, my dad handed me and Chuy each an empty Folgers can. These were our buckets.

"Don't be lazy and buck this up," my dad said. "We can't sail if we're underwater."

Normally we would've laughed at my dad's joke, but I was feeling somber after a peculiar week with John, and Chuy was terrified of the boat sinking—an experience he'd already once survived. Two years earlier, my dad took Chuy cruising on an equally shitty boat. They'd parked to swim, but when they prepared to return to the dock, my dad forgot to raise the anchor. As he floored the motor to sail away, the boat spun like a wooden top before going nose up, Titanic style, and sank. At some point during the chaos, my nephew's fight-flight-or-freeze response kicked in, and he jumped ship. While my dad bobbed around in his life vest collecting his wallet and other buoyant odds and ends, he scanned the area for my nephew, and spotted Chuy on a nearby boat.

"I've never met anyone who wants to stay alive more than you," I told Chuy as he dumped water from his Folgers can. He'd only paused to wipe sweat from his eyes.

Chuy furrowed his brow at me. "And?"

"It's just an observation. It's endearing."

"En-what?"

"Sweet," I said. "It's nice to see."

"Okay," he said, and filled his bucket once more.

I moved a seat closer to my dad, and said, "I need some parental advice. What should I do about John being MIA?"

Earlier that week, during John's hand job no less, he shook the whole room by blurting out, "Oh my god, Michelley. I love you."

Slip of the tongue, I told myself and ignored him.

But then John said it again more clearly, "Michelley, I do love you. I really, really, really love you."

That time I felt absolutely galled.

How could John think he loves me, I wondered. He barely even knew me. I'd been fairly open with John about certain things at the start—mostly my family—but our long talks had dried up after John and I started skipping dinners. Nothing too deep had ever taken place in those pre-session five minutes, making John's declaration feel delusional. I handled the situation the only way I could think to, by saying, "Thank you for sharing that with me," and continuing with the task.

"It's fine if you talk, Shell," my dad hollered over the boat's engine. "But you've gotta talk *and scoop!*"

He steered toward the west, and our bodies slanted with the boat. I collected an inch or two in my can and emptied it over the side.

"You don't love John?" my nephew asked, a stripe of sunscreen on his nose.

I'd amended the story for my audience, glazing right over all the sexual details, and spoke only of the "L-bomb."

"No," I said. "I don't."

My nephew looked perplexed. "How come?"

I studied the water. It was blue against the white rock but muddy in our boat. I wanted to say, *Because this is an arrangement.*

While it was evident from the beginning that John yearned for something more—a genuine connection, a sense of being desired, listened to, and cared for—those were not things he could buy. At times I felt guilty, questioning whether I was doing John a disservice by allowing him to financially support me instead of someone else, but then I'd quickly dismiss these thoughts. Regardless of whom John hired for physical contact or company he would always be paying for counterfeit affection. Deep down, John must have been aware of this, although, the more I thought about it, he clearly preferred living in blissful denial. My distaste during the sessions had also become increasingly difficult to hide. I would try to muster warmth, but surely my aversion to John's body was obvious through my silence and inability to hold eye contact. I wanted to put on a better show to keep my job safe, but it's simply the way my body responds when it's unhappy. I call it my "going stiff."

Lucky that even as vacant as I was, John still declared that this sex was the best of his life. What he must've meant was that it was the most

exhilarating sex of his life. Not in terms of the actions or chemistry between us (I was there, it was not *good sex*), but for John, the eroticism lay
in the notion of being intimate with a woman half his age. My arriving
at those hotel rooms all dolled up and granting him access to my body
unwittingly validated John's belief that his money could buy anything. I
knew John did not actually love me, but he did love what I represented
about his wealth—and therefore, him.

On the boat, my shoulders were turning pink from the sun. I shrugged
them at my nephew. "Love is special. You don't just feel it for anyone."

"I hope you didn't tell John that," my dad said with a laugh.

There was a silent moment. We three listened to the water splashing
the boat. I thought that I ought to be feeling happier. I knew what might
do the trick. I opened the cooler again and unwrapped the Snickers. I
took a bite then passed it to my nephew.

"Give me some," my dad yelled over the sound of the engine.

Chuy tossed the candy his way. My dad missed, picked the bar off the
floor, shook off some water, took a bite, and said, "Germs are good for
you." With his mouth full, he went on. "John's not going to fire you if
you don't say you love him back, is he?"

My nephew looked concerned.

"I don't know," I said. "But it gets worse."

After John said that he loved me, we finished without incident. As
soon as John was dressed, I stood by the motel door, anxious to leave,
but he wouldn't stop lollygagging. John paced back and forth between
the restroom and his empty briefcase, which he rummaged through as if
expecting a little white bunny to appear. John had already paid me, so it
wasn't my envelope he was hunting for. Finally, he broke the silence. "I
need to talk to you about something."

"What's going on?" I asked, expecting John to add *must say "I love
you"* into our contract, but it was much worse. "The company I work
for is shutting down," John said. "Eventually everyone will be let go. It's

a gradual process. Most employees don't know yet. We begin the first round of layoffs next month."

John sat on the edge of the bed and stared blankly at the wall, while my whole life flashed before my eyes. But rather than the one I had lived, it was the life that could've been. Ease and comfort. Debtless and healthy. "Oh, god," I said, dropping beside John. "It's over."

"Oh. Oh no. No," John said, rubbing my shoulders. "I have a lot of savings. There's nothing to worry about on that end."

"We can keep seeing one another?" I asked, catching wind of my own desperation. I didn't care about turning John off. The man just said he *loved* me. He probably even liked this emotional display. "Even when you lose your job?"

"Yes," John said. "I'm telling you because I've known about this for a few weeks and I've been scoping out the job market. I sent my résumé to a recruiting agency and I've had a few companies interested."

I started laughing. What an odd assortment of feelings! To be so disturbed one second, then terrified of the loss, desperate and relieved at last for the continuation of our arrangement.

"Unfortunately," John said, "there isn't a whole lot available within my salary range here in Colorado."

"Oh." *Pay decreases?* Then it hit me. "You're moving?"

"It's a possibility," John said. "But I wanted to talk to you about it first. Would you still see me if I moved?" He paused for me to consider. "These things are slow. It might not even happen for a few more months or even next year. I might even take a few months off in between jobs. Just rest a little. But if I do move, I would pay for the flight and all your travel expenses, of course."

"Yes," I said. "I would definitely keep seeing you." I did not stop and think through what that would mean. I had just felt the backsliding end of the arrangement and now I would do anything to keep it. Plus, John said it was still a way off into the future. Maybe I'd have enough money saved by then to quit. Who knew. It didn't matter in that moment. I just didn't want to lose him now.

"Great!" John leaned in to kiss me and said, "I love you, sweetie."

"What will your kids do if you move?" I asked. Two teen boys in high school. John said they lived with him during the school week and his ex-wife on the weekends. Would they move in with her? Did she have the room for it?

"Oh." He paused to think. "They'll stay in Littleton. In my house."

"Without you? Two teenagers will live in your house without you?"

"Well . . ." I could almost see John's brain doggy-paddling around. "My eldest son drives, so he can take his brother to school."

"What about their mom?" I asked, confused. "Why can't they stay at her house?"

John hadn't expected this question. His voice wobbled. "She'll still live in her house, and they'll still go there on the weekends."

"Just to clarify," I spoke slowly, "your teenage kids will live without a parent in your house while you live in another state. Even though their mother lives right up the street?"

John puffed his cheeks before releasing the air with a mouthy POP. "Uhh . . . yes. That . . . is . . . exactly what they will do."

A sneaking dread rose in my chest that the "ex" in John's "ex-wife" was a convenient fiction. If I'd had a say in it, I'd have preferred to be the sugar baby of a single man. Although not totally unpredictable, it was still disappointing for me to imagine John lying about being married. It seemed like every relationship I'd ever seen or been part of had its own terrible betrayals. I tried to deflect from letting John confess this secret to me, because I wasn't sure how either of us were meant to respond. I just peered at the clock on the bedside table. "Well," I said. "Shall we?"

"I haven't heard from John since," I said to my dad now, chewing on my lower lip. I usually heard from John nearly every day. We'd parked the boat a few dozen feet from the reservoir's edge and were bobbing about as everyone prepared to jump in the water. "Can you believe this?"

"What's the issue?" my dad said, perplexed. He was rubbing sunscreen on his belly.

"Well, clearly John is married," I said. "His *children* cannot live in a house *alone*. Don't you think?"

"Why can't the kids live alone?" my dad asked. "All John has to do is keep paying the bills and giving them money to order pizzas. Two teenagers can't order a goddamn pizza for themselves?" He looked bewildered. "Millennials are all made out of sugar."

My nephew started laughing. He had tossed his Folgers can to the floor and was now pulling his water wings from our bag. "Will you help me blow these up, Auntie?" he asked.

"Sure."

As I puffed into the hot plastic, I thought of the time my parents left eight-year-old me, my eleven-year-old sister, and my twelve-year-old cousin Ellie home alone during a Category 4 storm. Hurricane Floyd. September 1999. For most of the day, we bundled up together in the living room watching back-to-back episodes of Jerry Springer. Paternity tests, weird phobias, some guy screwing his girlfriend's mom. Suddenly our screen turned black. My sister, deeply rattled, turned to Ellie and cried, "How are we gonna survive without TV?"

"That's kind of irresponsible parenting, don't you think?" I said to my dad. My nephew was older now than I was then, and no one would leave him without power.

I slid Chuy's water wings up his arms. Up next, his tube.

"You're going to float to the moon with all this on," I said.

"Oh, sorry, princess," my dad mocked. "Momma and Papa had to work. What was so hard about the three of you sitting safely inside eating Chef Boyardee without a parent? What would we have done if we were there? Opened the can for you?" This turned into a familiar lecture. "Do you know what I was doing at nine years old?"

"Working!" my nephew said. "Just like I've been working all day on this boat."

"Oh no! I wasn't just doing a little bit of work for a luxurious boat ride," my dad said dramatically. "I was breaking my back picking god-damn potatoes to pay the goddamn rent." As a child and eventually a teen, my dad worked alongside his five siblings and parents on migrant farms in Idaho. His father would pluck all the kids from school as soon as harvesting season began and they wouldn't return until the work was done months later. "One summer," he told us, "I outgrew all the pants I took with me and my mom refused to buy me new clothes when we got home. Everyone at school called me 'high waters.'" That same year the principal pleaded with my grandfather to stop taking the kids out of school because they needed an education. My grandfather replied they needed the money.

Sometimes I look at my body and think about all the DNA inside of it. A need for money has always wound up the ultimate problem in my family. This was the reason my dad and my mom understood my deci-sion to touch John for what felt, to us, like actual wealth. This was why, when I told my dad that John was not the kind of father who would leave his kids alone to order pizzas and he had to be married, my dad covered Chuy's ears and playfully mouthed, "So you're not just a sugar baby anymore, you're a mistress?"

I covered Chuy's eyes with my hands so he couldn't read my lips. He giggled sweetly. "Yeah," I whispered. "I think so."

We both let go of Chuy's head. "Okay, buddy. You're out of jail," my dad said.

I emptied my lungs into Chuy's tube again. My phone pinged from within my bag. I leapt for it at once.

"Relax," my dad said. "It's not the president."

"Who is it?" Chuy asked.

"Your mom," I said. "She wants to know what time we'll be home. I wrote back, *4ish.*

"So what if John's married?" my dad asked. "Had you wondered before?"

I nodded. I'd had my suspicions, briefly. Nothing John had said or done in particular made me feel this way. I'd just assumed that anyone willing to pay for sex would probably be willing to have an affair too. But then he complained about his divorce so often, with such specificity, and he never had any problem texting me or sending me pictures of his life. Eventually, I simply believed him.

"It doesn't feel great," I said. "There's a big difference between being a," I looked at Chuy, "*girlfriend* to a lonely single man and being involved in someone's big, elaborate affair. I'd feel so bad. I could get over it, of course. John is strictly a job to me and the whole dynamic isn't exactly kosher, but I'm worried *he's* having second thoughts now."

I paused and looked at my nephew. Such a sweet little guy. "What if John went home from the La Quinta last week, looked at his kids and thought, *I can't believe I'm paying their future inheritance to some twenty-four-year-old girl for,*" I mouthed the rest, "*blow jobs?*"

My dad frowned. "You know what an inheritance is? Unnecessary. Rich people act like that's a guarantee. I hope you guys don't expect anything from me, because I'm going to spend every last penny before I die."

My nephew laughed, but I wasn't in a playful mood.

"That doesn't solve any of my problems, because we're talking about John," I went on. "Not you and me." Whenever I paused to think about John's radio silence, it seemed possible that he simply hit his limit of deceit.

At the start of this arrangement, I'd been focused on the stress of the sex and my reputation, but the further I trekked into this situation, the harder it was becoming to cope with the distress of constant secrecy and lies. It was wild how this one hour a week with John had turned all my other days deceitful. I was as lonely as I'd ever been with friends, and physically suffering from stress-induced chronic migraines and lack of appetite, but in every other way, my life was basically the best it'd ever been.

"A wife?" I said. "How, on top of everything else, could John deal with hiding me from his wife?"

My dad shrugged. Perhaps it conjured a memory. "What's your mom got to say about it?"

I'd withheld this recent development from my mother because of the way she, too, benefited from my arrangement. If I lost the income, she'd lose the small amount of money I'd been able to give her each month. "She doesn't know," I said. "I've only told you."

My dad seemed flattered by this. "Well, Shell. The worst thing that could happen is that he fires you and then you can either go back to the strip club or Whole Foods."

"I know." I'd already considered this. If John called it off, astute decisions would have to be made about how I'd cascade back into poverty. I'd have to immediately halt my student loan payments, so I could instead buy a car flat out. This was imminent anyway, as my ancient Honda had barely delivered Chuy and me to Pueblo.

"I want to buy a new, used car," I said. "But what if my friends ask me how I could afford one?" I collected water from the floor and emptied it out. "Is it believable to say I won ten grand off a scratch ticket?"

"Dubious," my dad said, taking a quick swig from his Mike's. "But why do you care? Your friends should mind their own beeswax. My friends don't ask me about things I buy."

"That's because you don't have any friends," I said. My dad has always maintained that friends are too much work for the payoff. *They just make life harder.*

"I don't care what you buy," my dad went on, "but let me give you some advice. Do not put your money into a bank. A savings account only appreciates *point zero one percent per year*. Point zero! You could make more collecting pennies off the sidewalk."

"Are you suggesting I keep my money in my safe forever then?"

He shook his head no.

"I'm suggesting you invest in gold bars, or at least gold coins." He started to speak in a hushed tone. "My radio show said gold is the only way to assure your money doesn't lose its value once the aliens take over."

"That's one idea," I said. "But I think I should just stick to my original plan and pay off my student loans, as much as possible anyway."

"PFFT!" my dad spat. "Don't bother! If I were you, I'd spend that money however I wanted. Let your loans disappear when the internet goes dark."

My nephew hooted in the background and stepped into the middle of his water tube.

"Damn. Those sure are some fancy shoes you've got on," my dad said, nodding at Chuy's feet.

"Thanks," Chuy said, grinning. "They're my new Air Jordan 10 Shanghais."

"Cool," my dad said. "You should take them off to go swimming. You don't want to get them even more wet. I know those were EX-PEN-SIVE."

I shot Chuy an "I told you so" look, because I *had* told him to leave the Jordans at home. Why would he risk soaking his new $200 shoes in mucky water? I asked. He should only wear them on the court to stretch their life. Chuy rolled his eyes and tightened his laces. The Air Jordans were of special concern to me because they had been purchased with money I'd hoped might wind up in my mother's savings account. I'd scolded her when I first saw them, "The money I give you is for bills!"

"Oh, Shell, relax!" she'd said. "I used *my own* money to buy them." I'd wanted to say that regardless of where the money came from—me or her own paycheck—she couldn't afford to blow it. But, why bother? My mom would've returned the same rebuttal, *You can't tell me what to do with my money.* I left the conversation dismayed and walked outside to call my dad in private.

"That was nice of her," he'd said.

"What about her mountain of debt?"

"If your mom's not worried about it, why should you be?" Before I could respond, my dad said, "That's one of those questions you're supposed to think about, not answer."

"Rhetorical?"

"Is that what the fancy college students call it?"

"Grandma said it's good practice to dress for the job I want," Chuy told my dad now, meaning an NBA player.

"Well, today your job is a sea skipper," my dad said. "So, take 'em off!"

"Aye, aye, captain!"

"Are you crying?" My dad asked, shocked, when he looked my way.

"Yes," I said. No more sunny days! No more breezy afternoons! No more thinking about anything other than money! Back to my old reality.

"I got too ahead of myself," I said, wiping my eyes. "I thought life was going to change. I thought I was going to get out of debt. But if it's going to end, I'm going to need even more student loans this year. It's stupid, but I thought I was going to set myself up for a whole new life."

My nephew came up to hug me. "It's all going to be okay, Auntie." It was a sweet gesture, but what'd he know?

"You're getting too ahead of yourself now," my dad said. Never enough sympathy in his voice. "You don't even know if John is married. Maybe it's not what you think."

"Yeah, right," I said. "Usually, I'll get a selfie of John or a picture of his lunch. But it's been radio silence." I blew my nose into Chuy's discarded shirt.

"Ew," he said. "That's disgusting."

"I packed you a fresh one for after," I said.

"Still."

I did it once more. "Sorry," I said. "My nose is blocked."

When my dad and nephew jumped into the reservoir, I stayed on board to cry, and, as my dad reminded me, "scoop water from the boat."

I kept at my task. Scooping and scooping. An easy enough chore, as I was more in my head than anywhere else. I debated which John might find more insufferable: deep loneliness or deceiving those around him? But the answer wasn't black and white. Just like it wasn't for me when I weighed financial insecurity with the latter. I couldn't fathom losing the money. Nor the whiplash I would experience reentering the insecurity. How taxing the day-to-day would become again when I was waiting for one tiny little thing to knock me off my feet. The thought alone was distressing.

My iPhone pinged again. I looked down at my phone and, *iMessage from John Linghu* exploded on my screen like confetti. For the first time all week, I felt hopeful. I dropped my bucket and opened to a lengthy message.

Hi sweetie. I have some bad news I need to tell you.

I withheld some information from you. I hope you can forgive me... My kids are not as young as I told you. The kids have both already graduated undergrad. One lives and works in Portland, the other is finishing his master's in Boston. I'm sorry to have deceived you!!!! I didn't want you to think I was too old for you. :,(:,(

Relief flushed through me. I went dizzy, like I'd cookie binged my blood sugar sky high. John hadn't been having second thoughts about the arrangement. And he wasn't even married! He was just lying about his kids' ages. Something I did not care one lick about.

I texted back right away. *Hi! Oh, I don't care how old your kids are! I was worried you were married and the kids would be living with your wife! :0 It doesn't make me think you're too old. Thank you for telling me!*

He replied: *Oh no! Sorry to make you worry, sweetie. I am NOT married! I'm so happy that you aren't bothered! I've been thinking about your face all day. Sometimes it gives me a boner :0 :) Does 6:00 p.m. work for you on Wednesday?*

I imagined John at work, admiring my photo. Windows all around. Him twirling half circles in his swivel chair. Elbows resting on the padded armrests. Polo pressed to perfection. A tiny lump pushing up against the crotch of his khakis below the desk.

"John isn't married!" I called out to my family as I jumped off the boat. The frigid water knocked the air out of my lungs, but it only made me feel more alive. When I came up for air I was no longer crying.

"What are you yellin' about?" my dad asked.

"John isn't married," I said again. "I'm still employed! I'm still rich!"

Chuy kicked his feet and splashed me. He was all goggles and cheeks and front teeth. "Yay, Auntie!"

"Well good for you," my dad said. "But you can't just jump ship on your duties." He swam over to the boat and pulled himself up the ladder. "We still need someone to scoop water. You're just like all the other rich people," my dad said playfully. He shook the water from his black hair. "You're safe, so you let the rest of us drown."

I floated on my back. The sun was hot. I had never been happier. That was untrue. I had never been more relieved. I hummed to myself. Everything was more or less the same as it had been a week ago. Aside from John's impending move, which I still wasn't ready to think about. These things were slow, he'd said. He wanted some time off. The move might not even happen until next year. In the meantime, what did that matter? I would be paid just the same.

"Let this be a lesson," my dad said. "This gig is nothing more than a lifetime." What he meant was that sugaring was just a blip in time. An era.

Impermanent. *We all live many lifetimes inside our one life* was a proverb of my dad's own creation. It was what he'd said to me when my parents' marriage ended. "Shell, your mom and I lived a whole lifetime together, but now we're both in our next lives apart." It made sense to me. My dad was a person who'd had a big fat existence. One that stretched decades before he'd ever met my mom. He'd lived a lifetime enlisted in the military, and before that as a Kmart cashier, and before that as a ranch hand, and before that as a boy who picked potatoes to help pay rent.

"What I'm trying to say," my dad said from the boat, Folgers can in hand, divorced and still chugging along, "is this rich life you've got right now is one lifetime, but it's not your whole life. Don't get yourself confused."

I turned over to my belly and paddled my legs. My dad was right. Before I'd ever been a sugar baby, I had been a dancer. And before that, a bagger. And before that, a bartender. And before that, a dishwasher. I felt suddenly worried about my next lifetime.

"Dad, when this is all over, do you think I'll ever meet someone that could love me in spite of John?"

My dad nodded. "Life is hard, Michelle. You're just a kid, so you don't totally get it yet, but everybody does things they're not proud of at some point or another."

I tried to envision looking someone in the eye and saying *I slept with someone for money* without them looking away. "I'm not hopeful," I said. "Unless I meet someone completely unhinged."

8

Teacher's Pet

I began my final semester of college days after Donald Trump's inauguration. It had taken many by surprise, but I'd long since predicted he'd win the election. Throughout his campaign Trump had said horrendous things. Calling Mexicans rapists, being caught on tape declaring he could grab women by the pussies, and so forth. But our country was built on racist ideologies, and while it'd become less socially acceptable to outright say prejudiced, sexist, and xenophobic things, Trump came in as a tornado, unapologetically terrible, and in his monstrous crudeness people saw themselves and voted in their own likeness.

When I arrived back at school, there was an air of despair, but also of rebellion. I was grateful to be in a blue state. I was grateful to the one hundred thousand people I marched with downtown just two days before, surrounded by pink hats and loud, rambunctious voices in protest. The majority of those in attendance had been women, but there were a handful of men. My newest professor, Dr. Wes Elliot, had been one of them.

That's the first thing he said as he stood behind the podium in our Sociology of Deviance course. "For far too long women's movements have lacked male participation," he said. "It's important we break out of these gendered barriers and acknowledge that women's issues are the people's issues." I appreciated the opening speech's feminist flair. Women and Gender Studies was not a particularly large department, so to accrue all necessary credits, I often took classes in different departments. Sometimes Chicano/a Studies, sometimes Psychology, and sometimes, like Dr. Elliot's class, Sociology. Not all professors were so progressive.

During roll, after Dr. Elliot called my name, he caught my eye and smiled ever so slightly. "Hey," he said, an airiness in his voice. "Haven't I seen you before?"

I was positive he had. Professor Elliot was lanky, naturally slight, and though he was starting to gray, still quite blonde, all of which gave him a youthful quality. Upon second glace his face was handsomely mature. Etched with fine lines and a trimmed beard. He wore his hair to his shoulders or occasionally pulled up in a bun. Whenever I'd seen Professor Elliot around, navigating the halls, and, once, at a nearby brewery, during, of all things, Drag Queen Bingo, I always thought of Kurt Cobain.

I blushed. Not expecting this shared recognition. Certainly not expecting the displayed acknowledgment of it. In my life, it was always me doing the reminding. Yes, we've met. We had a class together. We were in grades six to twelve together. You dated my cousin for four years. "Yes," I said, shyly. "Just around campus."

"Ah, of course." Professor Elliot tapped his pen on the podium edge and smiled. The whole class saw. "Well, I'm happy to see you here."

★

After roll, Professor Elliot insisted the class participate in an icebreaker. Normally, I hated such activities. I wanted to be an invisible student who listened and took notes and submitted my work, earned the grade and remained as good as anonymous, but something had come over me this day. I wanted to be seen. Specifically, I wanted Professor Elliot to see me.

He stood before the whiteboard, uncapped a red marker, and wrote the question *Who am I in my dream life?* It echoed the question I had first asked John at Penthouse: *Who are you in an alternate reality?* I took this as a sign.

Each student would have to answer this question out loud when it came our turn. I nervously sat waiting, as I heard my classmates speak their deepest desire—to be an actress, to be rich, to own a business, to travel the world. I had the same wish I'd told John. "In my dream life, I am a writer."

"What kind of writer?" Professor Elliot asked me.

"Literary," I said. "In my dream life I've written novels and memoirs. I've written essay collections and scripts."

"I'm also a literary writer in my dream life," he said smiling in earnest. "I went the academic route for the security of it, but I've been working on a fantasy novel the last ten years." He laughed a little in embarrassment. "Maybe in ten more years it will see the light of day."

Before moving on to the next student, Dr. Elliot paused. He looked thoughtful, misty. "I took a writing workshop back in undergrad. I'll never forget some advice my professor told the whole class." Dr. Elliot coughed, then put on a deep and dramatic voice, before saying, "The writing industry is cutthroat! It's a shame, but the best thing you could do for your writing is probably to kill yourself. If that's too extreme, then at least do yourself a favor and write for the purpose of entertaining. Think of yourself as an *entertainer*. Not an artist."

"That advice is so old white guy," someone said and laughed.

"Oh no, I hope I didn't just age myself," he said, playfully covering his mouth and widening his eyes.

It was finally the next student's turn, and then the next. I couldn't recall what anyone after me said. My head had gone fuzzy wondering if what I thought was transpiring was true. It was the spark that lit a forest fire. I recognized it at once.

★

"You all know who you'd be in a dream life, so I want you all to ask your-selves what you're willing to do to achieve those dreams," Professor Elliot said at the end of class. He had turned all our sour moods around, by reassuring that yes, while the cultural moment was grim, our lives were still ahead of us. "I'm a full professor," he said. "That was another dream of mine that I actually achieved." He paused for the class to laugh. "I was once right there where you all are, trying to imagine my life, trying to make a difference in the world, and now I get to come to campus and learn alongside evolving generations of students." Dr. Elliot was telling us that the most important thing to our success was to have a goal. "The number one reason I'm successful is not because I'm the most talented or smartest guy in the world—although that's up for debate—but because I commit myself to my work," Professor Elliot said.

He asked us to consider ways to rearrange our own lives so that we could begin prioritizing our dreams. "No one is going to champion your life more than you are. So, take yourself seriously."

In my younger years, writing was an integral part of my daily routine. I'd approached it with a religious devotion, filling journals and crafting scripts that I'd beg my sister and friends to perform. I'd even completed two manuscripts, now dead and gone: a Sapphic poetry collection that I'd read from at weekly open mic nights and a memoir chronicling a road trip to see Britney Spears perform in Chicago.

As I grew older, I lost my momentum. Or rather, life's demands took priority. Balancing homework, a full-time job, helping my family, and maintaining a social life became an arduous juggling act. I no longer had the mental space to write. Meeting John changed that. I had more time available to me without need for an hourly job or friendships, and writ-ing about it had proven itself to be the perfect outlet. Think of yourself as an entertainer, the professor had said. I suppose that made my life the entertainment.

★

A week later, at the La Quinta Inn, I found John aglow under a lamppost. During the dark winter months, we'd meet in the parking lots and walk together. "I have a little treat for you," he said and opened his gloved palm to reveal a tangerine. "Something to brighten this gray day."

The company John worked for had officially shut down back in October, and it was clear he was further starved of social interaction. This had resulted in his becoming ultrawarm toward me. On the contrary, I had been feeling stiff since November when Donald Trump officially won the election.

The evening the results were announced, I stood in the living room with my mom and Chuy, all three of us in tears. Though I had bitterly anticipated this outcome, I was unprepared for how devastating it would be for my eight-year-old nephew.

"What's going to happen to my daddy? Will he have to go back to Mexico?" Chuy asked through sobs. My mom and I shared apprehensive glances.

"I want to call him," Chuy said.

When he pressed the phone to his ear, the screen slick with tears, he repeated over and over, "Te amo, Papa. He can't make you leave. Te amo."

The next night, I told John this story after he confirmed that he'd voted for Trump. I hoped the image of my nephew might fill John with regret or at least make him acknowledge that something terrible had just happened with this election. Instead, John grew defensive. "I've always leaned conservative," he said, then began referencing Trump's business and tax stances—things I had always been too poor to care about. "So, sue me," he said, rubbing my arm, "I like money. It allows me to buy high-quality things, *like my Michelley*."

This was a phrase John used often, stripping away my humanity until I was a literal *thing* he could buy. I was always cross with myself for letting these comments slide, but how could I defend myself? Hadn't I willingly entered a transactional relationship with John, implicitly treating my own body as a commodity? I found myself incapable of admonishing John for his remark, and instead, I turned my attention to the bigger picture.

"Are you insinuating that you care more about lower taxes than you do people?" I asked.

"I work very hard for my money," John said, his defensiveness apparent.

"I understand. And you are already very rich."

"I'm not *that* rich," he said, dismissively.

"That's something only rich people say." My voice began to tremble. "You're not Jeff Bezos, sure, but you've got *several million* in the bank. You're making enough in the stock market that you don't even need a day job." I pressed my finger into his bare chest. "You're driving a Lexus, and you're supporting two kids *and me* on your one salary. You're doing pretty all right." I paused for effect. "It's disgusting if you think a lower tax rate is more important than basic human rights."

John's eyes widened, surprised to see me being anything other than docile. I knew I ought to shift the conversation to lighter topics. (I was his sugar baby, after all. The subordinate in our power dynamic.) But I couldn't stifle my anger. I was furious at John for feeling so entitled to money that he refused to look at the people anguishing beyond it. Take me, for example. I was right in front of John, suffering, forcing myself to suck his dick to crawl out of debt. *Oh, woe is me*, I thought. The internet had gone wild after Trump's election, and the consensus was that if your partner supported Trump and you didn't leave them then you were also what was wrong with the world. John wasn't my partner, but I was in business with him, and our exchange confirmed much of what Trump stood for. I was choosing money over my own well-being.

I couldn't think about my own hypocrisy, however; I just needed to make a point.

In the upcoming weeks, I'd complain to my dad about John's politics, and how lousy I felt being a Republican's sugar baby. Sometimes I wondered if I should even quit. My dad would tell me this was an inane thing to get hung up on. Did I not think the people running his job were awful too? "Even fancy-ass Whole Foods, a supposed do-good grocery store, is just another corporation, banking billions in profit each year," my dad said. "The CEO doesn't care about people, and they never cared about you." So, I could throw myself a pity party, my dad said, just because John wasn't a generous people-loving anti-capitalist, or I could acknowledge that I'd likely never not worked for one anyway.

But that night in La Quinta, I was desperate for John to acknowledge that this panic was real. Lives were at risk. "Millions of people felt the very same fear my nephew did on Tuesday night. People will be deported. There are countless kids—Americans, if that makes a difference to you—that will lose their parents."

John threw an exaggerated look at the clock. "I think we should change the subject. You look very sexy tonight." He lifted my hand and placed it on his limp dick.

"Isn't that awful?" I asked him. My eyes went hot, like everything bad inside me had caught flame. It wasn't that I thought I could change John's mind, but I thought he might at least acknowledge the menace ahead of us. "I can't do this until you tell me you understand that Trump being elected is a tragedy and you were complicit in that."

"I understand," John said, hollowly, and then placed his palm atop my hand to begin working himself by proxy.

I harbored great shame over what I did next, but eventually I fell to my knees and got to work.

Now, in the La Quinta parking lot, I took the tangerine from his palm and smiled weakly before we crossed the asphalt, mindful of the odd patch of ice. We passed a housekeeper. John said hello but I, as I often did in these compromised moments with him, looked away out of shame. Inside, we peeled off our layers. Gloves, coats, snow boots.

"Sweetie," John said cheerfully, patting the bed beside him. "I have some news about Titan."

A few months after John received word about his company closing, he reentered the job market. He'd applied to be a cloud manager at Titan Inc., a cloud storage corporation out in Washington, DC, and had already had a handful of interviews with the hiring managers. His fourth was this last week. Around interview three we both accepted a move out East as a real possibility, and so John mapped out the potential new rules. Once a month I would fly to meet him for a "romantic" four-day weekend, which would include "one pleasure session per day" for $4,800 total. While John would receive sixty-eight additional hours of my company each month, my salary would remain the same.

Message received: John didn't think of our spending time together as a part of the work. The money he paid me was exclusively for sex. Back when I asked John if we could skip dinners (which we never picked back up), he didn't try to pay me any less. And a couple of times over the last year, either John or I'd had to cancel, and there was never any pay during those weeks. John wasn't just giving me the cash because he wanted to "take care of me." He simply paid me the agreed upon amount for sex. Four pleasure sessions meant $4,800.

I could comprehend that logic, but sex wasn't the only part of the job. After John dropped his love-bomb on me last summer, he said it nearly every time we met. When it became probable that John was moving to DC, he began fantasizing about our time together. Romantic boat rides on the Potomac, walking tours of the National Mall, nice restaurants. It took its toll to constantly meet John's physical needs both public and private. Moreover, like our previous dinners and brief pre-session chats, I anticipated that the responsibility of keeping our conversations lively would fall to me. Top all that off with sex four days in a row? I'd given myself a handful of migraines just thinking about it. But there was one sure perk. After my four consecutive days with John, I'd have the next twenty-six days of each month completely free.

"I got the job at Titan!" John said.

"Congratulations!" I said, putting on my best voice. "I know that it's a highly competitive position. They've seen something really special in you."

"Thank you," John said, and pulled me in for a kiss.

"So," I said. "When do you move?"

John was suddenly all business. "Titan is moving me out to DC in three weeks. It'll be a big transition with finding a place to live and getting all my stuff across the country, but I'll be paid a big relocation fee." He paused to rejoice. It was a moment for us to acknowledge what hard work, education, and careers can do. "*And* they'll set me up in a furnished condo for up to two months. It's a five-star complex." John swiped through photos of the condominiums they'd proposed. Smack dab in the heart of Alexandria, Virginia. A suburb outside of DC. The units were identical. White marble countertops, stained hardwood floors, modern square couches, and beds made with $200 pillows. It looked nice. I told him so.

"It'll be a big help while I house hunt," John said. "I've been looking on Zillow, but I'm not familiar enough with the area to consider anything online seriously. Once I'm there, I'll hire a real estate agent," John went on. "And I'll hopefully buy a house within my first month."

I nodded. Suddenly quivering. I tried to play it off as being cold and reached for my scarf. John stopped me. "Enough with the house babble," he said, unbuckling his belt. "Let's celebrate."

★

As I drove home that night, I tallied the pleasure sessions, fifty-four thus far. I could reach fifty-seven before John left for DC. When I first agreed to the arrangement, I told myself sixty-two weeks and then I would walk away. Because, at the time, $75,000 sounded like enough money to change my whole life. But as I neared the finish line, it clearly wasn't. In the last thirteen months, I had paid for my last three university semesters out of pocket ($13,000), chipped away at my student loan debt (originally $35,000), finally bought myself a car—a 2012 lime-green Ford Fiesta at 32,000 miles—($6,500), given my mom small offerings every month, and spent $18,000 surviving the day-to-day with groceries, phone bills, tanks of gas. If I quit the arrangement after our fifty-seventh session, having made $68,400, I would walk away with $6,000 cash and $12,000 in remaining student loan debt. And then what would I do? Go back to earning minimum wage? Somehow get some kind of career I didn't feel passionate about only to make less money and work forty plus hours a week?

Aside from just survive, what I really wanted to do was write. Professor Elliot's lecture had prompted me to take my dreams seriously. If not now, while I had John, I knew I'd never have the chance. So, I wouldn't quit the arrangement just yet.

What are we willing to do for our dreams? Life is always a compromise, I thought, thinking of Professor Elliot's lecture. And maybe DC wouldn't be so bad.

★

During class a few weeks later, I shyly placed an assignment on Professor Elliot's desk. The second step of our semester-long project, where we picked a stigmatized deviant behavior and interrogated the social structures around it that made this behavior "deviant."

I had picked stripping as a profession and wrote that I knew a few women in these roles (not me, of course) whom I could interview throughout the semester. I wanted to highlight that while society often demonizes these women as slutty and money hungry, out to shake their asses for Prada bags, women could choose or fall into these roles for financial survival.

After I'd submitted my topic, Professor Elliot stopped me in the hallway and said, "Your first submission was great. It's evident that you're a writer. You're the only one who used scene and dialogue." He smiled. "I can't wait to read more."

My cheeks went hot, thinking about the scene I had created. Breasts and thongs and dollar bills at a strip club. "Thank you," I said.

"Do you have any creative projects that you're working on?" he asked. We'd begun walking toward the courtyard and talking. It felt intimate, like a scene in an old movie. "If so, I'd love to take a look."

I took too long to answer, thinking about my creative work about John. I couldn't share that.

"Only if you want to share," he said, flashing his palms in a *no big deal* kind of way.

"I don't have anything in great shape right now," I said.

He looked a bit disappointed. Like he'd gone out on a limb to connect with me, and I'd shut it down.

"But I'm working on a short story. So, give me a few days?"

He smiled and said to email it to him anytime, that he'd keep an eye out for it.

I wasn't sure what on earth I'd send. Everything I'd been writing for the last year had been about John. Even if I called the story fiction it seemed indecent to send to Professor Elliot such sexually explicit material. But then I read his feedback on my assignment. Little notes of encouragement written in the margins and four lines at the very end. *Intriguing topic. I think you're on to something here. But this perspective is boring. Go beyond defending this "deviant" behavior with survival need and instead focus on why society has deemed this work morally bad. Explore the question: Why do I feel the need to defend this type of work at all?*

I felt a bit scolded. I'd worked at the clubs enough to know that not everyone was there out of need or a lack of better options, but that wasn't the point I was trying to make. The point was that *I* had been there for those reasons. I was trying to process my own experience. But when the initial sting wore off, I understood what Dr. Elliot was getting at. He wanted me to ask what made stripping morally wrong to the culture. *Where'd that idea stem from anyway?*

In those questions I could find relief. Dr. Elliot understood that this kind of work didn't devalue someone. It didn't make them bad. Fueled by the possibility that someone out in the world could understand my choices and not think poorly of them, I shaped up a twelve-page story of an anonymous sugar baby killing her sugar daddy in a La Quinta Inn because she's so repulsed by the transaction and can't handle it anymore. I figured killing the sugar daddy would make it clear this was a fiction story and couldn't be traced back to my own life. I simultaneously wanted to know that my secret could be accepted and yet never actually known.

It was the first time I'd seen Dr. Elliot since I sent him the story, and now I was feeling deeply embarrassed. I wondered if he'd mention it.

"Nice 'Girl Power' tattoo," Dr. Elliot said, pointing to the ink on my arm as I laid my assignment on his desk. His finger was close enough to my skin that I felt the heat of it.

"Thank you," I said.

A smile rose all the way up his face. Soft freckles ran across the bridge of his nose. "I like it," he said. Other students were rushing around to turn their assignments in. A boy bumped into me and my forearm brushed the professor's. "Sorry," I said.

"Don't be," he said.

When I returned to my seat, the girl beside me asked, "Was he just flirting with you?"

"I don't think so," I said.

She shook her head, "Yeah, he was. I saw it. These fucking pink-pussy-hat men," she said. "They think they can get away with anything as long they call themselves feminists."

She saw it, I thought. He *was* flirting with me.

So, I can't say that I was surprised when, later that night, I received an email from Professor Elliot. The subject was "Buffalo '66," the name of a film. The body of the message was economical: *Michelle, come to my office tomorrow. I have a film that I think you'll like. It'll help your story.*

★

When I stopped by his office the next afternoon, Dr. Elliot came across as uncharacteristically shy. "Hi," he said, quietly, turning away from his laptop. The overhead lights were off and sunlight poured in through the window behind him. This left him dark and indistinct while I was illuminated. Suddenly self-conscious, I scanned his bookshelf as an excuse to turn away. He had a mix of academic and literary books. *We Should All Be Feminists* by Chimamanda Ngozi Adichie and textbooks on sexual deviance and crime among them. When I spotted his own book—his name glazed on the spine—I picked it up and said, "The dream!"

"While it was quite an accomplishment," Professor Elliot said, "publishing an academic book isn't quite the same dream for me as a novel." He straightened in his chair, crossing his legs, and interlacing his fingers across his knee. He was a very effeminate man. This, in its own way, made me feel more comfortable with him.

When I'd first told my sister about Dr. Elliot's email, she looked confused and asked, "But aren't you a lesbian?"

"Well, yeah. But he's a *professor*." I hadn't dated, slept with, or even kissed a man since I was a teen (aside from John, who didn't count), and I'd honestly never expected to again. It wasn't any vendetta against men. I'd just always been more attracted to women. Dr. Elliot had something indistinct and special, however. I couldn't name it, I told my sister. Couldn't put my finger on what it was exactly, but he was very beautiful and held control in the classroom. People fawned over him. They respected his mind. Anyone in that class would've jumped over an email from him. And yet, Dr. Elliot was reaching toward *me*. It made me feel chosen. At that time in my life, lonely and breaking all the rules anyway, to feel chosen was more than enough. What did it matter if he was a man?

"Let me see his picture," Bianca said, lying down on her bed.

I searched the university's website for his department and found his faculty photo. Wes Elliot smiling and warm against a nature backdrop. Bianca studied the photo, trying to see what I saw, but alas, could not. "He's not really my type." I wasn't offended. Bianca's type was short men built like brick houses with names like New York and Mr. Caponee. "And he's old."

I studied his face. He didn't look *that* old.

"You're lovin' these middle-aged men, aren't you?"

"Ew," I said, recoiling. "Please don't lump John and my professor into the same 'middle-aged' category. Age has nothing to do with it. John is a lonely Trump supporter paying me for company and Dr. Elliot is a very intelligent and successful professor. He sees real potential in my work. He thinks I'm smart."

My sister shrugged. "Whatever you wanna tell yourself."

In his office, Professor Elliot considered me for a long moment, retrieved the DVD from his bag, and slid it to the edge of his desk. "I think you'll enjoy this film. It's thematically genius. Your writing reminded me of it." He turned back to his laptop, signifying that I should go.

"And Michelle?" he called after me, in a jovial voice. "Do share your thoughts after."

★

Buffalo '66 is a good film. It follows a man, Billy Brown, on the day he gets out of prison as he kidnaps a dancer, Layla, and forces her to pretend she's his wife in a lame attempt to impress his parents. Parents who clearly never loved him. It doesn't work. Enraged and hurt, Billy drags Layla around on all his revenge schemes, trying to get back at various people that had wronged him. To simplify the plot, Billy realizes it isn't blood he's after, but to be loved for who he is. In the end, it's a romance. I understood why Professor Elliot had suggested I watch it. The film was a clear example of character growth and dual desires—one surface and one deeper. I emailed him a thank you for thinking of me.

WE: *Tell me, truthfully, what'd you think? Did you find the film helpful?*

MG: *I did. Truthfully. I liked that scene of Christina Ricci tap dancing at the bowling alley. I found the surface and deeper levels of character desire really well done. I like to think of the john in my story as someone like Billy. A man who thinks he wants something simple— sex with a young woman—but really, he wants to be loved. It's sad for someone to not know the difference even within themselves, but it's good in a story.*

WE: *That scene. I love it bc it's so unexpected. & maybe you're smarter than most, but I think a lot of us are like Billy, like ur story's john. We think what we're looking for is a quick fix. Something immediate. A pill or a girl to kiss, but it only ever offers momentary relief. So, people repeat behaviors. Another pill or another girl to kiss. Same cycle. What I think is sad is that for most of us even getting someone to love us isn't enough either. That feeling*

*of relief might last longer, but I doubt Billy Brown went on to live
happily ever after with his girl. Don't you think?*

Thus began a correspondence that spanned two days. I don't know
why I was self-conscious about each message. Pasting my words into
Grammarly and deleting all my comma splices before sending them when
his own punctuation was slack. But I wanted to impress him. No, I didn't
think Billy Brown and his girl went on to live happily ever after, I wrote.
My mom loved my dad for who he was and that wasn't enough for him.
With that, we messaged back and forth quickly about our childhoods and
our families and our ex-lovers and our favorites of everything: color and
books and songs. Professor Elliot was open and answered any question I
asked with thoughtful, long-winded responses. He came across pensive,
and a bit sad, different than his upbeat personality in class, which I mistook for emotionally generous. Sensitive. Kind. A lover.

The last email Professor Elliot sent me contained his phone number.
The entire ten digits. He asked me to call.

"Hey," he said warmly upon answering. "I don't mean to say there's
anything inappropriate happening between us—I mean, we're just two
people having a conversation—but the university would frown upon our
friendship. It wouldn't matter if you were a guy," he said, annoyed, "but,
of course, they think anything between a man and a woman, especially a
young woman, is cause for concern."

Looking back, I'd note Professor Elliot's carefulness with his words.
How he skirted around the "inappropriateness" that was, in fact, palpa-
ble. How anytime we were not one-on-one in person, he spoke as though
I were tapping the line. But on this day, I simply mumbled my agreement,
slightly disappointed, slightly confused. Wasn't something murky happening? Wasn't this flirting?

"That being said," he went on, "would you mind deleting our emails?
I don't want to risk the university seeing."

"Sure," I said, happy to comply. Hoping if Professor Elliot found me obedient, he might feel safe enough to have our conversation in person. It was a trick to make me feel as though I had at least some control. Like how far this flirtation advanced was up to me. I believed it. I worked to show him how considerate I could be.

"Oh, and while we're at it, a few more things." Professor Elliot began listing off "favors" that sounded a lot like rules. I wasn't allowed to text him. If I wanted anything, I needed to call. I couldn't tell anyone about us speaking. *No one at all*, he hammered. It was grueling work to become a professor and if he got in trouble over any unsuitable conduct, which wasn't unsuitable at all, well, there'd be a lot of consequences.

I fought the urge to tell Professor Elliot how good I was at keeping secrets. My whole life had become one. I was as isolated from people as I'd ever been. Aside from my parents, who were totally cool, I had no one to even tell. I knew better than to admit that. It would terrify him. "Not a problem," I assured.

"Okay. Now that's all out of the way," he said. "How about tomorrow evening for a drink?"

★

When I caught Professor Elliot eyeing my ID alongside the bartender, I told him I was twenty-five. Not at all embarrassed by our age gap. Professor Elliot told me he was in his "early mid-fifties," but being out with him felt different than being out with John. There was still a clear air of judgment about our age disparity, but the chemistry between us made up for it. Being at a bar with him was not financed. By appearances alone that much was certain.

I found myself suddenly shy when we tucked into a corner table. I knew so much about him from our emails, but when I looked at his face, I still only saw my professor.

"What name should I call you?" I asked.

"My name is Wes," he said, "but you'll keep calling me Dr. Elliot."

"Even tonight?"

"No, not tonight, babe,'" Wes said, then laughed. "Oops, sorry about that. Slip of the tongue."

"Cool."

"You know," he said. "I tried to picture your face so many times over the weekend, but I'm realizing now I actually forgot what you looked like."

I took a long drink from my vodka soda and wondered if I should be offended. It was rude, but at least he'd been thinking about me. "I guess you should study my face right now. So you don't forget it again."

Wes placed his chin into his palms and scanned my features. "Done," he said. "You will forever be in my mind."

I smiled and then finished my first drink too quickly. Wes noticed, and said, "You're nervous."

I nodded, caught and embarrassed.

"I actually came to the bar early for a pre-drink because I was nervous," Wes said. Then he downed his beer and ordered us another round.

Within the hour Professor Elliot was complimenting my maturity for my age. Adding that the years all start to feel the same at some point anyway. "Lifestyle is really what ages us," he said. Wes had never been married and didn't have any children, so his life, aside from his research and his university job, didn't really feel all that different than it had in his late twenties. "Oh, except that sex for the sake of sex is boring to me now," he said, his tongue swollen from the alcohol. "Now I think sex is about closeness."

It was a good opening to tell Professor Elliot what sex had become for me. That the only sex I'd been having was with John. Sex I was being paid for. Sex that I loathed. Sex that was slowly ruining me. Not noticeably, but with invisible damage that made me wonder if I'd gone bankrupt inside. What kind of person can live a double life? I sometimes wondered. What kind of person can keep so many secrets?

"Where'd you just go in your head?" Wes asked from behind his drinking glass. I almost told him the truth but decided to withhold. His foot kept "accidentally" grazing my ankle and I suspected we were close to prolonged contact. I didn't want the truth interfering with the night's plot. Instead, I leaned in closer and asked, "Can I fix your shirt cuff?"

Wes draped his arm across our table, fixing his eyes on my hands as they worked to fold and unfold the cotton. I ran my thumb along his forearm. He had an old, faded tattoo of a clover in the crook of his arm.

"Tell me about this tattoo," I said.

His fingers wrapped around my elbow. Electric. He looked grateful to have been asked this question and launched into a story from the early 2000s. When he'd been living in Texas for graduate school with a serious girlfriend. He told me about their sex. How when they fucked he was sure she was the one. He could picture her in late age, mourning his death. But when they were clothed and somewhere less amatory, like the grocery store, for example, he saw her alcoholism. Her two DUIs. Her shaking in the morning until she drank her first breakfast beer. Her barreling toward disaster. Heartbreak was imminent, Wes said. But still, he persisted.

One day their cat, Clover, went missing, and he convinced himself that if they found him alive, it meant they would make it, but if the cat had died, it would symbolize the end of their relationship. "I spent the whole day hoping Clover was dead," he said. His ex found Clover in the field behind their house. Coyotes had killed him.

"Michelle, do you think that Clover being eaten was the world communicating that my relationship was doomed?" he asked me. "Or do you think it was just the way things happened?"

I was a girl that believed in fate. In signs. I thought of how John had arrived in my life, and how Wes had come to me with just as much ease. A therapist would one day call this phase in my life "nose blind to chaos," but I could only see it as a star-crossed meeting. "A sign," I said. I ran my finger across the clover tattoo. "Obviously you think so too."

I watched Wes watching me, and I wondered who'd be brave enough to turn the page.

I was not a total lamb. I understood that our being at a bar together was inappropriate. I figured we were both fetishizing the teacher-student power dynamic. And I could've guessed by all those news headlines about other young women, regurgitated and cliché, that I'd be the one to get hurt. But I was a sugar baby. Alone in the deepest pit of lies that I'd ever been in. Yes, Wes would be yet another secret, which might've done me in if it were anyone or anything else. It must be said that for the last year, John and I shared a clandestine world that he couldn't honestly define to save his life. He had no playbook. No rules. We navigated boundaries that should have been rock solid and crystal clear, but his were neither. As this new secret was opening up before me like a Venus flytrap, it was a relief to be *in it* with someone who took charge, told me to delete the emails, played coy on the phone, only revealed his cards when no one else could see them. Professor Elliot appeared to be no novice. He seemed to know exactly what he was doing. I was naive enough to feel a sense of safety in that. So, when three drinks deep, Wes finally placed his fingertips under my chin, told me I was beautiful, and asked me outside, I said yes and followed his lead.

★

In the parking lot, Wes pressed my body against his car and kissed me. His mouth was rough with beard and urgency, but his fingertips were supple and soft and lingered on my clavicle, my earlobes, my wrists. When I slipped my hand inside his shirt, I felt acutely aware that this skin was not John's. I could be present in both mind and body. I could enjoy this experience. I let myself imagine the blood pumping through Wes's heart. Through mine. Two distinct currents, separate yet momentarily entwined. And for the first time in a long while, I felt like I belonged to myself.

I suffered an instantaneous obsession with Wes. Our meeting felt inherently scandalous because he was my professor, I was his student, and he was kissing me. A man who did not believe sex work was immoral was kissing me. A bright mind who said my own work *showed promise*. No money was exchanged. That was enough. That was plenty.

I thought about Alanis Morissette as we moved into the back of Wes's car, because I once read an interview in which she said she'd spent her early dating years with men twice her age. They had all been in the music industry. Men she admired. I had always wanted, in any way possible, to relate to Alanis. I envisioned a world in which I sat down before her and said, finally, *me too*.

Wes unzipped his jeans, pulled out his cock, and said, "I want you to see me."

★

Wes's apartment was in a gated complex in North Denver. "Recent breakup," he explained regarding the lack of decor. He'd only just moved in. He let her keep it all, so he was starting from scratch.

The bedroom was just as simple. A bed, a dresser, and a side table with a single candle on it. Wes lit all three wicks and the flames sent our shadows jumping onto the wall. His bed was unmade, which made me think that he had not intended to invite me over. I wondered if the night had gone better than he'd expected. That what he'd predicted was average, but what happened was genuine connection. I would've asked, except he was already undressing me. And although I'd done this once a week for months now, I felt as though I hadn't touched another body in years. Wes pulled me onto his bed. Wes kissed my thighs and eventually lowered himself between them. We were as close as two people could be. I wanted him. I was there in my body. I stayed there.

★

Afterward, we lay in Wes's bed, watching our silhouettes flicker on the wall. The fluid, gray shape of his hand traced my hips, pausing on a thick scar on my right thigh. "What's the story?"

"Cutting when I was thirteen," I said, eager to tell Wes anything he asked. After a year of secrets, any truth I could spare was bursting at the seam of myself. "I stuck a pair of scissors into my leg. It was an accident, really. I wanted blood, but I didn't want my flesh to split. I saw the pale fat in my thigh and never did it again."

"That must've been pretty deep." He grazed the scar with his thumb. "I bet you were scared. Couldn't tell your parents, could you?"

"I was scared. I thought I needed stitches." The scar ran two inches long and half an inch wide. "I probably did need stitches."

"Tell me, Michelle." Wes's voice was a whisper. "Have you ever wanted to die?"

I almost laughed. It was such a tortured question. Who was this dark man that appeared so jolly and hopeful in class? Still, I answered. I didn't want to be unkind.

"No," I said, truthfully. "I've wanted to be different, of course. Thinner, prettier, smarter. But I've never wanted to be dead. Have you?"

"I've wanted to be dead way more than I've wanted to be alive."

I combed through Wes's long hair, which was finer than expected. "Even now?"

"In this moment, right now, with you? No. But tomorrow, yesterday, next week." Wes looked at me. "Sometimes I'll sit down and wonder what, if anything, I'm still bringing to the table. Most days I can't think of much."

"You don't have to earn your spot here, you know. You can just be," I said.

"You're an optimist. I'm not." Wes leaned over and grabbed the candle. "Sometimes, when I'm really thinking about suicide, I lay very still in a dark room and imagine that's what death would feel like." He blew out the candle for the same effect now.

In the silence, I laid my head back and let my eyes adjust to the dark. I felt changed. Not new exactly, but like I finally existed in a way I'd always been told that I needed to. So desired that the rules had to break.

"I've only ever felt this way with the women I've loved," Wes said. Then, quickly, "Don't think that means anything."

But of course it meant something. There would be a whole story between us.

"Remember," Wes said, leaning over to his lamp. "When you see me in class." Click. "You pretend." Light on. "That none of this ever happened."

9

Virginia Is for Lovers

"**D**o you have daddy issues?" my dad asked when I gave him an update on Wes. We were having lunch at Chili's, a few weeks after the fact, awaiting our 2-for-$20 entrées. He took a long drink from his lemonade and looked disapprovingly at me.

Although slightly offended, I was aware that my father had never asked if I had daddy issues when I spoke about sugaring. Meaning he must've seen sex work for what it was—my job—which was fundamentally different and separate from romance. I felt so sentimental about this that my eyes watered, but I faked annoyance to hide it. "No," I said. "I'm merely a grown adult speaking to another adult." And then I explained the situation the same way Wes had lain it out a few nights earlier, over what had become our nightly phone call.

"It really ticks me off to think I could get in trouble for what's happening between us," Wes had said. "What's wrong with it? We're just two people attracted to one another. Yes, you're my student, and there is a *teeny-tiny* power dynamic, but what cards do I hold over you? One measly grade on your transcript? Pfft!"

"It's absurd," I said, tucked away in my mom's closet for privacy. I was learning to be agreeable with Wes as a means of soothing. After that first night, Wes had been hesitant to see me again, but his fears seemed to hold water. Wes told me that one of his professor friends had recently been fired for forcing a kiss upon a student in his office. This friend had misread the signals, Wes explained. "It's not always that obvious," he said. "Right now, you're young and pretty and everyone is receptive to your advances, but wait until you get older and you'll see for yourself." I was concerned with what happened to the student, but I also wanted Wes to know that I didn't relate to her experience. I had wanted the kiss. I'd be open to another. Still, I tried to be sympathetic to Wes's anxieties as he told me this man's career had dissolved overnight. "I wouldn't be surprised," he said sadly, "if my friend kills himself."

Nearly every time we spoke, Wes would slip in some comment about building trust. "I have a lot at stake," he often said. "My career, my reputation. Deep down I know you wouldn't do anything to get me in trouble, but I need reassurance." So, each night, I'd work to intuit exactly which anxieties to soothe. One day I might've told Wes that I was happy with everything that happened between us that first night. The next, that I could keep a secret. My life did not depend on him. I could be as easy as he needed. In fact, I could be needless. I could shrink myself into any shape that fit into his world. I never stopped to consider how all this bending could potentially harm me. I was too focused on not letting this camaraderie with Wes slip out of my fingers.

It was also true that our nightly call had made me feel less alone than I had that entire last year. And more seen. More prodded, more known. Supported in my writing. Every time he rang me, I felt more like a real person. I didn't need to see Wes out in some bar just to go home with him. I was already a body to somebody else. It had been almost a relief to be reduced to a mind and a voice in the ether. So, even as Wes's fawning requests for reassurance turned our dynamic into a game of earning his trust, I happily obliged.

"I'm twenty-five years old," I said, trying to sound sure of myself. "My frontal lobe is fully developed. I can make my own decisions."

"I'm glad to hear you say that," Wes said casually. "And no offense, but at your age, the school classifies you as a nontraditional student. Speaking from a *strictly biological standpoint*, you're practically an old maid." While his comment may've seemed out of character for a man that went to the Women's March, the more I got to know Wes, the less filtered he became, and he had sharp edges that often reminded me of his blind spots. "Although," he went on, "you're still way too young for me to consider dating seriously."

I felt the sting of Wes's swift rejection even as I knew this wasn't going to be something serious. I couldn't ask more of Wes even if I wanted to, because I was involved in an arrangement with someone else. This, in a roundabout way, made Wes feel like a godsend, because he was a safe bet. As long as he kept his distance and didn't want anything with me, I didn't need to tell him about John. And anyway, Wes had told me he was fresh out of a breakup with a long-term on-and-off girlfriend. Totally unavailable, except every night for a two-hour phone call.

Still, my being labeled an "old maid" was distressing because my success as a sex worker was reliant on my youth. I was able to make ends meet because John wanted to sleep with me. Strippers often spoke about "aging out" at the clubs, but I thought that moment would come a little later in life, maybe around twenty-nine or thirty. It's when I assumed I might age out of sugaring as well. Had I been misguided? Now twenty-five, was I already on my way out?

"I only say that because age gaps between lovers have been protocol since the beginning of time," Wes went on. "On a primal level, all bodies want to procreate. Men simply don't age out the way women do. It's sexist, I know. But Mother Nature is sexist."

At Chili's, my dad scoffed at my retelling. "If Mother Nature is so sexist, then why do you think it's gross that moneybags wants some young tail? He's younger than your grandpa professor."

"John is like two years older than Wes," I said. "And it's about his desperation. John *pays* me." We both cringed. "But Wes and I have chemistry. It's special between us."

"If it's so special," my dad said, digging his heels in, "then how come he doesn't want to see you again?"

"I already told you! He doesn't want to lose his job."

My dad blew air through his lips. "You know goddamn well that's an excuse. If this guy with his fancy degree had any common sense whatso-ever, he would know that your phone calls could get him in just as much trouble. There's cell tower dings, and cell phone records, and ah!" My dad lost his train of thought when my own phone started dinging. Once, twice, four times. "Who the hell is texting you," he asked, "while we're at this fancy restaurant?"

"John," I said.

★

John was headed off to DC that very week. I wouldn't see him again for a few months, until he was settled into whatever home he'd buy. I was not in the dark. John had been keeping me in the loop throughout his house-hunting process. Sending links to various options because I would "live with him part-time," and because he "valued my opinion," discount-ing that I would merely visit four days a month and I hadn't so much as rented an apartment.

With every batch of homes John sent I'd click through thumbnails, unmoved by the brick fireplaces or various tile backsplashes. "Why con-sider anything other than proximity to Titan and the price?" I'd asked him. When I received no satisfactory answer, I began texting back, *I like the cheapest one.* He'd respond with some diminutive objection, *You're*

so flexible! I think I'm a little bit too spoiled for wall-to-wall carpeting.
John was also "too spoiled" for accent walls, fewer than three bathrooms,
a kitchen sans island, or any home that needed so much as a lightbulb
replaced. *I want my house to be completely move-in ready,* he eventually
texted. *I've decided to buy new.*

The link was for a brownstone listed at $725,000. "Dang," my dad
said. "Sancho has serious money!" I nodded. My father and I scrolled
through the listing—four bedrooms, crown moldings, hardwood floors
in the living areas, carpet in the bedrooms, beautiful, of course. I
exited and returned to my messages. *What do you think of this layout?*
John asked.

:) :) <3

Is the fourth bedroom around a good size for your future writing office?

John had never asked this question before, but as I neared my May
graduation, he had been upping his insinuation that I focus on my writing. "You don't have other plans, do you?" he'd asked during our last
meeting. I shook my head. I did not. "I think you should dedicate your
life to being an artist," John said. "I'll fund you." This wasn't so much
support as it was insurance for our arrangement. Divorced and with his
sons long since moved out, John was lonely, and he wanted someone
around. Even though we didn't know one another deeply, he liked the
idea of me graduating college and moving across the country and into his
place. He also knew that I would've needed a good reason to do so, hence
his recommendation I take the artist's route since I wouldn't make any
money elsewhere. I'd have to fund my author dreams through blow jobs.

Normally, this idea would have destroyed me—John paying for the
long-term company of someone half his age to remedy his loneliness,
and I selling my life to sit behind a computer and type stories—but as I
thought of my alleged biological old maid status, I felt grateful I still had
John. I renewed my promise to myself to take my writing seriously. The
chance was *now.* It would never come again.

Just then, a sizzling sound approached. "Hell yeah," my dad said. "Earth to Michelle. Here come the fajitas!"

★

Eight weeks later, on a Thursday in April, I made my first trip to Virginia. John was overjoyed to see me and kissed my face twenty times before we'd even loaded my suitcase into his car. "I have to confess something," he told me as we merged onto the freeway. "I haven't seen a single soul outside of work since I've been here." He laughed nervously and squeezed my hand. "You're giving me life!"

I smiled weakly, nervous about the weekend ahead. My role as John's sugar baby was evolving. I was not visiting him merely as a body for sex, but as a stand-in companion for everything. We'd eat meals together. Watch TV. Talk for hours. I hoped I could handle it. "Now you're here, I finally have an excuse to check out the amenities at the complex," John said as we waited for the gate to open. He pointed to the right. "The pool is heated. In case we want to take a romantic dip later."

Thanks to a Zillow video walk-through, I'd long since known about the heated pool and countless other details about the complex. I'd even compiled a list of complaints about John's new place. Excessive. A four-bedroom, five-bath, three-story home. Far too big for one man. What was *so* special about crown moldings? Or mahogany floorboards? John had no need for a den. Or bathrooms on every level—that was just ridiculous. But when we finally stepped inside, I caught whiff of something I'd never encountered before. Fresh-cut wood, was it? Filtered air? Dryer sheets? I imagined a candle of the scent, aptly named *$700,000-$800,000 property*. I dragged out an inhale. *Damn*, I thought, against myself, *that's fucking good*.

On the ground floor was a large den that led to a lower deck. Beyond that was a strip of forest, preserved for the level of separation it provided neighbors. Red maples and sour gums and dogwoods on the verge of bloom. I had grown up around Virginia's blossoming trees. It felt like home.

I walked, a little less rigidly, toward the French doors for a closer look. That's when I noted how bare the room was. Not even a roll of toilet paper in the connected bathroom. "Have you ever been in here?" I asked.

"Maybe during the walk-through," John said, bashfully. "Seeing as I don't really need it, I was thinking this could be your office. Where you can work on your author dreams."

My author dreams were feeling a little more possible, thanks to Wes. Three weeks prior, I'd had to present my semester-long project on stripping in his class, which, admittedly, had been a little disastrous. With Wes's guidance, I changed my angle. I was now presenting on stripping as a job that many people did not because they loved the work, but because it was a well-paying job. Some hated it, just as some hated their office jobs, but it was just work. When Professor Elliot first opened the floor for comments, zero hands were raised. With a little coaxing, "Come on, whatever your thoughts. Even the ugly ones," a man eventually volunteered. "I guess I'm a little confused why some of these women wouldn't just get a *real* job," he said. "Especially the ones who allegedly hate it so much." This comment broke through any hesitation the others initially felt and soon people were sharing whatever crossed their minds. "It's a safe space to say what we think, right? Well, I feel like strippers just want to take the easy way out," said a girl. "Anyone can just take off their clothes." And "I don't know how much I agree with the pro-sex work movement," an older student said. "I've got a sixteen-year-old daughter, and this sets the bad example that selling your body is okay."

I hadn't expected such disapproval over a presentation on stripping in a deviance class. I knew I couldn't walk into that room and announce that I was a sex worker without being persecuted, but I had been hoping that this was a safe space for anonymous women in my research to do so. I squirmed every time one of my peers made a judgmental comment, taking their words personally. *I* was a woman that needed to get a real job, and *I* had taken the easy way out. *I* set a bad example.

Professor Elliot had been assertive in the conversation. Sticking to shop talk while trying to stop the class from spiraling into nonconstructive comments. "We've clearly hit on a nerve," he said. "Let's try and think of where this judgment stems from." Only one woman came to my defense, claiming that people hated strippers because it was a female-dominated field that financially benefitted off men's loneliness and that sexism was one of the issues that landed Donald Trump in the White House.

"He loves sex workers. Just look at Melania Trump," someone snickered, cutting her off.

"Grow up," the woman said.

That class had been largely demoralizing. I wondered what I'd been doing the last year, writing so much about sex work. Even if I claimed it was fiction, people still had a sour taste in their mouths about the topic. It was all useless musings.

Fortunately, Wes had given me a one-on-one creative writing consultation the weekend before. Though our nightly phone calls had become routine, this marked only our second time ever meeting up. He had invited me out to drinks, then subsequently to spend the night. When I awoke, I found Wes sitting in his living room, reading a new story I'd sent him. This one was about a sugar daddy offering his sugar baby a spa day instead of something useful like extra cash. He didn't acknowledge me when I walked in. Too enthralled, I told myself, as I poured a cup of coffee and memorized the room. Now this was modest. A mammoth maroon sofa and a suede armchair. Three bookshelves, one of them lined with DVDs.

Eventually Wes finished my story and flicked at the stapled corner. "It's raw, Michelle. Honest. Good. It reads as true to real life." The sun had been slow to rise that morning and was finally peeking through an east-facing window. I sat, feeling vulnerable, waiting for Wes to say more.

"You know, a lot of fiction is based off our real-life experiences."

I took a deep breath. Here was the connection I had been dreading and yet here was my opportunity to be honest. Brave. I decided against it. "Have I ever told you that I stripped?"

"Michelle," Wes said, a bit cross. "You know you haven't told me that you stripped."

"I don't really go around talking about it much."

"Why is that?" Wes's voice lifted. He sounded genuinely curious.

"I feel kind of bad about stripping."

Wes, in his element, wanted to know what "bad" meant and if I had moral qualms about having taken off my clothes for a crowd. I explained that the issue wasn't so much about being nude, but rather that it'd felt as though I had two options: tell my friends and hear the rumors about me being a slut, or not tell friends, and slowly crumple under the weight of being a liar.

Wes nodded his head knowingly. "An ex of mine used to be a stripper. She'd occasionally sleep with a few of her club regulars for some extra cash." I felt immediately relieved to hear there was someone out there that had done what I had. Not just some anonymous username on Reddit, but a real woman that Wes knew. "My ex told a few of her close dancer friends about her johns and these girls were terribly judgmental." He frowned his disapproval. "Her best friend was always 'my body, my choice,' whenever someone called her a slut for being a stripper, but when my ex admitted to giving a blow job for some extra cash, this woman said, 'Whores like you are why dancers have a bad rap.'"

Wes laughed. "Can you believe that? These women truly believed they were better than her because they only showed their pussies and didn't let anyone touch them. There's no hierarchy of purity." Wes pushed his hair back to meet my gaze. "I'm just happy she had me around. I told her not to listen to those girls. It was a smart business move. She was already in the sex industry so why should she have limited her income to lap dances?" He looked at me dead in the eyes. "Now she's paid off her master's degree."

I thought back to a conversation I'd had with my dad in his speedboat last summer, when he told me that one day we'd all look back and realize we'd done something we weren't proud of. Perhaps my father had been wrong. Maybe you could figure out that the reason you weren't proud of what you did was because of what the world told you it had meant about you. Maybe the world was wrong.

Wes took a long drink from his coffee, then casually asked, "You ever slept with someone from the club?"

Since entering the arrangement with John, dissecting my experience had been confined to my writing and my family. While I'd been happy to tell my family general information about John, I always omitted the hard parts—how the sex was dissociative at best and repulsive at worst, or that the secrecy was making me feel incredibly lonely—never wanting to bother them with my discomfort. And whenever I'd considered telling my friends about John, I'd felt a sinking feeling in my stomach, sure that what had happened to Wes's ex would happen to me. It was a total wonder to realize that I might be able to confess it all to my professor. That of all the people in the world, he might actually get it. "I did," I said. "I mean, I am. I have a sugar daddy."

It happened all at once: the curtain I'd been hiding behind began to unspool as I told Wes about the weekly meetups, and how I'd gotten stupid lucky when penetration turned into weekly blow jobs because John couldn't hold erections with a condom. "It's a relief," I told Wes. "But still not ideal."

"Ya," he said, nonchalant about the whole thing. "That makes sense."

I could've cried over this emancipation from my own cage, but not wanting Wes to think I was too emotional, and therefore "unsafe" to see outside of class again, I explained that the arrangement had become more serious, with John moving out to DC and all, but the money—

now $4,800 a month, I clarified when Wes asked—felt impossible to walk away from. It wasn't as though I'd been able to save much of the cash when forking it over for tuition and a car and my student loans.

"You're being really smart with your money," Wes said. I felt moved by this recognition. "I'm a college professor and I still have $80,000 in student loan debt." He told me that he'd been paying the debt off for twenty years. "I've already paid nearly twice the amount that I borrowed. That's not an exaggeration; I've already paid over $120,000. I thought education was the answer, the way to get out of poverty," Wes said, "but I'm worse off from it. My student loan debt feels like a financial prison." The room fell quiet. It was a classic American story. I knew without John I'd have been echoing the same sentiments my whole life. It was sad to hear about but also validating.

"If there was any market for me to be a sex worker, I'd do it," Wes said, his face open. I felt a closeness to him because Wes understood my need. He understood that sometimes it takes these decisions and routes to be free. Wes made me feel like I had chosen right to compromise my body to change the course of my life.

"I think this is really good for you, Michelle. Not only are you getting yourself out of debt, but this work clearly inspires your writing." He took a sip from his coffee. "Every time you see this John, and you feel like you're suffering through the sex, you should think of it as research," Wes said, referencing my short story. "It's a win-win. You have the time and space to write, and to have your life writing the story for you. It's lucky."

I looked down at my feet. *Lucky* felt like the wrong word. A self-compromise that was turning out to be worth the risk was more like it. I felt a bit miffed by Wes's cavalier attitude, but maybe there wasn't enough vulnerability in my writing or sharing for him to understand that. "I think what you have here is bigger than a short story," he said. Winning me back. It was the flap of a butterfly's wing. "If you blow this idea up and really expand, give the reader a backstory, find a larger arc, and give the girl good reason to kill her sugar daddy in the end, you could have an actual novel."

★

As I was standing in John's den now, I was thinking about what Wes said. A good business move. And a good story. Could be something more. Bigger. A book. "It is a beautiful view," I said to John, in what could be my office, a little swayed.

"Wait till you see it from the top deck."

John lugged my suitcase up the first flight of stairs, which opened into a colossal kitchen. The black marble-countered island was the length of an SUV, and while it could've comfortably fit six stools, there were none. "You're my first guest," John said. "I haven't needed seats yet."

"Doesn't all this empty space make you feel more alone?" I asked.

John looked around and then back to me. "Well, maybe it could use some feminine touches."

To move the conversation forward, I asked John to show me his fridge contents. He opened the door to reveal a fresh-off-the-assembly-line empty interior. "Are you sure you're not a robot?" I asked. "One that survives by being plugged into an outlet?" John laughed and pulled open a false cabinet that concealed the trashcan, overflowing with greasy brown paper bags and takeout containers. "I usually get delivery," he said.

John ushered me through the dining room, where a collapsible pic-nic table was topped with three Apple monitors, into the living room. Thus far, the most inviting space thanks to the eighty-five-inch TV and big comfy sofa, which, when I pried, John admitted had cost $1,400 and $5,000, respectively.

"It sorta feels like you're a realtor giving me a property tour," I said.

"That sounds like a good intro to a porno," John said in his yummy voice.

I faked a paltry laugh. I had somehow forgotten why I was there for a moment. Now, I felt suddenly sure that my body could not go through with it.

But I had done it fifty-seven times before. There was good reason to do it again.

I had not been paid a penny since our last hotel session eight weeks ago, further confirming that John did not just want to help take care of me out of the kindness of his heart. I'd profoundly felt the disruption in income. In just two months, I had watched my money begin to dwindle away. I had been wrong. Fifty-seven nights of sugaring had not been enough to change my whole life. I was not sure anymore if there was an amount that would be enough. Because regardless of how much I could save, once I walked away from sugaring, every dollar spent would come from an un-replenishing pot. I needed something significant beyond John and the arrangement. A future-future plan. I wasn't sure yet what that could be.

"Well, then," John said, in a steamy voice. "Would you like to see the top story?"

John hauled my suitcase to the third floor, where there were two more bedrooms, two full bathrooms, and a second large empty living space. The master suite contained only two pieces of furniture: a king mattress laid directly on the floor, and a moving box, flipped upside down as a bedside table. John once recommended the book *The Millionaire Next Door*, which, if I understood correctly, was just two hundred pages of two men harping on about poor people being poor because they lived beyond their means while rich people became rich through their modest spending. But this was not simply a rich man's frugality here. This was psychopathic! Especially considering that on top of the box was a collage of selfies I'd sent John over the last year. I imagined myself on my very own *Forensic Files* episode. An up-close frame of John's collage before cutting to my mom's interview. "Shell should've known right then," I could imagine her saying, "that she was in danger."

"It would be nice if you slept in here with me," John said, "so we can cuddle. Or, if you want your own space, you can sleep in one of the spare bedrooms. I have an air mattress we can blow up."

Not having the air mattress prepared seemed like a strategic move on John's end, but the hassle didn't sway me. "I sleep better alone," I said. "Sorry."

"That's okay," John said, a little perturbed, but he quickly cheered when he began rubbing my shoulders. "Oh sweetie, I'm so happy you're here." He kissed the back of my neck. "I've been jacking off to your pictures all month."

I looked once more at my many selfies. All the same face. The same pursed lips. Shocking that John hadn't requested a little variety— smiling with teeth perhaps, or something sexier, given what he used them for. An intrusive clip of John masturbating played in my mind. My stomach grumbled. "Give me a minute to . . . uh . . . freshen up," I said, then hightailed it to the restroom.

I'd been having anxiety-induced IBS since the night before. An ailment I discussed with my mother earlier that morning as she was driving Chuy to school and me to the airport. My mother's car was in worse shape than my old Honda. Broken door handle, duct-taped glove compartment, jack-o'-lantern of a dashboard, and the driver's-side visor was "secured" with a bungee cord. But it did, at least, run. I knew my mother could empathize with my IBS plight. Both of our bodies doubled as our emotional barometers. Sad? No appetite. Nervous? Rancid sweat. Anxious? Well. The last places on earth I wanted to have diarrhea were in an airplane lavatory and in my sugar daddy's brand-new house. "What if my belly gets so sick," I said, "that I have to be hospitalized?"

My mom patted my knee. "Oh, honey. I know what you need."

Her left hand gripped the steering wheel, while the other rummaged through crumpled receipts and lollipop wrappers inside her purse.

"Stop sign!" my nephew yelled from the backseat. "You're *supposed* to stop!"

As my mom's car crept across the intersection, I assured Chuy that this was called a rolling stop, and while a cop might consider it illegal, as long as there wasn't one around, it was perfectly fine.

"Bingo," my mom said, at last, as she raised a bottle of Xanax in the air. "How many pills do you want?"

I paused to gauge the dread in my body, which was astronomical considering I was flying out of state as well. What if I ran into someone I knew at the airport? Or worse, as I was boarding the plane? What if they sat next to me? Or what if the plane crashed, everyone on board died, and, in the subsequent investigation, the whole world discovered my double life, blamed the accident on my karma, and then the entire planet hated me? "Can I have the whole bottle?"

"Oh, Shell." My mom chuckled as she performed the magic trick of steering completely with her knees, while shaking a few onto her palm. "I'll give you six."

After I funneled the little orange tabs into a Tylenol container, I turned toward Chuy, who was swinging his lunch bag around like a lightsaber.

"Tell me something nice," I said. "I need support."

"You can do it, Auntie!" Chuy cried, though he had no idea what "it" entailed. He released his seat belt to lean forward and wrap his arms around my shoulders. "Here's a hug to take with you!"

I squeezed his fingers, which were short and thick with youth. Eight years old. Way too young to say what I most needed to hear, which was, "Shell, you don't have to do this," so that I could say, "But I need the money," and then he could say, "Okay, but know that this will not be your life forever." Then, I wanted the Universe to paint me a clear finish line, not too far off, with a happy life visible just beyond it. One in which I could write, not be poor, and stop feeling like a rotten liar who lacked something fundamental (like a soul).

What really happened was that I kissed Chuy's hand, and said, "You smell like peanut butter."

"Thanks," he said sinking back into his seat. "I had a Reese's for breakfast."

Back in John's bathroom, I popped a Xanax and looked into the mirror. The flight had dried my skin. I searched in my bag for my setting mist and spritzed while thinking how much my feelings about the arrangement oscillated. One minute, I felt as though I could never leave the security. And the next, I was certain I couldn't go through with the sex. But that was the contradiction of the arrangement. It was simultaneously the best and worst thing to ever happen to me. *But it's really not so bad*, I told myself. *At least there isn't any penial penetration.* I smiled. That helped. *I will not be a sugar baby forever.* I felt sure of it. *I will have countless lifetimes after this. But for now, I have a job to do.*

After I rinsed off in the shower, I returned to the master bedroom, where I crawled onto John's mattress. John stood naked in front of his own bathroom mirror, rubbing his scalp and humming. To enforce a level of separation between myself and the moment, I remembered Wes's research advice and observed John from the perspective of a writer taking notes. *He swishes mouthwash around, spits it into the sink and doesn't rinse the basin. John uncaps his deodorant, tucks the stick under both armpits, then trails the bar across his chest, up his neck, and out to the tip of his chin.*

I'd always assumed John wore cologne (an expensive brand, given the way it clung to my skin), but it had only been Speed Stick. Just when I began to feel sorry for myself—*I don't know this man at all!*—I wondered how I could've ever believed that I *had* known him. John and I had spent less than a hundred hours together total, and now in one weekend we would nearly match that. I had never seen John's house. I had barely seen the interior of his car. Before today, I did not know what kind of toothpaste he used or how little food he kept in the fridge, that he did not believe in proper furniture, or that he used deodorant in place of cologne.

Every oddity felt like both a surprise and, given my anxiety, a threat. A shadow crept across the ceiling, glacial and distorted. It terrified me beyond belief. What could it have been? A racoon on a fence? A passing car, most likely. But no logical answer could calm me. Totally irrational thoughts filled my head. What if my dad had been right about the aliens? What if they took over tonight? My dad would have *never* mistaken deodorant for cologne. My dad, I thought, had street smarts.

Just as I was preparing to steal John's Lexus and drive home to Aurora, his feet padded against the blossomed marble tile, and then he was there, lifting the sheets off me. "Oh my gosh," he said, as if he hadn't seen my body fifty-seven times before, in an identical position, in identical circumstances. *I have done this before*, I told myself, trying to relax. *And the world is not on the cusp of an alien collapse.* John kissed my mouth. His tongue like a tadpole. Slimy and instinctively en route to the back of my throat. I opened my jaw and reluctantly accepted the offer. The scent of Speed Stick, once tolerable, good even, now pungent. John's chest hairs prickly against my breasts. My formerly calloused skin, shed during those weeks without use, was now baby pink. Raw. It felt like that very first time at the Marriott. How, terrified of being murdered, I'd hidden my hairs in towels and planted my fingerprints on the wall art. Sixteen months later and here we were. John pressing his cock into my mouth. Spittle dripping down my chin. John's hand sliding down my stomach, in a straight vertical line like he was splicing me open. I leaned back on the sheets and imagined all the fragility that existed inside me. Blood and guts and digesting pretzels from my flight. Inside John too (minus the pretzels). I almost felt moved. We were human, how magical. But then John's fingers entered my body and I did not feel magical anymore. *You've done this before*, I told myself again and tried not to breathe. *What if I turn blue?* I wondered. I had an ex-girlfriend who thought blue was a boring color. "The sky is just so much lovelier during sunset," she'd once said, meaning it was less lovely the rest of the day. I was off in my head, wondering what a good alternative color for the sky might be—I came up blank—when John broke the Unspoken Rule of our arrangement. The one that made me feel as though I wasn't selling my whole self. The one that made these pleasure sessions feel remotely manageable. "Sweetie," he said, "can I fuck you?"

It was the entire ocean crashing in a single wave on top of my head. I hadn't fathomed this would ever be on the table again. Not after a year of only blow jobs. And not *now*, when John was already milking me for "quality time" in another city. He must have prepared the condom beforehand because in seconds he had one ripped open and rolled down his penis, which stayed erect. When he lowered himself between my thighs, my belly howled like some terrible creature. I imagined a full moon. My skin ripping off to reveal my fur hide. I shook, violently, like it just might happen. If John noticed, he ignored it. "I love you, sweetie," he said, as his body moved in and out of mine. Be present, I told myself, *for the story*. "I love you," John said again. "I love you. I love you."

But it wasn't just a story. It was my life. I closed my eyes, entered the time machine of my mind, and left John there alone.

Two hours earlier: when John picked me up from the airport. The humidity, so different from Colorado's arid climate, had draped my body like a hug. We rolled down our windows and sailed west along the highway. John gripped my leg. I placed my palm over his hand and turned to observe the pines that walled the road, thinking fondly of my childhood. "I've missed Virginia," I said, and then told John a story.

When I was seven, my dad, my sister, and I had been sitting on our couch in Newport News watching *Child's Play*, the original Chucky movie. It must have been summertime because only the screen door was latched. "My mom," I told John, "saw the three of us sitting wide-eyed with the blanket pulled up over our noses, so she grabbed one of my baby dolls, snuck out the back door, ran around the house, held the doll up against the screen, and rang the doorbell. We all screamed bloody murder. My sister was so scared she started crying." I smiled, re-membering. "My mom thought it was so funny that she peed her pants on the porch."

John laughed generously.

"Tell me a story about your parents," I said after.

"Oh gosh," he said. "Let me think. My parents aren't as playful as yours."

"Few are," I teased. "Did you have strict parents? Did they give you a bedtime and curfew and whatnot?"

"I don't know if they were strict, precisely, but they had really high expectations," he said. "I had to do well in school, and I had to choose a lucrative degree path so I'd eventually be able to provide for a family."

"Your dad must be happy with you," I said.

"No," John scoffed. His brow furrowed in a way I'd never seen before. "Nothing I do is ever enough for my father. It never has been. Never will be."

I couldn't relate. My family was always proud of us, even when our accomplishments didn't really seem to warrant congratulations. Once, when I worked at a clothing store, I scored 100 percent on an employee training module. Ten questions quizzing what one ought to do in case of shoplifters. "Smarts run in the family," my mom had said, and she took me, Bianca, and Chuy out to dinner (charged to the Discover). As much as I loved chastising my parents for not having any expectations for us, it did give me the freedom to be myself. Perhaps John was trying to do the same for his kids.

"You've broken the cycle," I said. "You're a great dad."

"Thank you." John smiled. "I try really hard to have a good relation-ship with my sons. I never wanted them to feel pressured into a job they didn't like because of money. They knew they'd be taken care of, so they could go after their dreams. Funny, but they both took lucrative routes anyway."

I felt both critical and envious of John's children. They could've been anything—artist, educator, activist, *writer*—and yet they each chose a direct route to money. I wanted John, with his abysmal pockets, to take care of me without asking to be fucked in return. But that made no sense. I was not his child. I was a girl he'd met at the strip club. I would not receive his "support" without it being what he considered an equitable amount. I looked out the window. Green, green, green.

John went on, "That's the one thing my dad did for me that I wanted to continue—paying for school and living expenses. In school, I could focus my attention on my studies, and even that was a challenge. That's why I am very impressed that you were able to work and maintain good grades *before we got together*."

John first began hinting at our "togetherness" back in November, when we celebrated our "one-year anniversary." He would tell me he was grateful for me. That our *relationship* had changed his life. He was happier. The most sexually satisfied he'd ever been. He said he appreciated that I was nice to him. I was the best girlfriend. I did not then, and hadn't once since, responded to the claim. I just kept quiet, which I hoped might make it clear that I did not agree. I'd told Wes about all of this during one of our calls. "He knows he's gaslighting himself, right?" I said. "It's not like John can truly believe that he's in love with me. It stresses me out to think that John might consider this a genuine relationship." I had lost all self-consciousness, and Wes had essentially appointed himself as my sugaring mentor. He had a robust knowledge on the subject, thanks to his ex. I felt grateful for it. Less compartmentalized.

"John doesn't care about the truth," Wes said. "He cares about the narrative." He sighed, displeased. "To be frank, Michelle, it's not *all* John's fault that he's pushing the boundaries of the arrangement."

"What do you mean?" I asked, taken aback.

"You've let John get away with basically anything he wants," Wes said. Sometimes he seemed exhausted by my naivety. "You've already sold the

narrative to him. It's too late now to change it without rocking the boat."
Wes must've sensed that he'd been too harsh. So he added softly, "Let
John buy his narrative. Let him call it love. You know the truth."

"Was it a big deal to your parents when you got divorced?" I asked
John.

"Oh god, yes," he said, exasperated. "End-of-the-world big deal. When
my ex-wife and I first started having problems, I used to call my mom and
tell her about it, and she would just say, 'Deal with it, John.'"

Despite the pressure, John insisted that his divorce had been worth it.
Once he and Patricia had children, they shared nothing outside of parent-
hood. No passion. No grown-up time. They were a family, but Patricia,
John felt, saw him as a flesh-and-blood ATM. How sad, then, that John
sought out an arrangement. A situation that was guaranteed to reinforce
this same feeling. Maybe that was why he refused to acknowledge it plainly between us.

"Do you at least feel appreciated by your sons?" I asked, optimistic.

John grimaced. "No. I actually don't think I ever have."

"Does that bother you?"

John chewed his lip. "I don't even think about it. I've always thought
of providing as my duty."

We rode in silence for a while.

"Do you feel appreciated by me?" I asked.

"I do," he said. "You always say thank you," he said, nodding at the
road. "And I feel that you truly mean it."

"I do mean it," I said. "Meeting you has been the best thing that's
ever happened to me." My voice went wobbly. I felt emotional about the
whole thing. Sixteen months ago, I lived a completely different life. One
of so much need. So much struggle. So much stress. And now, it was
breezy. I noted the leather seat under my legs. The hushed engine. The
smooth ride. What, with some continued self-compromise, was possible?
This salary, free time, an office, the time to write a book. I could hear

Wes in my head, "You're a lucky girl, Michelle." That feeling came again, clutching at the coattails of John's wealth, *I could never leave this.*

But that was two hours ago! Here I was now, under John's naked weight, wishing the whole thing away.

"I love you, Michelley," John called out as he came in a great huff and collapsed on top of me.

10

Graduation

'll congratulate you when you get a job with that expensive piece of paper, my dad texted. It was May, and I was in DC on official sugaring business, now a college graduate. I had eluded the tradition of joining my class in walking across a stage, and instead, opted to receive my diploma via mail, which my mother had opened that very afternoon. She sent a snap of the degree along with the celebratory emoji. I forwarded both to my father. *Bachelor of Arts,* I wrote. *It cost me $48,000!!*

The lack of fervor made sense. Sure, this college degree was the first in my immediate family, but we, as a collective, didn't know what this degree would ever amount to, if anything. We did know, however, from the rhetoric, from the national debt, from the fact that so many millennials had bought into the same narrative—*go to college!*—that my degree wouldn't guarantee me a seat at the table. I could still end up bussing said table. Or, if my dad had it his way, delivering the tables via 18-wheeler.

The only future I could see clearly was the immediate. I had spent the day writing a description of John's bathroom-cabinet contents, and he was now on his way home from work, eager to pick me up for dinner. It was day two of my second visit to DC I was one penetrative session down (three to go), and $4,800 cash was awaiting me on Sunday. My degree, in that moment especially, felt secondary to sex work. My arrangement was the smartest decision I had ever made. My arrangement was the vein toward a better life. My arrangement was providing me the chance to take my writing seriously. A text banner dropped on my iPhone. John and I were going to dinner. *Pulling up in 5!* he wrote. *Meet me outside. :)*

★

As I waited for John, I got a call from Wes. I hit decline. Things were rocky between us. After I'd returned from my first DC visit, Wes went MIA. He stopped answering my calls and never bothered to return them. It was odd to sit in class with a ghost. I couldn't just raise my hand ask him what was going on or where he went. He'd give me a look sometimes, like, "Be cool. Don't do anything stupid." But I felt his absence like an amputation. My friend. My confidant. My every single day "Hi, how are you?" vanished and yet he was right in front of me, behind a podium. *Just tell me what happened*, I'd try to telepathically say from my desk. *Did I scare you away?*

It all made sense when one day Professor Elliot showed up to class with a colossal hickey on his neck. I felt betrayed by the indecency. After months of following Wes's rules, I couldn't believe that he wouldn't even give me a heads up. I knew I wasn't his girlfriend, but I certainly wasn't nothing. After class, I dropped by his office. Per his guidelines, I needed to have a legitimate question prepared, but standing at the door and seeing the mark up close, round as a golf ball, purple as a beet, my mind flatlined.

"I've just totally forgotten what I came here to ask," I said.

"Well, if you remember it, feel free to shoot me an email," Wes said through a gritted smile.

"All right," I whispered. "Thanks."

That evening Wes called, irate. "What did I tell you about coming to my office without a legitimate reason?" He used language to deflect it all onto me. "I feel unsafe when *you* break our rules. I want to be able to trust *you*, but moves like that make me question if I can."

Trust? Moves like that? Wes should've been scolding himself. I'd planned to ask about the hickey and remind him how well-behaved I'd been in class, even though he didn't offer me the same courtesy. But I cowered at his anger and told myself I was in the wrong. Wes wasn't mine. He'd made that clear from the beginning. "I'm sorry," I said. "I just wanted to see you. You've vanished on me. Where did you go?"

Wes sighed. "Look, Michelle. I need to tell you something. Katrina and I are back together. We're trying to figure things out." Katrina was Wes's ex-girlfriend. An off-again, on-again whirlwind relationship for four years. She was his age and in the same place in her life. There was real potential there for forever, he told me. I should've been able to figure this out myself, but I hadn't seen it coming.

Wes put on his sweetest, most sorry voice and reiterated how, even though we had a *genuine connection*, and he *thought about me often*, and he couldn't help *stealing glances at my pretty face in class*, it was best if we were just friends. Plain and simple.

"Of course," I said. "I understand."

"I know you're good at playing reserved, but I'll just say this, I'm sorry if this is hurtful, and it's okay if it feels like a betrayal, but mature emotions require us to be able to feel hurt while also recognizing that no one did anything wrong. We both knew what we were getting into, didn't we?"

"Yes, we did." And this didn't feel untrue.

"So, you can feel hurt, but you can't get mad and go telling on me," Wes said.

"I'm not going to tell on you. Really, I get it."

"I thought you would. Because it's not all about sex between us, right?" Wes asked. "I've always felt that we had a real emotional connection."

It was precisely true. I tried to hold on to the fact that I didn't need or want romance right then. And, we never even fully had it. Mostly some kind of over-the-phone voice affair. What I needed from Wes were the intellectual and emotional pats on the back, and the regular and consistent reassurance that I hadn't ruined myself with John. I needed a friend. So, I said, "Yes. Of course, we do."

★

Healthy Heart was a four-star, $$$ restaurant that John found on Yelp. "It's 100 percent vegan," he said as we turned into a shopping center.

"What kind of three-dollar-sign place shares a parking lot with a GameStop?" I asked. We laughed.

John linked his fingers between mine as we walked across the blacktop. My palm was swampy from anxiety. This was only our third outing in DC, and because we hadn't publicly stepped out together in Denver since my arrest anxiety kicked in last spring, each time we braved the world, stress hormones would ooze from my pores. "Sorry," I said to John, as we both wiped our hands on our pants. "It's the humidity."

Much to my relief, Healthy Heart was tiny and quaint and nearly empty. The walls had been painted red and cream, which I supposed was meant to emit the feeling of "barnyard chic." This was amplified with framed cow and pig portraits. "These pictures are making me hungry for a burger," John whispered playfully. But I had just watched *What the Health* for the third time, so I didn't find his joke funny at all. "Do you know," I said when we took a seat, "that eating animal products can raise your cholesterol?"

My comment was pointed. With John off at work, I had spent the day happily alone. Per her daily request, I called my mom to confirm that I was still alive. "Search John's house while he's out," she said, peeved that I hadn't done this during my first visit. "Search for what?" I asked. "Oh, I don't know, Michelle," she said sarcastically. "A damn gun!" So, with my phone pressed to my ear, I wandered John's house, hunting for weapons, cameras, poison, tarps, or anything else that suggested danger. "All clear," I told my mom, at last, as I ended my investigation in the kitchen. "But John did leave me sixty dollars with a note that says, 'Buy yourself some groceries. *Heart.*'"

"Oh no. You're not done yet," my mom said. "Go look in his medicine cabinet, then read me the names of his prescriptions." I obliged, and climbed, for the fourth time that morning, two flights of stairs.

"Cardura and Lipitor," I told her, holding the orange bottles in my hand.

"Oh, I take those same ones," she said, disarmed by this likeness. "Those are just for high blood pressure and high cholesterol."

"All animal products are bad for cholesterol?" John asked sincerely. "Or just eggs?"

I rolled my eyes dramatically. "*All.* I think."

"Welcome, my friends," a server caroled through an Eastern European accent. "I'm Ilana and I will be your server tonight." As a former server myself, it was obvious to me that Ilana was a professional. Before even handing us menus, Ilana had upsold seasonal iced teas, Healthy Heart's newest appetizers (bruschetta and stuffed mushrooms), and a thirteen-dollar dessert. "We have *the best* chocolate lava cake," she said. "No refined sugar. It's made with dates, so it's actually good for you!" She elbowed John's shoulder. Incredible form, I thought, remembering a time I had been secretly shopped at California Pizza Kitchen when I was eighteen. *Very monotone, not friendly,* the report had said. My boss frowned the entire time we went over my feedback. "Do you like your job, Michelle?" she had asked me. I made $7.25 an hour. Of course, I did not. "But the cake takes twenty-five minutes to cook," Ilana said, her voice a few octaves away from doom. "So, if you want it, you have to order it now."

"We'll take two," John said, without confirming that I wanted one (I did), and winked.

"I'll put that order in *right away*," Ilana said, pleased. "And I'll grab your iced teas while I'm back there."

When Ilana walked away, John and I turned toward the window and commented on the world outside. *Look at that kid skateboarding. Oh, he fell. Is he hurt? No. Just a skinned knee. Is that his dad?* "Yuck," I said, "is that dude wearing a MAGA cap?"

"Uh-oh," John said. "Look away."

To John's dismay, I often brought Trump into our conversations. I'd run through the latest news headlines to be sure that John knew what *his* president was up to: Trump signs an executive travel ban on predominantly Muslim countries, Trump signs an executive order to dismantle climate laws set by former president Barack Obama, Trump tweets more fake news claims. It was always depressing.

I frowned. "Do you ever wear a MAGA hat when I'm not here?"

John laughed. "Pfft, no!" Then quickly began skimming over Healthy Heart's menu. "I know you don't like the president," John said, feigning distraction. "But what are your feelings about his wife?"

"I have no real feelings about Melania," I said. "I don't know enough about her. Although, from some of those candid pictures I've seen, I assume she hates Trump too."

"I bet she's pretty happy because Trump is crazy rich," John said.

"I don't think being happy and being 'crazy rich' are the same thing," I said. "You know, there's a famous study on this." The study[1] I was referring to was conducted by psychologist Daniel Kahneman and economist Angus Deaton, published in 2010. "Money can make your life better to an extent," I told John. "Which makes sense. I feel so much lighter since I've met you, I can eat cake and afford to fix some kind of life mishap. I can go to the movies and buy popcorn without worrying about it. People just need enough money to live comfortably without feeling

---

[1] Daniel Kahneman and Angus Deaton, "High Income Improves Evaluation of Life but Not Emotional Well-Being," *PNAS* 107, no. 38 (2010): 16489–93, https://doi.org/10.1073/pnas.1011492107.

stressed out all the time. But, if I were making a salary like yours," I said, taking a small jab, "I wouldn't actually feel any happier."

Last night in bed, when John's guard was lowered post-sex, I pried about his income. "God, I just can't get over how nice your house is," I said, twirling his chest hairs around my finger. "How much is your Titan salary, anyway?"

"It's an obnoxious figure," John said, grimacing. "I'm worried that if I tell you, you'll think, 'Oh my god, what a jackass.'"

"I won't think that," I lied. "I benefit so much."

John smiled. "Well, part of my salary is in stock," he explained. "So, it's not a straightforward answer."

"I'm just going to guess a number," I said, "and you tell me if it's high or low."

John nodded.

"One million."

John tossed his head back and laughed. "Oh, gosh. I wish! Much lower. Within three years—stock values upholding—my salary will hover around $500,000."

I tried to be calm, but $500,000? That was nearly four times what everyone in my family earned combined, my sugaring salary included. "Do you think your job warrants half a million dollars a year?"

"Well," John said, his nipples erect from the air conditioning, "I work all the time, and I do have a master's degree."

To give John some perspective, I began telling him a story, with a few minor omissions. Once, my professor, a PhD and author, held a Q&A "during class" (really, a personal phone call). "Do you think it'd ever be possible to fund my life through writing?" I'd asked, toying with prospects. "Or should I just give up hope and pursue another career?"

"There's a micro-possibility," Wes said. "But for most, supplementing writing with teaching is usually the best answer." High school or middle school had the most job opportunities, but academia—with a whole lot of hoop jumping—was possible too. "How much money do you make as a professor?" I asked.

"And what do you think he said?" I asked John in his bed.

John tapped his chin. "Hmm. $200,000?"

"Eighty," I said. "Before taxes."

"The whole 'Education is the answer' argument is bullshit," Wes told me again, just as he had the morning I confessed to him about sugaring. "I've been trying to climb out of poverty my whole life, and, somehow as a result, I've spent my whole adult life trying to climb out of debt." I told John this, too, but stopped before the juicy part; that within a week of my final grade being posted, Wes had proposed that I join a side gig he and his girlfriend were running together.

"I find guys off Craigslist for her to sleep with for cash. I post the ads, upload the naked pictures of her, arrange the jobs, write the emails, do the sexting, confirm the price, and then drop her off at the john's house," Wes said. "Then I wait outside for her to finish. It's a lot of work, so she pays me 20 percent of what she makes."

"What are you asking me?" I said.

"Sometimes these guys want two girls. It's all safe," he said before I could answer. "There's always a condom. Sometimes the guys'll pay just to watch the girls go down on each other. I know you're into pussy and haven't had any in a while. It'd be a quick way for you to get laid and make $200."

It was an unbelievable leap. Wes, my professor who, as of one week ago, was a man who was too afraid to see me outside of class for fear of losing his job, was now offering to take nude photos of me and post them on the internet. He was saying he'd drop me off at these men's houses and wait outside for me, as I fucked his girlfriend, or she and I fucked some guy together. And all he wanted was 20 percent. Forty bucks. I would need to sleep with ten men for him to make a single student loan payment. Where did that fear go? I wondered. Were the regulations so loose at universities that as soon as a student is no longer on a professor's roster, all rules cease to apply? Did the consequences simply expire? Or now that Wes saw a financial opportunity, did he stop caring about being so careful?

Although I found it hurtful, I'd be lying if I said I was entirely surprised. Wes had always endorsed sugaring as a good business move, but he never understood why selling my body felt like such a grave compromise. One that I couldn't fathom repeating with anyone other than John. I believed that everything that had transpired with John had aligned with magic precision to change the trajectory of my life, but Wes would shake this off to push his own Deviant Sociology Professor prerogative with sex work. "Sex is just sex, anyway," he always said. "Make a profit where you can and make as much money as possible." Which was fine as an idea on its own—we all have our own boundaries with our own bodies—but Wes refused to validate that there were things I felt capable of doing and things I did not. "Michelle," he said, harshly, "what's the difference between selling your body to John and someone off Craigslist?"

This sort of pushback had grown exasperating. Ever since he'd gotten back with Katrina, Wes had grown prone to lecturing me on my morality, which he spoke about as simultaneously wildly loose and frigid. Wes, as progressive as he played around sex work, boiled it all down to one factor: a person either found it acceptable to sell their body or they found it unacceptable. I was the former. So, I should get off my moral high horse and pocket the cash from whoever was willing to pay. Having a say in the matter was no more than some lame attempt to convince myself that I was a high-class hooker. *What do you think?* I could imagine Wes asking me. *That you're better than me or my girl or anyone else in this world?*

I didn't want to give Wes reason to launch into another lecture, so I proposed a number far beyond what any Craigslist john would pay. "Two hundred is pretty cheap," I said. "I'd consider it for $1,000."

Wes scoffed. "You think too highly of yourself. Believe me."

"Of course money doesn't buy happiness," John said now at Healthy Heart. "My sweetie is so smart! That's why I love her. But I will say that it does buy things that can make us happy, like . . ." He raised his eyebrows at me.

Injured by Wes and John's gross insinuation that I'd been bought, I felt suddenly frantic to acknowledge that I, too, had a say in this arrangement. That while John had paid me for sex, my heart or my sense of self had never been on the table. I had stuck true to that. And while the decision to sleep with John had been hard, over and over and over again it had been hard, I chose it for myself because it was worth it. Sugaring existed at my absolute maximum capacity for what I could give of my body. Sex in exchange for money that I needed to change my life. Money that I had spent on concrete things like student loan debt and filling my teeth and helping my mom buy groceries. Regardless of what either of these men wanted out of me, neither Wes nor John was going to convince me to go beyond my own limitations.

"John, do you actually think money can buy someone who will love you?" I said, bitterly.

John grew visibly uncomfortable. "Not exactly. I don't think money can buy *love*." He grabbed my hand across the table. "But I do think it can get your foot in the door."

I pulled my hand away, and then Ilana arrived just in the nick of time. "So," she said. "What looks good?"

After we'd licked our lava cake ramekins clean, Ilana delivered our tab: $128. A shocking sum for two people but worth it according to John. "Did you enjoy everything?" she asked.

"Yes. I love this place," I told her. "I wish I could come here every day."

"You should!" Ilana said with earnest excitement. "We change the menu all the time."

We two began chatting. Ilana was a vegan. And like me, she had seen *What the Health* and *Cowspiracy* and wondered if I had watched *Fed Up*. I had not, I told her, but I would add it to my watch list. John glanced awkwardly back and forth between us, looking for a doorway into the conversation, but neither Ilana nor I was particularly interested in providing one. When I asked, Ilana said she was twenty-three years old, and she'd moved here two years earlier from Ukraine to be with her husband. She said it was a nice town, but quiet and very *buttoned up*. I told Ilana that this was my second time in the city, just visiting John, who had recently moved here to work for Titan.

"My husband also works at Titan!" Ilana cried. "And his name is also John!"

We both turned to my John, who looked glum. Well, here was his way in. "Do you know my husband?" Ilana asked. "John Gibbons?"

"No," John said, stiffly. "Not off the top of my head. But I'll look him up on the employee database when we get home."

We, I thought, mocking in my head. *We are not a "we."*

★

On Saturday morning, I discreetly popped a Xanax while John drove us to the National Mall. Last night after dinner, I told John that I needed an itinerary for our weekend. "I'm a planner," I said, though, truthfully, I wanted to ration my replenished stash of Xanax. "I'm also a homebody, so don't feel like you have to entertain me," I added. "I'm happy to stay at home."

John smiled, and said, "I was thinking it might be nice to do something fun together."

"Okay." I could do this. But what would 'something fun' constitute? "What are your hobbies?"

"Money," he said and laughed.

I tried a different angle. "What do you usually do with your free time?" He just shrugged. In the four months that John had been living out East, he'd only left his house to go to work and run errands. "I have," John said, at last, "been wanting to drive into the city and see all of the national monuments."

So there we were. On a Saturday in mid-May, strolling the National Mall, gawking at monuments—which repeatedly surprised me with their size—and remarking, every now and again, on the beautiful foliage: a rosebush, an oak tree, a perennial bloom. John possessed an unexpected patriotism. He thanked men in uniform for their service and even teared up at the marker where Martin Luther King Jr. stood to deliver his "I Have a Dream" speech.

I rubbed his back, mimicking what a girlfriend might do. "Do you want to talk about what you're feeling?"

"My parents immigrated here from China in the '50s," he said. "They left their home country because they wanted to give me a good life. They wanted me to have the American Dream." John turned toward the reflecting pool. "This country," he said, "has so much opportunity."

I found myself baffled by contradictions. While King may be historicized in heroic terms, the America that he spoke to in 1963 was largely against his message. He was assassinated because of the hatred he fought against. How could this nation truly embrace King's dream even now, in 2017, when we had an openly racist, sexist, and xenophobic president—one whom John had voted for? I stopped myself from challenging him. John's parents were Chinese immigrants who had worked hard to support him through college. He was a living testament to the American Dream, and now he was passing the Dream to his kids, and in some totally fucked way, momentarily, me.

We contradict ourselves. We contain multitudes. Just like Walt Whitman said. John, Wes, and me. I could grant a man access to my body, then attend the Women's March in downtown Denver. My professor could propose pimping me out on the internet after assuring me that I had a bright future ahead of me. I could need that reassurance so bad that I'd cling to his belief in me instead of cutting him out of my life. John could work his whole life away trying to provide for his family, just to end up paying for the intimacy he'd neglected. And I could take advantage of John's loneliness, while he knowingly took advantage of my financial desperation.

"Did I tell you that Luke is moving?" John said. "He took an internship with the social media platform Chirp in California."

"That's incredible, like unbelievable," I said, and then sought a gentle way to check that John and I were on the same page—that the "dream" was not accessible through dedication and hard work alone. I settled on, "Is that internship paid?"

"No," John said. "I'm supporting him. But I'm happy to do so, my boys work hard, like their daddy."

"It's not *just* hard work," I said, bristlier than I'd meant to. "I know your kids work hard. You *have* to work hard to land something like a Chirp internship, but do you think that either of them would've been able to *accept* those offers if they didn't have you paying the bills?"

"Uh . . . I know that things are unfair," John said, with all the weight of an empty potato chip bag. "But I have worked very hard and so have my kids."

A drip of sweat trickled into my eye, which annoyed me way more than it should've. "My dad has worked hard his *whole* life," I said. "He started working at eight years old, and he'll be working past the age of retirement. But it's not the same kind of 'hard work' that this country finds respectable, and it's not the kind of 'hard work' that leads to any kind of opportunity or status."

"Well, if he had gone to college," John said.

I cut him off. "My dad could barely finish high school because he was plowing fields. College wasn't even in the realm of possibility." A frog emerged in my throat. I swallowed it down, but it only hopped around in my stomach. "I wonder who my dad would've been if he'd had money and opportunity," I said, almost to myself.

"I'm sure he has a lot of unrecognized potential," John said. "But I'm sure he's proud of you for recognizing yours."

"You think he's proud of me for selling my body?"

"That's not fair," John said, cross. "You were already in school when we met. You were already setting yourself up for a good future."

"This is what you don't get. This lifestyle I have with you is not real. Your house is not mine. Your car is not mine. Your money is not mine. And when this arrangement is over, this illusion of security will go with it."

★

The drive home from DC was tense. But John, eager to reconcile before the evening's sexual events, sought out some emotional foreplay. "Oh. I meant to tell you," he said good-naturedly, as he merged into the left lane. "I looked up Ilana's husband. John Gibbons."

I took the olive branch. "What does he look like?"

John passed me his iPhone, which he had used to take a photo of his computer, he explained. "So, forgive the pixilation." I gasped at the picture. It was an ancient sir. One with a white comb-over and saggy jowls. I guessed that he was in his early to mid-sixties. "You're *positive* this is Ilana's husband?" I asked.

"He was the only man by that name, John Gibbons, in the system," John said.

I was stunned. What was their story? How had this man landed someone as young and beautiful as Ilana? Was it possible—I felt my heart jolt at the mere thought—that Ilana was *like me*?

A car cut us off. "Asshole," John and I mumbled under our breath at the exact same time.

"You should lay on the horn next time," I said. I had grown up a defensive city driver. "And instead of swerving so much, just hit the brake a little." I was also a skilled backseat driver.

My phone buzzed in my lap. Wes Elliot calling again. We hadn't spoken since the Craigslist debacle. I wasn't sure if I wanted to speak to him ever again. I hit decline and counted the telephone poles we zoomed past, while thinking about my desperation to crawl out of debt, and how, despite Wes's misguided approach, I could empathize with his own desperation to do the same. He could've been kinder about my boundaries. He could've just accepted my no and moved on. I shook Wes out of my mind and returned my thoughts to Ilana. "Does John Gibbons make as much money as you?"

Ilana's husband was also a manager. "So, yeah," John said, "I assume he makes something similar. Maybe more. He's been there a while."

With half a million dollars a year, Ilana's John could afford to take care of her financially, and yet here she was, serving. Perhaps she worked nights at Healthy Heart for time away from John Gibbons. I imagined trivial details of their life together: laundry mixing, hairs in the sink, the stench of sweat, dirty dishes, clutter on the kitchen table, required sex. A kind of cage. But also, a kind of mindless freedom. If I looked at it the right way there was a message here. Ilana's life with John Gibbons could just as easily be my life with my John. I heard Wes in my head, *You lucky, lucky girls. Take it. Write with some security.*

"I don't know what your plans post-graduation are," John said suddenly, as if he had just read my mind. "But we could get married, you know?" He rushed ahead. "I love you so much. Whenever you're here, I feel so much happier. So much more alive. I'm not just working twelve-hour days but actually getting out and enjoying my life. I think we could have a lot of fun together. And there will be perks for you, of course. You wouldn't have to worry about money ever again. My house would be your house. This car could also be your car. *What's mine is yours.*" He began listing off the possibilities like a game show host. "I wouldn't be too needy either. Just sex maybe four or five times a week. But," he said, sort of shy, "I would like to kiss every night."

It was jarring. I felt bad for John. I knew his life was lonesome without me here. I was grateful for the time I spent away from John. Trying my hardest to put our arrangement out of my mind. Meanwhile he was always counting down the days until I was back. But John was also being manipulative. This offer—marry me for security, marry me for a chance to focus on writing—was a worse kind of manipulation than anything he'd ever offered me before, because it was deeply *informed*. There was a real dream of mine at stake. How could John believe that he loved me when he would barter what I wanted most in the world in exchange for giving him my *entire life*?

I shook my head. I would never marry John. Though, if I'd asked my past self if she would consider sleeping with a customer for $1,200, she would have said *hell no*. It wasn't as though I had fallen down the rabbit hole all at once. One compensated, sexless dinner had slid into the next, and the next, and so forth. Each step forward was so well lubricated with cash, it was hard to feel as if John had pushed things too far. My vision began to blur. Little squiggles started up in my eyes. Black and white and menacing, like a king snake slithering through my brain folds. "I'm getting a migraine," I said and cupped my eyes.

"Don't answer my question now," John said. "Just marinate on it. Know it's an option."

★

I arrived at the airport on Sunday afternoon with $14,800 in my purse. After the morning's pleasure session, John fanned two envelopes in my palm. The first envelope contained my monthly pay, $4,800. The next was a total surprise. "I'm proud of you for graduating college," John said, as I drew five stacks of hundred-dollar bills, each wrapped with a

$2k collar. Ten thousand dollars. "I didn't have to work my way through school," John said. "But you did. You fought really hard to succeed."

While I believed that John was proud of me, I knew in his world a bachelor's from a public university wasn't an accomplishment deserving of $10K. The cash wasn't about my graduation. It was an opportunity for John to flaunt what life could be like with him. He, as my husband. Me, as his wife. The cash was a calculated move, and I was still beyond grateful. I owed $8,000 more toward my student loans, and thanks to this hefty carrot, I would free myself of the debt that only a year and a half ago I had been sure would plague me into late life. Tears rimmed my eyes, but I didn't give John the satisfaction. Couldn't have him mistake relief for hope. I thanked him the way he wanted. With a kiss, then another. "Think about what I asked you," John said as he sent me off through security.

I celebrated my purse full of cash at an airport bar. Cheersing a shot of vodka against my vodka soda. Tipping 100 percent. Needless to say, I was not sober when I called Wes.

"Oh, Michelle," he said, remorseful upon answer. "I am so sorry about the other day. I don't know why I thought you might be into that silly idea. You're not a big casual sex gal. You're more into connection, so I get that the Craigslist johns don't appeal to you." His tone lifted. "It's really no skin off my teeth. It was going to help you way more than me. So, whaddaya say? Let's just forget about it?"

This was not a real apology. It wasn't sincere and Wes didn't take any accountability, but I folded. I had grown so deeply dishonest blurring my own sense of morality that I believed anyone I let inside the walls I'd built would've had to have a dark side too. How else would they have accepted me?

"What are we even talking about?" I asked. Wes laughed in his lavish way.

"I read your story again the other day," Wes said. "I really think you should consider graduate school."

"No way, no more debt," I said, quickly. Traumatized by the work it had taken to, at last, become free of it. I patted my thighs. Said a silent thank you to my body. But then Wes interrupted me, saying there are these things called MFAs. "MF-what?" I asked.

"Master of Fine Arts in Creative Writing," he said, tickled. "And some of these programs are funded." Sometimes, Wes told me, students teach classes at the university, which covers tuition plus a small stipend. Usually just enough to get by on.

"I almost applied to MFAs," Wes said. "But I went the safer academic route, and I wonder all the time what my life would look like if I hadn't been so scared."

There was a long pause. "Michelle? You're a writer. Take it seriously."

The gravity of his voice convinced me that I needed him. Professor Wes Elliot. For his guidance. His support. For his solitary faith in my writing. At the airport bar, I drank from my cocktail, smiled to myself. For the very first time I saw a concrete way out of sugaring that could lead me to a life I wanted. I'd lose the luxury of the sugaring money, and I would hurt John. Leave him right where he started—all alone. But for my dream, it might just be worth it.

Part Three

Wake Up

11

Exit Route

*N*ovember marked seven months since John moved out East. In the twenty-eight days we'd spent together, John tried, repeatedly, to up the ante on our arrangement by turning our handshake agreement into holy matrimony. After his original proposal in May, I'd returned to Virginia a month later, where I delivered a well-marinated and gentle-but-firm *No* to his offer. It was not an easy line to deliver. I'd spent the weeks prior wondering if John would end our arrangement right there on the spot. If he'd realized that he was looking for more than just sex for hire. That he wanted real intimacy. Love. A whole life with someone. If he might finally admit that money was never going to be the answer to that. I would lose the security, but there was no other option. I couldn't marry him.

That didn't happen.

Instead, my *No* registered to John only as *Convince me*. Every subsequent month, after the wheels of my Southwest flight touched the tarmac in DC, I'd walk down one moving sidewalk after another, past baggage claim and outside to arrivals, where John would be parked at the curb, down on one proverbial knee, with his palm open, extending a ripened deal.

"If you say yes," he told me back in June, "I'll take you shopping once a week!"

"I don't need weekly shopping sprees," I said, indifferent after my original no had been disregarded. "I need healthcare."

John took the feedback seriously and spent the summer revising his case. By August his proposal included medical, dental, and eye insurance. In September, an extra salary to write my stories. In October, after I finally let him in on MFA prospects, John offered me a paid writing tutor. "Essentially," John said, "your own private MFA. Here at home in Virginia."

While John believed each additional clause was sweetening the deal, I had seen it clearly from the start. He was proposing more money, which he could paint any way he pleased: a desk in a den, a trip to the doctor, a makeshift MFA—the Sugaring Edition of the life I would've wanted for myself.

"Why do you want to marry me?" I finally asked him. "Not why do you want to be married, but why *me* specifically?"

He paused, searching himself for the answer. "You're kind," he said. "And a lot of fun! You want to travel the world, and that's what I want to do after I retire." He was sincere when he added, "I don't want to do it all alone." Then he laughed out of nervousness. "I really don't want to live and die all alone."

I felt bad for him. I wasn't in love with John, but we had been in one another's lives for two years now and I cared about him. It would've been impossible not to. Maybe he'd accepted our relationship for what it was and thought he could live his whole life this way. I couldn't fathom it. As the propositions began to stack on top of me, and John grew more and more anxious by my rejections, I accepted it for what it was: John was losing interest in an arrangement that wasn't going anywhere. He was looking for long-term, pseudo-serious companionship. Either I gave up my entire life, partook in John's fantasy and married him for a lifetime of security, or I quit sugaring.

★

"I have a plan," I told my dad. We were driving four hours to Alamosa, Colorado, where my abuela Corina recently moved into an independent living community. He wanted to check out her new place to be sure she was settling in. I'd originally planned to join my dad because I wanted to see my grandma, but now I had another motive. I'd conceived of a way to leave John without returning to poverty. This idea was reliant on my dad's help, or better said, his participation. I needed his approval to buy a million-dollar life insurance policy on him, something I understood as relative to investing money in the stock market or real estate, except without the risk, and, seeing as life insurance policies were broken down into low monthly payments, something I could afford.

The idea had come about that very morning, on my drive to pick up my dad in Colorado Springs, while I was on the phone with Wes. He'd had an incident with his carbon monoxide detector the night before. "My upstairs neighbors had a leak that saturated the wiring in my ceiling," Wes said. His voice ragged from exhaustion. "The damn thing beeped all night long." I extended my sympathies, but Wes said it was all fine. "I just kept thinking, damn, I wish I had a kid. Because if I died this way, they could cash in on some good life insurance policies."

Outside the windshield were new developments. Apartments popping up between South Denver and the next town over, Castle Rock. The word *investments* came to mind, and then I thought about what Wes said, life insurance policy. Wishing he had a kid to pass it on to. I wasn't in the business of insurance policies, but seeing as everyone on true crime TV were willing to murder over them, I figured they were a pretty safe bet. Buy a big enough policy and it could provide long-term security. My wheels were turning. There was only one certainty in life: everyone was going to die. My parents, woefully, included. "Is it possible," I asked Wes, "to buy a policy on one of my parents and make myself the beneficiary?"

Wes assured me that I could if they'd pretend to have gotten it on themselves. Then, having caught on to my plan, Wes added, "If you do this you should give me a cut of your policy. I'm the one who gave you the idea."

I floated the idea to my dad, trying to be gentle yet practical. "It's like giving me an inheritance without having to save or spend a penny of your own money."

"Hmm," he said. "If I say yes, I don't have to do or pay for anything at all?" my dad asked now as he zoomed past a Toyota Camry.

"Nope," I said. "Just do the physical and sign up for whichever one I choose. I'll cover all the costs."

"Well, then sure," he said casually. "Why the hell not."

I let out a dramatic sigh of relief. As morbid as it may have seemed, this brand-new possibility of eventually coming into an inheritance via life insurance gave me hope that I'd be able to leave this arrangement behind without fear of taking a lower paying job, because it would mean that my next era of poverty would be temporary. And I *really* needed something concrete to pull me away from John's escalating proposals. The last time I visited John two weeks ago, his tactic had shifted. "I've been thinking about your mommy," he told me while shredding a hot pita. We were having dinner at an upscale Mediterranean restaurant. "How you said she won't be able to retire." John paused. "If you marry me, she can."

I swallowed water backward down my windpipe. John patted my back, but I dodged him and, when I recovered, presented my most evil glare. "What did you just say?"

John grinned, a *gotcha!* grin. "You heard me. I would pay all your mom's bills. I would take care of her."

I wanted to remind John of a conversation we'd had back in October. We had been in his car, listening to talk radio. The MeToo movement had caught the media's flame, and we heeded a recent update: *The New York Times* released a story in which Ashley Judd detailed Harvey

Weinstein trying to coerce her into sex for a film role. "Yuck!" John said, dramatically, turning the radio off. "It's so gross that creeps like Harvey Weinstein took advantage of these girls under the guise of helping them." He sighed a great heavy breath of disgust. "It's unfortunate that we've created a culture in which girls feel like the only way they can be successful or help their careers is by sleeping with someone like *him*."

I was dumbstruck by John's hypocrisy but understood almost immediately why he had placed levels of separation between Weinstein and himself. When John offered his loaf of bread, I had been a stripper ("depraved") rather than a Hollywood actress ("prestigious"). But I still questioned how John could be so blind to the underlying dynamics of the sugaring system. Had I been overly generous in assuming that John truly comprehended the implications of his actions? I could almost hear Wes's voice echoing in my mind, asserting that I had enabled John enough to shield him from facing the truth within our peculiar ecosystem. His delusion was my fault.

But, again, that was the catch of an arrangement.

I couldn't have drawn attention to the truth without risks. Sure, I could've said, "John, you know what you're doing is not that different from Harvey Weinstein," and then risked losing the money. Or I could've said, "Interesting," and let the muddled situation get murkier, payment still included.

At the table, I chose passive aggression and said, "My nephew and my mom are a package deal."

"I'd take care of him too," John said. "I was actually thinking that we could start a college fund for Chuy. And what about your sister?" Then, the deal was supersized. Everyone would be upgraded to leased vehicles. Car insurance, eye and dental, groceries, spending money, and even rent. My mom would never have to worry about anything for the rest of her life! It was a bear trap under hundred-dollar bills.

★

"Hey now, that's a pretty good deal," Wes said, when I'd called him from the airport after that November visit. I'd had the instinct to withhold information about John's marriage proposals from Wes before this, but the offer had become too big. I could no longer wrap my arms around it alone.

I was hoping Wes would say that I had my head on straight. I was smart to resist John's marriage offers. I wanted to be financially secure, sure, but I wanted freedom and a life above board at some point even more. I knew Wes wouldn't say that, of course. He was not nuanced about John.

"I think you should take it."

"No way," I said. "A whole life with John? I'd rather die poor."

"You're being kind of rash," Wes said. His voice was cool. I imagined him with a toothpick in his mouth. "There's no harm in saying yes. It's 2017. Marriage doesn't mean forever. You could marry John, get your finances all bundled up, have your mom retire on his promise to fund her, let him pay your nephew's way through college, and *then* leave him."

I shook my head to myself. "If I marry and divorce John, my mom will be in a vulnerable position if the scheme doesn't work out. She can't quit her job for a few years, then return to the workforce, even older than before. And my nephew is only nine years old," I said. "If I married John, I would have to commit to the role for the next twelve years."

Wes groaned at my rebuttal. "You would write this into a prenup." Wes laid it out bare for me. I would only need to be married to John for about a year. In the prenup, I'd make sure that John promised to cover the cost of my "lifestyle" in the case of a divorce and write my family into the clauses. John would be contracted to provide our quality of life until he died. "God," Wes said, stunned. "You're so fucking lucky. You should really start buying lotto tickets."

Was this really how it worked? I knew that John's ex-wife was living off money he paid her, but their situation was starkly different. They'd had two children together, and were, therefore, already amalgamated. I was deeply ashamed of this secret arrangement. When I walked away from sugaring, I intended to forget the whole thing ever happened. A marriage would make that impossible. I imagined the paper trail. A certificate. A divorce announcement. Alimony. A lifestyle that would've required an explanation. "When I leave sugaring," I said to Wes, "I want to leave it all behind."

"Oh, come on," Wes said, growing aggravated. "So what if you have to check in with John every once in a while? You'll be living on his dime. It's a pretty easy trade. Just think about it. You'd be able to hole up in some writer's paradise for a year or two and churn out a novel without thinking about money once."

When I didn't cave, Wes paused to switch tactics. "If I'm honest, Michelle, you're being selfish. Your mama has been working hard her whole life. You don't think a year of getting paid to be fucked is worth all that security for her?"

Retiring would be life changing for my mother. Since the day she entered the workforce, she expected to labor until she died. I held the power in my hand to help her. Something I had spent my whole life trying to do, but with the opportunity before me, I felt immobilized. "I don't know if I could do it," I said. "Even for a year."

"Oh, come on," Wes said, practically begging. "I'll help you. You'll only have to suffer through one year, which is a tiny fragment of your life, but plenty for the court system. Then we'll file for divorce and spousal support, and you and your mama will spend the rest of your lives financially secure."

The terminal felt suddenly chaotic. A child screaming in her stroller. The PA system paging Mr. Jerome Taylor to gate B49. Some cash register dinging behind me. My stomach clenched into a fist. It was too much responsibility at too much cost.

"And, of course, you'll give me a yearly cut for walking you through it," Wes said, finally showing his hand. "Something tiny. Five percent."

★

On the flight back to Denver, I really thought about it—John's offer, that is. Though I'd gotten used to wielding my family's poverty around, I was unprepared for how effective it'd be when John used their status to manipulate me. *My poor mom*, I thought, and returned to a memory that had branded itself in my brain. Back in Newport News. Her driving away from my grandmother's house in a U-Haul, crying. If I really focused, I could still feel reverbs of her distress. Even as an eight-year-old, I believed that my mom, who saw Colorado as the right decision for our *family*, was making the wrong decision for *herself*. She may have been our mother, and Bianca and I may have been her children, but my dad hadn't seemed too concerned about the family unit when he decided to move, I told her, so we couldn't think about the unit either, only ourselves. My mom could not be swayed. I knew then at twenty-six what I had not known at eight. My mother loved my father. And, probably more importantly, she could not raise two kids on her single salary. This was why I felt my mother's current struggle in Colorado was, at least in part, my fault.

But here was the opportunity to right it all.

My mom could stop worrying about everything. The rent, the light bill, food, her car, her prescriptions. She could quit her job. She would have money to visit her family in Virginia. After all those trials and tribulations, loneliness and heartbreak, and that one terribly tough decision to move to Colorado, I could make it so all of this had been leading my mom to financial freedom. Marrying John would have made it all worth it.

The flight attendants passed pretzels down the aisles as Wes's words played in my mind. *Why not just do it? It's selfish to say no.* The guilt of derailing my mom's old life had been terrible enough, and I hadn't truly had a say in that move. This decision would be all mine. If I chose not to marry John, I would have to live with the knowledge that every bad or hard or financially stressful thing that would happen in my mom's life could have been different.

I began to cry, politely as to not disrupt the passengers I sat between. The woman to my left offered her napkin. I thanked her and wished she might ask me how I was. I would've told her the truth. That I was standing at a fork in one of life's roads, and I had two options: I either drag myself away from sugaring, damning my whole family to hell in the process, or I become the sacrificial lamb and marry John.

★

Oh, but here I was now. Two weeks later, watching my dad spit sunflower shells into a Coke bottle, with this newly cultivated *third* option. I started allocating everything I'd do with the money off a life insurance policy on him. If I invested in a hefty enough plan, I could pay for Chuy's college, I could send my sister to trade school, and I could even help fund my mom's retirement. The leftover would be used to aid all our lives modestly and securely *forever*.

My dad nodded his head. "This is a pretty good idea. Bueno, Shell. How'd you get so smart?"

I explained that early on John told me that the best way to make money was from money. He'd suggested either investing in the stock market or real estate. While owning property sounded simple enough, I couldn't buy a house without first being approved for a loan, and sugar babying wasn't exactly observed by the IRS.

The stock market, too, proved problematic. Once, in DC, John set his laptop on his picnic table and walked me through opening a Vanguard account. "What will happen to the money I invest?" I'd asked John. "It'll accrue value over the years," he said. "You have to just put it in there and forget about it." John didn't understand that what he often referred to as my "nest egg" was everything I had. The building blocks for my future and how I was surviving day-to-day. I needed a way to grow my money, while never losing access to it, which is what made a million-dollar life insurance policy the best option for me. There was a monthly premium, so I'd be able to allocate my "nest egg" to a separate account and set recurrent payments for x number of years. I wouldn't lose the lump sum, meaning I could always access what remained of my savings.

"Did you say a million dollars?" My dad's round eyes dilated, and then he retreated into himself like a turtle. He was thinking.

All around us was pastureland. All of it the color of sand. We passed two horses, and then two more. "Mira, caballos," I said. I'd been practicing Spanish on my Duolingo app.

"It's the right word," my dad said, "but you sound white when you say it."

"I am white," I said. When I was younger, I would use my pale skin to hurt my dad, taunting, "I'm probably not even your kid," whenever I wanted to antagonize him. The last time I said this I was ten. "You really think you're not mine?" he'd asked. The corners of his lips drooped, injured. I felt bad about it now. "Well, half white and half Chicana."

"You know, Shell, I've been thinking." My dad sounded as though he'd been gnawing over his proposition for a few days rather than just a few minutes. "Life insurance policies aren't cheap. Especially if you want a high payout. I think you need a partner. Someone to split the costs with."

Although it'd be nice to have two policies—one on my mom and one on my dad—I knew I couldn't afford both. Unless I had my dad's help. "You want to split a policy on Goldie?"

"Well, yeah," my dad said. "But not right now. Your mom isn't in the best health, but people don't just die from being sick anymore. Modern-day medicine prevents it. By the time me or your mom dies you're going to be an old woman yourself."

"What are you trying to say?" I asked.

"I think we should start with a policy on Grandma Corina."

"Genius," I said. I hadn't even considered her an option.

As my dad and I drove farther south—two fools with no clue about the fine print of these things—we developed a fruitful plan. First, we would split a moderate policy for my abuela. After she passed, we'd use the money to invest in a larger policy on my mom (presuming that, because of her health concerns, she'd die before my father), and then I would use the profit from my mom's passing to buy a million-dollar policy on him.

"If your mom goes first, I'm going to get a little piece of land in San Luis," my dad said. This was where he'd grown up, in the house my grandma Corina had just been forced to leave thanks to a sunken roof. "And I'm going to get miniature goats and pigs to live there with me."

My dad sounded like me when I first agreed to John's arrangement offer. My list had felt very practical. Time to write sat at the very top, small and sharp like the *sweets and fats* brick of the Healthy Eating pyramid. Stacked on top of a paid-for education, and, on top of that, dental work, a functional car, a sense of financial, and consequently, overall, well-being. I wanted emancipation from a poor life, and I figured that was nothing more than a math equation.

What I hadn't understood then was that an influx of money for a limited amount of time wasn't enough to change my whole life. It was like being hungry. How you could eat yourself full, and like magic, after your body burned it all up, you're hungry again. This life insurance policy wasn't going to solve everything, but it would be better than a marriage to John. I saw only one hiccup in our plan. "Do you think grandma will agree to it?"

"I don't see why not," my dad said. "Everyone has to die. It won't even affect her."

I shrugged. "I guess you're right. I just don't want to hurt her feelings."

My dad turned his face to me. "Do you think Corina is made of sugar?"

No, I did not. I didn't even think sugar was an ingredient. Corina didn't give hugs or bake cookies or say much of anything other than "estás gorda," (you are fat), but this was nothing personal, my dad had told me—as she'd never said she loved him either, nor happy birthday—even as a little girl, her nickname had been "chica mala" (mean girl). All this to justify that my grandma wasn't someone who'd feel sorry for herself for having to die.

Fine, it was very morbid of us, we admitted to one another, but we were all going to die, so why not use the tragedy for some security? "I'll do the same for my own kids one day," I told my dad. "And I won't even make them front the cost themselves."

"Pfft," he said. "Yeah, right. You just wait until you have kids, and you'll see how much you want to pay for all their shit."

My dad's parenting had always included letting me and my sister know, repeatedly, that it was absolutely a hassle to raise us. We were made of sugar and we lacked enough money to take care of ourselves. My dad, while happy to dish out advice, did best when we did not *need* him. For example, when I was twenty-four years old, I found myself with a blown tire on the side of the highway, with no mechanical help in sight. Because I slept on my mother's couch, my trunk had become a storage unit, with my spare tire buried underneath my winter clothes. I called my dad, panicked, and asked him what to do. "It's not rocket science. You have to take all the shit out of your trunk and put it on the road, so you can get the spare tire out," he said, sternly. "And let this be a lesson to not be such a pack rat." I was crying and offended, but I followed his instructions. "Okay," I said, eventually. "What do I do next?" "Get off the goddamn phone with me," my dad said, "and google a how-to video or article. Something with pictures." The sky opened up with a loud crack. "Oh god," I said, howling. "It's pouring." "Fantastic," my dad said. "You won't be hot."

It never seemed to matter how bad I had it, because, at some point in time, my dad had had it much worse. This was true but still felt minimizing. "Trust me," he'd said throughout my life. "I'm a better dad to you than my dad was to me."

Remembering this, I asked my dad why he hadn't been gentler to me the day of my blown tire.

"You were so stressed out," he said. "It was stressing me out."

"It was stressful," I said.

"You think changing a flat in a little bit of summer rain while you've got YouTube doing all the thinking for you is stressful?" he asked. "I'll tell you what's stressful. Back when I was a knucklehead kid, I was driving home, drunk as a skunk, and I got a flat. I had to pull over, but it just so happened to be right near a DUI checkpoint. A cop came up to me shining his flashlight in my eyes, asking why I was trying to avoid the checkpoint. 'I'm not avoiding nothing,' I told him. 'My tire blew!' Then I had to pretend to be sober while changing my tire in front of a policeman. Now that's stressful."

"Speaking of DUIs," I said, "for one of my classes, I had to research my family history, and I found an article about your dad.[2] It was about him trying to get his license back after being arrested for a DUI."

"Sounds about right," my dad said. "When I was a kid, my dad used to ask me if I wanted to spend the day with him, then he'd drive to the bar, go inside drinking all day, while I sat in the car waiting for him, then make me, a kid, drive his drunk ass home."

It was always worse for him. I didn't bother arguing.

---

2 Gurule v. State, Dept. of Rev., Motor Veh. Division. Justia Law, n.d.

On hour three of the drive, my dad and I came up against long swaths of silence. "So," he said, not deeply interested, just bored, "what's the deal with your grandpa professor?"

I shrugged. "I'm planning my escape from both of these men." I'd already been pulling away from Wes in micro-amounts. Answering the phone less, being less available, etc. He had taken note. "This always happens when I become friends with younger women," Wes told me just a week earlier at a bar. It was 2:00 p.m. and we were buzzing. "At first you girls all praise my 'wisdom,' because what you really want with me is a daddy, but, eventually, you all get sick of it. You stop wanting my honest advice and guidance—which is what a father figure should offer—because you actually want to be reckless. I can respect that," Wes said, tapping a finger on my wrist. The bone sharper than normal because I had been distressed by my whole life for two years at that point. "But it's hard to watch *you*, someone who has been offered such a dream deal, throw it away. And for what? Because you don't want people to know your little secret? Get the fuck over it."

It was true that I had wanted Wes's advice in the beginning. More than that, I'd wanted to be *seen* and then reassured that exposing someone to my life as a sex worker wouldn't always cost me closeness. But my relationship with Wes was just another stupid thing I had tolerated and entertained for too long. How could I ever explain myself? My arrangement had clear motives, but with Wes the only thing I'd wanted was to be cured of my loneliness. And while that might sufficiently explain the start, how would I ever defend why I didn't push him out of my life sooner? Why I was at a bar with him that very moment getting chastised? Never sticking up for myself. The answer does not get more interesting with time. Wes was my confidant. Wes believed in me as a writer. Wes and I talked almost every single day. The dynamic was messy, and he gave me bad advice around John, but I was a liar and what more did I deserve? Aside from my family, Wes was a crucial figure in my life in this era. He was who I had.

Now, in the car with my dad, I could see a way out from all of it. Graduate school felt like a portal that would transport me to a new life. I had done what I could. I'd edited my stories. I had submitted my applications. But Wes held the very last requirement. I still needed him—with his academic credibility and substantial support of my creative abilities—to submit his letter of recommendation.

"Well, when that's all said and done," my dad said, "I'll be glad to watch you drop his ass like a hot potato."

An hour later my Grandma Corina opened the front door of her new apartment. "Estás muy gorda, Mom," my dad said, beating her to the punch line, as he pushed the door open with his shoulder. His hands were full of our luggage, while I carried our sleeping bags. "Are you just sitting around eating all day, or what?"

Stepping aside, my grandma started to laugh. "Ee, no se. I'm never hungry," but her mouth was full of an ice cream sandwich. My grandma *was* chubby, but not *too* chubby. Her lips and nails were painted complementary reds. I had never once seen my grandma without lipstick. Nor without two-inch heels. I once told my dad that it was hard to picture my abuela picking potatoes with the rest of my dad's family. "Why?" he scoffed. "You think Corina couldn't slip off the heels and wear some tennis shoes to work? When you need money to eat, you're not worrying about your goddamn hair."

In the living room, all the furniture from the ranch had been packed up and unloaded in a condensed fashion. Two chairs, with wooden armrests that my cousins and I had carved our initials into, sat on either side of a sunken sofa. My dad chucked everything onto the living room floor, where we'd be sleeping.

"Well, Corina," he said, "aren't you gonna give us a tour?"

She shrugged. "Si, quieren."

My grandma's low-income apartment was five hundred square feet. A fraction of the size of her old ranch house, but it had the essentials: a living room, bathroom, kitchenette, and a perfectly square bedroom, which was almost the exact size of her queen bed.

"This is awesome for you," my dad said when he saw it. "Now you can't be hanging out in the bedroom all day getting depressed. You come in here only to sleep."

★

Back in my grandma's kitchen, my dad and I poked our heads inside her freezer, where we found nothing aside from stacked boxes of ice cream sandwiches. The fridge, on the other hand, was crammed with canned sodas, green chile, beans, eggs, a brick of cheese, and a cling film-wrapped plate of leftovers. My grandma offered us Cokes before we took seats in her living room. The TV was switched on to Telemundo.

"Bruno was here yesterday," Corina said. "He has a gringa girlfriend and he told me she has big titties." My grandma mimicked large breasts with her carpal tunneled hands. Bruno was my cousin. "He didn't know how to say 'boobs' in Spanish and I told him 'titties.'"

I whispered over to my dad, "Is that correct Spanish?" He shook his head no.

"Big titties, huh?" he said. "She sounds awesome."

"Do you remember his old novia?" Corina asked. "She was short and had big tits tambien. She dances at a club now."

"Which club?" my dad asked.

It was quiet long enough that we all started watching TV. My grandma stared at the living room floor in deep thought. I assumed she was trying to recall the name of the strip club.

"I'm ready to die," she said. "I don't care if it happens tonight or tomorrow."

"Oh Dios mío," my dad said. "Are you bored here or what?"

"I don't like it aquí."

"You don't like running water? And a heater? And being able to use the toilet inside the house?" This was a swing at the home my grandma had to leave. Their single-story ranch house had been built in the late 1960s on my family's land by the hands of my late abuelo himself. "My dad found these two white boys at the bar," my dad had told me once. "They told him they were carpenters, but they were just traveling drunks." My dad swore that my grandpa and the two men built the whole house with a beer in one hand and a hammer in the other. "That house only stood up for fifty-odd years," my dad had said. "Carpenters my ass." Admittedly, there was a slight tilt throughout the whole house, like the place itself was drunk. She would've stayed there forever if she had any say in it, but the roof caved in, a family of raccoons settled underneath the flooring, and there was no point in repairing the place, she simply couldn't take care of herself alone on the ranch anymore.

"I don't *want* to die," my grandma said. "Pero, when it happens, I'm ready."

My dad looked over at me and gave a "what the hell" eyebrow raise. We hadn't discussed a good moment to bring it up, but now my dad said, "Well, Corina, since we're on the subject of you dying, can I get a life insurance policy on you?" Adding, "I'll pay for everything."

Earlier that morning when I spoke to Wes, I had no idea what was in store for me. Now my dad and I were about to set ourselves up for good lives. We didn't have much information to provide Corina. Hadn't had much time to look into it, but we would once we got home to the computer. My dad didn't have a smartphone and I was all out of data. Just calls and texts for another week. But she, just like my dad, didn't even hesitate.

"Sure," she said. Her face as bored as it was a moment prior. She grabbed the remote to check the television directory; *Señora Acero* was up next. "As long as you're paying, what do I care?"

"Exactly, Corina," my dad said. "If you're not paying a cent, you got no reason to care."

We shared a triumphant smile.

I didn't want to appear too pleased in front of my grandma, but I could've cried right then. My whole life was going to change. I was never going to see John again. Oddly enough, the idea of this hurt, like a bee sting to the heart. I knew this was merely a trick of the mind, but as I reminisced on all that had happened between that first night I met John and this very moment, I could only recall the good. The easy conversation, the laughs, that joyous feeling of climbing out of a financial hole. I wanted to fly to DC once more, to take John's face into my palms and say, *Thank you. You have changed my life.*

My dad and I spent the rest of the night giggly like we were stoned. Camped out in the living room, we ate ice cream sandwiches and watched episode after episode of *Ancient Aliens* on my grandma's outdated satellite channels. Every now and again my dad would share a musing: *Do you think Antarctica is just a big frozen UFO? My belly hurts, I hope that ice cream wasn't expired. I think aliens have been on Earth longer than we have. Are we bad people for doing this life insurance thing?* Once, during a commercial break I, too, spoke and asked my dad more about his relationship with his father. "I don't think he liked me very much," my dad said. "You know, he never once said he loved me." I didn't say it out loud, but I felt my grandfather's resistance to my dad was like a slingshot; I received the release of all the love he'd held back from his son. At some point I started to doze off. Lulled by the blue light of the television. "Are you sleeping?" my dad asked, pulling me back into the night. "I think so," I said. "Okay," he said. "I'll stop talking. I love you. Goodnight."

★

Before heading home that Sunday, my dad and I grabbed a shovel and made a pit stop at my abuelo's grave in San Luis. The graveyard had no official caretakers, so it was often left to collect tumbleweeds inside its black iron gate. The cemetery was not beautiful. It was dirt and headstones. But it was free for locals to be buried there. Families were responsible for digging the hole and burying the casket, which I had blurry memories of my father and his brothers doing in 1997, when my grandfather died.

I had been five years old at the time, and the single other memory of the funeral I could conjure was at my abuelo's wake. The smell of embalming fluid, two faceless little boys standing at his casket beside me. "How'd you know him?" I asked the boys. "A family friend. What about you?" they said. "He was my grandpa." I wanted to claim him, this man that I had only met in my infant years, where the memories had all since evaporated. We had the same blood, connected through my father. The possibility of my ever being able to know him had vanished, taken by a semitruck on the side of an Alamosa highway. My grandpa had been drunk. Walking in the middle of the road. But that was not important. He was mine.

In the cemetery, the tombstones were obscured beneath the weeds. I followed along in my dad's footsteps as he cleared a path with the shovel. Burrs buried themselves into our shoelaces. Little balls of sharp edges, which felt even more ominous as the lightness that had trailed after my dad and I all weekend had disappeared. I watched my dad wedge the shovel into the dusty earth, pull weeds from their roots, sweep tumbleweeds away from my grandpa's headstone. I watched him pack the earth six feet above his own dad's casket, a feeble attempt to make it look nice.

Sometimes it felt like a true miracle that my dad had been raised in this tiny Catholic town, by parents who had never once admitted to loving him, and yet, without reservation, he had accepted my queerness, my sex work, and my vision for my own life. Perhaps there were unconventional parent-child dynamics in my home. Perhaps I could even be disappointed by those. But my parents saw me as my own person with my own free will and never judged me for anything I did. I was grateful for that.

"What a sad life," my dad said. He wasn't speaking to me. "For nobody to care enough to just keep it tidy. No flowers. Nada." I watched his face as he worked. The sunlight shone harsh behind him, making me squint. When my eyes adjusted, I saw that he was crying.

My father kneeled and said, "I love you, Dad." He cried harder after, enough so that my being there felt intrusive. I wondered if I'd just witnessed my father's first time saying he loved my abuelo. Maybe not. Maybe my dad had said it to him as a child, maybe he'd written it in a letter, maybe whispered it on the phone, maybe my dad had stood in front of my grandpa and proclaimed it to his face. All I knew was that it was too late for my dad to ever hear it back. I wanted the earth to open up. I wanted my grandpa to rise from his grave. I wanted him to look his son in the eye and love him the way I did.

I wiped at my own eyes and looked up toward the sky. The winter sun hung low, and the rays of light triggered little kaleidoscopes of colors to dance in my peripheral vision. "I'm having another one," I said.

"I think those so-called migraines might be alien activity," my dad said, not a lick of sarcasm in his voice. He kept packing the dirt. "Not everyone communicates with words, you know."

Back at my dad's house, we sat down at his kitchen table and googled health insurance policies on his "new" laptop—the used MacBook that John had given me at the start of our arrangement for my writing dreams. I'd handed down the computer to my dad with the same clauses—it's old, but it's still good enough for Safari—because John had bought me a newer laptop, a 2017 MacBook Pro. It was, as John had put it, "good luck for the MFAs, and a little taste of what life would be like as my wife." Life would be nice, I concluded. It would be resistant to viruses. Life would be high-speed.

We'd put no real thought into our plan aside from how we'd spend the money. We were high for two days off the dream, too excited by our future lives to stop and consider requirements beyond a willing candidate and payment. There were rules.

"Uh-oh," my dad said. His face theatrically shocked. He spun the computer screen toward me. I speed-read a list of qualifications. My grandmother, at eighty-two years old, was no longer eligible for a life insurance policy.

"Shit," I said. "We're too late."

It was like waking up from a dream. One second you're a millionaire blueprinting a ranch house and the next, *poof!*—you're back on your mom's couch. I closed the laptop and moved my attention to my dad, then beyond my dad, and then beyond that very moment, toward the future, which I believed more than ever before was predetermined and already on its way.

There would be an end to this lifetime as a sugar baby.

I needed to hold myself accountable with a plan, so when the moment arrived, I would leap and leave it all behind. Unwed. Alone. Broke. Free. Summer, I decided. July. The moment before I transitioned to graduate school or something new and completely blank. I signed my name in my emotional will. Prayed for some higher power to notarize it. The arrangement was now a countdown.

My dad and I shared a look.

I saw on his face that his own could-have-been lifetime had flashed before him, that he, too, was jarred by the bleak return to reality. We had only spent two days in the fantasy of wealth. That was enough to know we wanted more out of our lives. We'd both been wishing for it.

"Well, I'll be damned," my dad said, with a sigh. He put his hand on my shoulder in shared defeat. "There go my mini goats."

12

Shadow Self

A few months later, I tucked myself away in John's spare room, where a twin bed had replaced the air mattress, and returned to work on my latest essay. A comedy-drama about my and my father's failed life insurance swindle. This would be my first workshop submission, because I had, as of two weeks ago, received an offer from an MFA program at the University of New Mexico. It was February 2018, and the question of where life would lead me once I parted ways with John had finally been answered. I could hardly believe it to be true.

I'd been working in a coffee shop when I opened the email from the university's admissions department. The note was short and simple and to the point: *Dear Michelle Gurule, We are pleased to admit you to our MFA program. Please see the attached offer letter.* The PDF was crisp and professional. I read the words *full tuition remission, teaching assistantship, health insurance,* and felt ruddy with relief.

Still, it wasn't all glitz. The offer stated a $14,000 yearly stipend. An amount that would knock me back into the salary range of my life pre-John. It felt startling, like waking yourself up by chewing on your tongue. *At least I'll have my sugar savings to fall back on*, I told myself, knowing that if I hadn't, I would've needed private loans or a second job to join the program. Education, I continued to experience firsthand, was so much easier with resources.

I could hear John snoring across the hall when a notification appeared in the corner of my laptop screen. iMessage from Wes Elliot. *Hey*, he wrote. *Can you talk?*

Yeah, I typed. *Give me 5.*

For utmost privacy, I descended two flights of stairs into John's den. A room so unused it still smelled new.

"So," Wes said, anxious upon answering. "What's the deal?"

Wes was referring to his latest scheme, which I'd christened "Quit Sugaring with Severance Pay." Hashed out three days earlier. I had been at home, on my mom's couch, scrolling the internet aimlessly on my new laptop. I was logged into my sister's Facebook, which she sometimes let me do since I didn't have an account anymore. I'd looked up a handful of people—my ex, my cousin, then my cousin's girlfriend who had been posting publicly about a dispute they'd been in—and then bored by my sister's feed, I had an abrupt urge to type John's son's name, "Luke Linghu," into the search bar. I'd never looked into John's family on the socials. I tried not to think of him much when we were apart, and I was never deeply curious about John. I felt he was a safe guy, that's all that had ever mattered to me.

Luke's profile photo was a picture of him in California. Standing on a boardwalk, arms open. Kind of cheesy. I clicked through a few photos and landed on a family shot. Taken during John's recent Christmas trip to Vermont. The Linghus were huddled before an ice castle, with John kneeling in the center, and his two sons at his side. And there, to John's left, with a gloved hand on his shoulder, was Patricia.

I jolted up, startled and confused. John had sent me a staggering number of text messages from Vermont, showing me places he'd been with his kids. *Potentially romantic*, he'd hinted, *depending on the company.* Not once had he mentioned his "ex-wife."

I zoomed in on her face. This was the first time I'd ever seen Patricia. She looked expensive. With beautiful sleek hair, a bright wardrobe, and designer glasses. She styled herself like an art dealer.

It could be a friendly nonnuclear family situation, I thought, recalling the countless things John had said about them getting along well. I clicked on Patricia's, or "Pat's," tagged profile. It was very private, but she did have herself listed as married and was still going by John's last name. This wasn't necessarily proof positive either. My mom still used her married name. I inspected Pat's five public photos and gained that she was a ski bunny, ran a book club, and last summer she posted an old picture of her and John slicing into a red velvet cake in honor of their wedding anniversary.

My blood felt like water. John *was* married? What the actual fuck?

When I first suspected that John had been married near the start of our arrangement, I felt terrified of losing the cash, but I hadn't felt hurt. This time, I was surprised by how deep the news cut. I felt betrayed. I wasn't in love with him, but I had known John for years. I had slept in his house. He'd started calling a room upstairs *my* room. I knew John's birthmarks and eating patterns and he'd told me about his family and his fraught relationship with his dad. Once, after we did a self-help questionnaire that asked some basic questions—Who am I? How do I want to be perceived? Who knows me best?—John admitted that, while he knew it was sad, his answer was me. *I* knew him more than anyone else.

Beyond that, John had been proposing to me on repeat. Making extravagant false promises, claiming he'd take care of me and my family. I'd spent the last few months mired by guilt for not taking John up on his offer, both for my family's sake and John's—knowing how much he wanted a wife. Silly me. He couldn't even marry me if I'd wanted to.

Although I'd also withheld aspects of my life from John, I still found it difficult to admit that he and I were not real people to one another—more like *mirages*. The world we had built together was exactly the same.

Let the eyes settle, and, well, there's nothing good to see. I closed my computer, unfairly injured, and cried.

I'd called Wes to share the news. Our dynamic had only hardened over the winter. Wes disapproved of my snubbing John's marriage proposals. He believed I was throwing away a winning lotto ticket for a stupid cause—my "morality or fear of societal judgments, whichever, whatever," as he had put it. And he had been stiff when I told him my MFA news, saying, "I hope you can keep up with the others." With more and more distance, it was becoming clear that our power dynamic—as insignificant as Wes insisted it was—had put me in a compromised position. While all my other recommenders had written their letters to the University of New Mexico and wished me well, Wes made me feel as though, in the face of the immeasurable kindness of introducing me to the idea of an MFA, I had wronged him by not marrying John. Information about grad schools was not coveted. If anything, helping students apply to grad schools was a part of Wes's university job. And it wasn't as though Wes had written the stories that earned my MFA acceptance. He'd penned a single-page letter in support, which he'd asked me to edit. I was completely exhausted by Wes at this point, yet sharing my John-woes with him had become my knee-jerk reaction. I needed an outlet, but I would've been better off just speaking aloud to myself.

"To be clear," Wes said, "John doesn't know that you know he's married?"

"No," I said. "But I'll tell John I know about Patricia when I quit. That way he'll know that I figured out all his promises were empty, and he can't try to convince me to stay by offering my family anything." I took a small pause. I felt angry. "I've been gearing myself up for the end of sugaring for months, and now I feel so disgusted by his make-believe grandiose offerings, I'm considering washing my hands clean of this while I've got the guts. But maybe I'm being rash. Maybe I should grin and bear it until my summer deadline and make as much money as I can."

"Hold on. Would you really just quit without even trying to get severance pay?" Wes had been persuasive. More than any time before. I just said it myself: two-timing-John had been asking me to marry him for close to a year. Putting intense pressure on me—dragging my mom and kid nephew into it for absolutely nothing. John had been trying to manipulate me with my family's poverty so why not reverse the manipulation? "Let's see what John will do," Wes said, amidst a totally silent backdrop, "if you say yes to his proposal."

"No way," I said. "What if I get locked into an engagement?"

"Wishful thinking," Wes said. "But fine. If that's too scary, then just tell John you're *thinking about it*. Get a record of all the big promises he makes, and after a few months of John thinking you're really considering marrying him—in July, when you already plan to leave—you can say, 'I found out about Patricia, and now the life that I was counting on—that my mother and nephew were counting on—has evaporated. What are we supposed to do?' He'll feel so guilty about misleading you that he'll likely offer you a cash apology." Wes paused for a beat. "I bet you could get $100,000."

"Yeah, right," I said. "You're out of your mind if you really think John would offer me that."

"Here's the thing," Wes said. "For you and me, people who grew up poor, a hundred thousand bucks sounds like a lot of money, right?"

"It is a lot of money." I thought of my MFA $14,000 stipend. "Someone could live off $100K for literal years."

"Exactly. Years, plural! But to John, it's only a fraction of his salary. He made at least five times that last year alone." Wes sounded very casual. "And you told me yourself that John also rakes in cash from rental properties and the stock market. He has millions, honey. He won't be hurt financially by a measly $100K. But it could make all the difference to you, and your mama, and your little nephew, if you were generous with them. *And to me.*"

I knew that was coming.

"To you?" I asked, rolling my eyes to the back of my head.

"Yes," Wes said, not missing a beat. "You'll give me 20 percent for walking you through it. $20,000."

It sounded like a classic Wes Elliot scheme, self-interested and completely far-fetched. As if John would ever pay me $100,000 over the guilt of lying. I told Wes as much.

"Don't be so negative," Wes said. "No sense in not even trying. You're flying to DC in a few days. While you're out there, you might as well test the ice. All low stakes. Be extremely nice to John. Let him talk about your future together. Ask him how'd he actually help your family. Get concrete answers. Make sure John hears himself promising that you and your family depend on him."

I laughed, not meanly, into the receiver. Unsure of what to make of it all.

"Michelle, this could really make a difference to the lot of us. I'd be smart with the money, just like you," Wes said. The line was cast just for me. Wes knew what I hoped my family would do with any imagined extra cash. "I'd put it all toward my debt. This money could change my life. Just like it's changed yours."

★

"Well, tell me what happened," Wes said to me now as I sat on the carpet in John's basement. My reflection in the glass doors looked like a ghost.

I wasn't dead set on the scheme, as the outcome seemed unlikely, but the more I'd marinated on a $14,000 yearly income, the better a $100,000 apology sounded. It wasn't enough to take care of everyone in the ways I'd dreamed via the life insurance policy, but it could potentially serve as a Gurule-family safety net for a good long while. So, I had, admittedly, spent the weekend doing what Wes had instructed.

"I tried to get John to agree on specific things he'd do if I married him," I said. "But all his promises fell through." I told Wes that earlier that evening, John and I sat in his kitchen, eating bowls of strawberry ice cream to celebrate my MFA news. To my surprise, John had been extremely supportive of this new venture, saying, "The flights to DC can't be much longer from Albuquerque." Seeing a good opportunity to test one of John's promises—the lowest stake one in my opinion—I asked when my "author's office" would take shape. "It'd be great for me to focus on my writing before the program starts." Playing coy to his earlier wager, John explained that this office was not part of our arrangement, but rather "the marriage deal." A good lead into my next question, this time the highest stakes. "You know, I've been thinking more about it. If I marry you, will you really fund my mom's retirement?"

John's eyes burst open like umbrellas. "Did I say fund her whole retirement?" He chuckled. "I guess I got ahead of myself. Well, I wouldn't want to pay for her entire livelihood, but I'd be happy to help out." John paused to think of what exactly that meant. "Let's see, to offset her rent, your mom and nephew could live here with me." He put his spoon down and grabbed my hand. "With *us*."

"But *you* live in DC," I said. "You would expect them to move here?"

"Well," John said, smugly, "for free rent, I think asking them to move is a pretty good deal." He smiled. "Oh, and I almost forgot—your sister too."

While this sounded like spur-of-the-moment bologna, even if John was being genuine, my mom couldn't just pack up and leave Colorado, nor could my sister and nephew. But if John was already married then even this lesser bargain was total bullshit. I didn't understand his motive. Why ask me to marry him at all? Why make the deal so irresistible? Why be so persistent about it? I looked at John, who had traces of pink ice cream around his smile, and deduced there was only one plausible answer: This marriage deal, which John must've intuited I would've never agreed to, was just another part of the mirage.

I couldn't help but laugh at my naivety. Here I was thinking that I was about to ruin my family's one shot at financial stability and leave John feeling terminally lonely, and none of it was even real! I knew from the moment John spoke the idea into existence that I would never marry him, but up until this moment, I had been burdened by the guilt of that decision. I'd exhausted six pounds of my own flesh wondering how selfish I must be to pick my own freedom over the well-being of my family. And beyond that, I felt like a cruel little girl for continuing to accept John's monthly cash, while denying what I truly believed was his desire to be loved and married. What a heap of unnecessary stress.

"The scumbag," Wes said when I explained this. "I think we'll have to resort to direct blackmail." He was too quick with this rebuttal. Too pumped. I realized that this must've been his plan all along. "It'll be pretty straightforward. We'll collect all the photos you and John have taken over the years, plane tickets out to DC, bank statements showing the money he's paid you, and then put them in an envelope. You'll wave it in front of John's face, saying, 'Here's proof that you've been having a paid-for affair with a sex worker. Give me the $100,000 or I tell your wife.'"

"Whoa. I can't do that," I told Wes. "That's a horrible thing to do."

"Michelle," Wes said, upset, "remember what we talked about? $100,000 is a huge amount of money to you, but put it into context. How would you feel if someone asked you for $1,000 in exchange for not sharing your sex worker secret? It's not nothing, but would that ruin your life?"

"No," we both said over one another.

"Exactly." Wes went on, saying that his debt was like a noose around his neck. "And I've done a lot to help you this last year. I mean, you wouldn't even know what an MFA is if it weren't for me. It's a big deal. I changed your life. You're going to get to live your dream."

There was validity to his claim. I don't know if I would've ever taken my writing seriously without having met Wes. I came close once. When

I was twenty-one years old, I bought a one-way ticket to New York City because I wanted to join the writing scene. I thought *there* I could make it happen. A week before I was set to leave, Hurricane Sandy hit, and I took it as a sign: *Not now, stay.* For the next several years I wrote inside of an echo chamber. I had my cute little dream but knew real life was off the page. And then I met Wes. He believed in me, told me I was talented, and I worked one hundred times harder with the fuel of having one single person in my corner. I felt so grateful that I would've done almost anything to show my appreciation. But I could not bear the idea that instead of feeling happy for me, Wes felt that I owed him this grandiose final act.

"Blackmail is illegal," I said, trying to hide the hurt in my voice, hoping to scare Wes out of this idea. "*We* could go to jail!"

"Unlikely," Wes said. "As long as we're not sloppy about it, and you do everything in person without an electronic trace, then worst case scenario would be a he-said-she-said court case."

"I'm a sex worker," I told Wes. "I can't see a he-said-she-said court case leaning in my favor."

"Oh, it's nothing to *actually* worry about," Wes said. "John is too concerned with his image and family to let it get that far." Wes reminded me of a story I'd once told him. John and I had watched a movie in which a man kills himself before it was publicly announced that he'd stolen money from his church. Curious, I'd asked John, "What would be worse for you if you were caught up in scandal: your whole family finding out and your reputation destroyed or dying?" "My whole family knowing I was involved in a scandal," John said. "Definitely!"

"Listen," Wes said. "You don't have to make any decisions right now, but you're in DC for the rest of the weekend, so you might as well get some proof of your arrangement. Photos with John, etc. And find Patricia's phone number and email. It will be easy, trust me. I bet John has these things just lying around. You've just never looked."

★

The next day, John and I had breakfast at his kitchen island. Fresh fruit and oatmeal. I wished I could forget about Wes's horrible blackmail idea, but I couldn't think of anything else. "Is your family sad about you moving to New Mexico for school?" John asked.

I nodded and told him that the night before I flew to DC, I had been jolted awake at 3:00 a.m. by my nephew rustling for a snack. I joined him in the kitchen and watched as he dipped his hand into a box of cereal and stuffed miniature marshmallows into his mouth.

"I love them crunchy," he said, then offered me a palmful.

Chuy's youth suddenly felt precious. It must have always been precious, but I had overlooked how fleeting it is to have a child around. Once I left for Albuquerque, I would notice every microscopic change that happened to Chuy in my absence. The inches he'd grow. The peach fuzz that would coarsen his calves. He was my kid nephew, whom I'd never lived apart from. It was hard to imagine that he'd be a teenager when I returned. "I'll miss you when I move," I said.

"Me too." Chuy dropped the cereal box, wrapped his arms around my waist, and started bawling. It was a sleep-deprived, sugar-high, manic cry. He banged his forehead softly into my hip. "I'll miss you so much, Auntie."

John laughed, then wrapped his arms around me and feigned a cry, "I'll miss you too."

I playfully pushed him away and said, "Well, the flight time from Albuquerque to DC is basically the same as from Denver, right?" John seemed reassured by this, but I knew our time together would end after the summer.

Whenever I envisioned my life after sugaring, I felt in my heart that I would miss John. We had developed a relationship. I wasn't delusional.

There were things John and I had kept hidden from each other (more than I had even initially realized), but we had also shared parts of ourselves—our deepest desires and secrets, our ugly faces behind the polished masks—that we had never revealed to anyone else.

Even before meeting John my life existed in two separate worlds. In one, I was a student working at Whole Foods, and in the other, I was a desperate stripper longing for financial stability. John, too, lived a double life. He played a happy husband and father, but he was a man who'd been plagued by profound loneliness for years. John and I yearned for relief. I had pleaded to the Universe for some tide to turn and change my life. When John arrived at Penthouse, it was an actual answer to that prayer. We both held keys to the other's desires. We shook hands, called it an arrangement, and built a fantasy behind closed doors. We were both guilty of lying to those around us to keep this secret hidden, and we both lied to one another to keep fulfilling our desire.

This arrangement was never founded on honesty. I could forgive John for being married. I hoped he could forgive for me for all as well.

★

Later that night, after John had gone to sleep, I lay on his couch and watched *Forensic Files*. It was a grisly plot: A couple was shopping at Home Depot looking for a man with a husky build, intending to slay him and later stage his corpse to appear as though "the husband" had been killed (and unidentifiably disfigured) during a routine oil change. All in an attempt for the couple to cash in on a million-dollar life insurance policy.

TruTV often repeated episodes in quick succession and I'd seen this one a few weeks ago, soon after I'd found out John was still married.

"Only an arrogant person would think they could pull off murder," I had said to my mom, who lay beside me in the twin beds, nibbling on a cold Pop-Tart.

"Yep," she'd said. "I mean, with all these DNA tests, and cell phone pings, and surveillance cameras everywhere, I wouldn't so much as steal a loaf of bread."

Bianca barged into the room to announce that she was heading off to work. A few days prior, Bianca had slid on a patch of black ice and popped a tire on the curb. "I spent all my money on my new tires," she said to the room, to us, to me. "And now I don't have any money for gas."

I pointed toward the closet. "Take some cash from my safe."

"Thank you," she said, flashing forty dollars in her hand. "So, I can get some Subway too?" Then came in close for a hug. I patted her butt and rested my hand on the cheek.

"While you're both here," I said, "I have something to share." I took a dramatic breath. "I think I'm going to quit seeing John sooner than expected."

She and my mother gasped in unison. "But why?" my mom asked. My sister finished her thought, "Why would you walk away from the money?"

I couldn't get into the murky feelings of it all. I used the easiest excuse. "I found out John is married."

The blood sugar of the room plummeted. Thankfully, my mom kept candy on the headboard for moments like this. She reached into a share-size Wonka Mix-Ups bag, grabbed three pieces of taffy, and handed one to me and my sister. We took turns reading the wrapper jokes.

"What kind of tea is sometimes hard to swallow?" Bianca read.

My mom's guesses were fast and loose. *Iced tea. Hot tea. Unsweetened tea.* We all three laughed.

"Reali-*tea*," my sister said, chuffed. "Wow. Very fitting."

My mom nodded. "I sure will miss the money."

"We all will," I said.

In DC, *Forensic Files* went on. This Home Depot killer couple, like all killers on this show, made obvious errors. Email and text messages, even from a burner phone, were often the dead giveaway. This reminded me of Wes's advice. "The blackmail has to be done in person," he'd said. "Without an electronic trace." Wes was a loose cannon, but he was clever.

Earlier in the day, without certainty of what I'd do with any of the information I gathered, I followed Wes's instructions while John showered and collected evidence I could potentially wager against him. I took photos of myself in his bedroom, sitting at his desk, and in front of his house, with the number plate in clear view. Then I rolled up my sleeves and began hunting for Patricia's contact information. Quite challenging at first. Where did one keep contact information other than their phone and Rolodex (which John did not have)? I sorted through papers on his desk but saw only Con Ed bills in his name and unintelligible IT notes. Eventually, I wandered into the kitchen, opened a junk drawer, and in a little bowl full of thumbtacks and rubber bands was John's silver wedding band, 7-17-90 engraved along the inside. Twenty-seven years together. At least two of those filled with deceit. I pictured Patricia alone in Colorado, going to films, eating half sandwiches in cafés, and walking museums with audio tour guides all while John had been dragging me to the Lincoln Memorial and paying for sex. I was abruptly nauseous. Still, I could not let the guilt deter me. I had done wrong for two years. There was no undoing it now. I fumbled around deeper in the drawer and, like a heaven-sent sign that this was the right thing to do, came across a Walgreens photo envelope. *Patricia Linghu* printed on the sticker. Her Colorado address and phone number just below.

It was really *that easy*. Just like Wes had said it would be.

I ran into the bathroom and spat bile into the sink.

★

When the episode credits rolled, I called my dad. I needed to tell someone that I was considering blackmailing John. Not considering it too seriously, but with all of Wes's persuasion and, admittedly, solid tips, I wasn't totally against it either.

"Oh . . . my . . . god . . . Shell," my dad wheezed into his headset. He had just taken a sip of liquid and was now choking on it. My timing could've been better, but I hadn't expected a negative reaction. Given our co-conspiring around the life insurance policies, I was sort of prepared for my dad to ask if we could blackmail John as a father-daughter duo.

"Are you trying to get yourself locked up in federal prison?" he asked. My face flushed. "No!"

"You cannot blackmail John," my dad said, as serious as I'd ever heard him. "You're being money-hungry and silly now."

"You think?" I asked. I felt suddenly hot with shame.

"I do," my dad said. "You're either going to get yourself killed, or you're going to go to prison. Don't you have enough?"

I shrugged. "Does anyone ever feel like they have enough money?"

"I worried this would happen." He sighed. "Answer me this, did you fix your teeth?"

"Yeah."

"Pay off your debt?"

"Yes."

"Buy a fancy new car?"

"It's not fancy," I said, thinking of the cheap plastic dashboard. "It's a Ford Fiesta Hatchback."

"That car has zero issues," my dad snapped. "Not even a cracked windshield. It's *fancy*."

"Fine, it's fancy."

"And you're going off to yet another college, so what else could you possibly need that you'd risk prison for?"

"Sure, *I'm* in a better place," I told my dad. "But what about everyone else? There will come a day when Chuy needs help for college or mom will need money for something. She has all those health issues. It's so expensive to be alive."

"It's hard for most people to pay the bills," my dad said. "Should we all go out and find someone to con? It's not nice, Michelle. And it's not *you*. I get it. John lied. But that doesn't mean you have to go as low as him."

We let the silence hang between us for a long while.

"What I can't figure out," my dad said, "is why you've always been more worried about everyone else's lives, your mom's especially, than even they are. What's that about?"

Tears threatened to spill over, as I dove headfirst into that familiar wound of having ruined my mother's life. I told him that I just feel so bad that Mom left Virginia. I feel like she only stayed in Colorado after things went south between them for me and Bianca. Life in Colorado is so much more expensive. And, for her, it's lonelier.

"If your mom was so much happier in Virginia, then why isn't she there now?" my dad asked. "She could move back to Virginia tomorrow if she wanted but she doesn't. You and Bianca are adults.

"Yeah, because now she has Chuy," I said.

"Exactly! Now let me ask you this, do you think Chuy should have to take care of your mom's finances now? I mean, she's made the decision to stay in Colorado for him after all. Do you think if some sugar mama out there made a bunch of false promises to him about your mom being able to retire, and that was total bojive, that Chuy should risk federal prison just to make it up to her?"

It was a good question. It had never registered to me that my nephew and I played similar roles in my mom's life. I had always seen how much she sacrificed for him, and yet, it never felt as though he owed her anything.

"So, why do you feel it's your responsibility to take care of your mom?" my dad said. "And not just in a normal way. We all want what's best for her and Chuy. But would you really do something that you know is wrong just to make yourself feel better?"

At last, I could not hold back anymore. I began to cry.

My dad sounded stern. "Yep. That's what you need to think about. This blackmail is all about you. Not your mom. Not Chuy. Not playing Robin Hood. *You*."

"So, what am I supposed to do?" I was a glass of spilt milk.

"You give it a goddamn rest," my dad said. "You met your goals. Now, you take the money you saved, you do the best you can with it. You walk away."

★

There is a version of my life in which I shake Wes's hand and say, "Fuck it, let's do this." Where we con John, he coughs up $100,000, and in the process, he loses faith that anyone could care about him beyond his wealth. In this life, Patricia is none the wiser, and their life goes on exactly like it is. Money remains the cause and the cure to everything.

There is beauty in that life too. I could help my mom out. I could start a college fund for my nephew. Send my sister to school. Wes could pay down his debts. I could focus all my energy on writing.

That was not the version of my life I chose. In this one, I tiptoed down John's steps into the den. A room that would never hold a desk or my books or an embroidered motivational quote. I would eventually grieve it, along with all the other savory parts of the life John proposed. None of those promises had been precisely real, nor plausible for me even if they had been, but that was irrelevant, because I had peeked into a parallel universe, and I could not unsee that gorgeous flicker of a life in which everything would be better. Everything *best*.

Grief would come, but I had other things to do.

"Tell me something good," Wes said when he answered the phone, so softly that I wished I could.

My voice trembled over itself to get to the end of my sentence. "I don't think we should be in touch anymore." I listed a million reasons. All of them true, none of them candid enough. Our friendship was too complicated. He'd held too many roles that were all blurred and confused. Mostly I was not someone who would ever bend as far as he wanted. And so, the tension between us would never quite slacken. It was time that I did right by myself.

There was a pause on Wes's end when I finished. Sad to admit it, but I felt the smallest bit hopeful that he might reveal his true colors, and Wes would be made up of pastels. Baby pink and lavender. Hopeful that he might acknowledge his wrongdoings, apologize with sincerity, let this blackmail scheme go, and wish me well. *Farewell. Adieu.* We were friends, he might've said. And it's okay that now we are not.

"Can't you have your moral revelation after we get this thing over with with John?" Wes asked briskly, callous.

"I'm not going to blackmail him," I said, keeping my words precise. I wanted no room for negotiation. "I won't do it."

"Of course you won't," Wes spat. "Because you're a selfish person, Michelle. I was counting on that money, but you only ever think about yourself."

There would come a day, nearly two years later, when I would wake up to an email from Wes. The message subject would be "etc.," and I'd know before I opened it what it would say. Better yet, I knew what it would feel like to read. I'd paste the letter into a .doc to grasp the length. To see its girth. To read it like a piece of art—the way Wes clearly wanted it to be read. It would be captivating. Scathing. He'd spell out all the things that I did wrong. Note the ways I had betrayed him. How I'd held the power to make his life better and instead chose to leave him in ruin. How I had "never even looked back."

Wes had been kind to me in ways I least felt I deserved. He didn't flinch at my sex work. He never treated me like I was dirty or damaged. He believed I had talent, and he helped me believe it too. I had needed his support—more than I even initially realized. But over time, his support around my sugaring twisted into something more rigid, laced with demands. He expected me to behave differently—to see myself and sug-aring through his sociological lens, to let his "wisdom" shape the choices I made. Wes had conceived of a real way for me to line his pockets with John's money, but I refused to do what was needed to make it happen. And any remainder of Wes's kindness turned sour.

When I'd finish reading his email, a serene feeling would overcome me, like saving yourself from a wave by ducking under it. While Wes had aimed his words directly at my pinkest spots, his terrible accusations no longer rang true. I could see myself as clear as a bright, blue day. And in that same light, I could see Wes as he truly is and always was.

As I sat in John's house in early 2018, I didn't have enough distance for clarity, so I told Wes that I was sorry. I was truly sorry that I had hurt him. That I had done this to him.

"There will come a day when you'll regret this. Trust me. I've been alive a lot longer than you. You think you've got it all figured out. That the way to get through life is keeping your moral high ground, and I say 'your' because there's a lot of shit you do that the average person would call immoral." He was enunciating every word with cutting precision. "You think that that life will reward you for being 'good,' but that's not how it works."

I had been staring blankly at the wall, tears streaming down my face. I made sure to keep quiet so Wes wouldn't think he'd made ground, but I felt outright terrible. He told me that he had just one last thing to say. It would reverberate in my mind for weeks. I would wonder every now and again for years if he had been right.

"Life is hard," Wes said. "And life will always be hard. There will come a day when you or your mama or your nephew gets into some kind of money trouble, a broken-down car, an unexpected hospital bill, a root canal, and you'll look back on this golden opportunity—this *once in a lifetime* chance to give everyone a little bit of security—and you'll ask yourself, 'How could I have been so fucking stupid?'"

13

Isn't It Ironic?

"Who are you?" the woman sitting across from me asked. Her gray hair was neat and freshly cut. I let our bony knees touch. "I'm a liar," I said. Almost by accident. "I'm a terrible liar."

"Who are you?" she asked again.

I peered over to my right and saw Alanis Morissette standing fifteen feet away. Illuminated under stage lights in an auditorium that looked like a yoga studio. It was not a dream. No, this was real life.

It was March 2018, and I was in Northern California at a resort called 1440 Multiversity, where Alanis Morissette was leading a three-day self-help workshop. The cost of attendance was steep. Just over $3,000 for "tuition" and accommodation. John, generous enough to offer, footed the bill. Ironic, because I arrived withered and exhausted, praying that Alanis's wisdom would give me the courage to leave sugaring behind. "I remember the first day we met," John said when we were booking my spot. "You told me Alanis impacted the person you were." It was true. It was still true. And now she was providing me a chance to save myself.

I opened my mouth and said, "I'm only able to be here because I had sex with a man for money."

★

This confession had surprised even me. Just two hours earlier, I'd arrived at the resort prepared to keep up my facade. I was "in between things," I would tell people if they asked what I did for work. Wealthy people never pried—at least that's what I'd always heard. And wealth would've been the case for anyone at this workshop. Ringing in the end of my sugaring era, I had landed in the heart of luxury. The grounds were breathtaking in that effortless, affluent way—where the wilderness felt curated rather than wild. The trees and shrubs gleamed a rich emerald, each one pruned with surgical precision. Even the rocks seemed suspiciously perfect, as if nature had been airbrushed. The dormitory lodges, built to blend seamlessly with the towering redwoods, boasted black limestone stairwells and interiors modeled after million-dollar cabins. It was the kind of place I imagined Gwyneth Paltrow retreating to when she needed to realign her chakras.

I first tested the line on one of my dormmates, Annie. "I'm in between things," I said when she asked what I did. Then, before she could press further, I turned the conversation toward her.

Annie was a Pilates-toned blonde woman in her thirties. A fast talker from Martha's Vineyard who worked as a landscaper. "I'm a self-help fanatic," she said, "and an Alanis Morissette mega fan." Annie shook off a white fuzzy coat to show off a genuine *Jagged Little Pill* vintage concert tee that she'd bid for on eBay.

"Alanis Morissette impacted my life more than anyone else in the entire world," Annie said, looking dead into my eyes. She stopped to think for a moment, and added, "Well, positively at least. Alanis was a role model when I had no one but addicts."

I found this easy to believe. I wanted to tell Annie that, as crazy as it may sound, I was at this retreat thanks to going down on someone—just as Alanis had sung about doing in a movie theater in "You Oughta

Know." I never could've imagined at thirteen that sugaring was in my future, and that, to be frank, giving blow jobs would be so life altering. As I looked around the room, awed by the lavishness of the hidden storage and electric privacy curtains on each pod, I felt the aftershocks of sex work rippling around me. I thought back to the version of myself that had taken John's business card, and I imagined wrapping my arms around that girl to kiss her thank you. There was a life I had wanted all those years ago. In some miraculous feat, it had worked.

I didn't explain all of that to Annie. I didn't want to throw a wrench in our budding friendship by admitting a secret I still felt made me untrustworthy. Instead, I asked if she thought there was any chance of us getting one-on-one time with Alanis that weekend. If we ran into her on the campus, would it be okay to ask to grab coffee? Annie didn't think so, but when we looked over the itinerary, we saw there would be a group photo on the last day.

"When we start doing the exercises, I don't think we should do them together," Annie told me, suddenly very serious. "We have to resist making our self-work comfortable."

★

The partner I ended up with for this first exercise was in her sixties, with silver hair and silver jewelry. A reflection of the middle-aged, turquoise-adorned, white women all around us. It was not a surprising demographic. Everyone there would've needed disposable income and time. The people who had access to those two things were quite limited.

Misconceptions around my identity had always followed me like a shadow, but there in that room, I felt I could not bear another miscalculation. I needed it to be known that whatever financial cloak sex work had draped over me was false. I could not afford to be there. Not in that auditorium with its shined hardwood floors and spa water, nor at this resort, with its ornate landscape and luxury pods and infinity edge hot tub. This was not my life. As my dad would say, this was just a *lifetime*. A moment. And it was ending.

This must be why, at least in part, I confessed "I'm a sex worker" the next time my partner asked, "Who are you?" But, beyond that, it must've dawned on me that I'd stumbled on an opportunity to rid myself of my secrets in a place where no one knew me.

When Alanis introduced this exercise, she'd said the point was *unabashed reveal*. To put a spotlight on our shame. To make it seem smaller and insignificant. In the dark our secrets are monsters, but in the light, they're our truest selves, our humanity. As soon as I'd said the words outright—"I'm a sex worker"—I felt like I was revealing much more about who I really was, and I realized I wanted to be seen for that. For the struggle, the desperation, the lengths I had gone to.

"Who are you?"

"I am terrified of walking away from sex work."

"Who are you?"

"I am terrified of losing the money."

"Who are you?"

"I am someone who wants to live in the truth." It was against the rules of the exercise to expand, but what I meant was that sex work had left me terribly lonely. I didn't want to keep tallying white lies, avoiding friends, and dodging connection. Even my brief afternoon with Annie— laughing and sharing had shown me how much I missed genuine companionship. Still, I felt there was no world in which I could possibly come clean and be loved—in friendship or romance. I had spent years worrying about what people might think about the sex work itself, but even worse, I worried what they would think of all the lies I'd told to keep this secret part of my life hidden. *What kind of person does that make you?* I imagined people asking, while holding their arms up and backing away from me. *What kind of person has the stamina to lie for so long?*

"Who are you?"

I answered this time through my hands. "I'm worried that I'm a terrible person." I parted my fingers and watched for the woman's gaze to sharpen.

She only placed her hand on my leg and swiped her thumb back and forth, shaking her head as if to say, *no, no.*

"Who are you?"

"I am someone who didn't know what else to do," I said. "I am someone who still doesn't know what to do."

"Who are you?"

"I am hoping I can be okay without John," I said.

"Who are you?"

I paused for a moment, wondering what to say next. Really, there was only one thing I needed to share, and I needed to share it as many times as I'd had to hide it. "I am a sex worker. I am a sex worker. I am a sex worker." I practiced the feel of it in my mouth, like trying to eat an entire donut in one bite: sweet and soft, but potentially a choking hazard. "I am a sex worker. I am a sex worker."

My partner, good on her, kept her eyes level with mine, as she asked the same question, "Who are you?" and I gave her the same, brick-like answer. "I am a sex worker."

It was astonishingly relieving, considering that one of my greatest fears was that the response I most longed for—understanding, empathy, *non-chalance*—would only be possible from my family. I would sometimes think of Wes's ex's friends, the peer feedback on my stripping presentation, and any other example of cruelty I had in memory as proof that my fear was founded. Even though I had already confessed this truth—fifteen times at this point—I still looked at my partner and waited for the whiplash of her judgment.

It was starting to dawn on me, in this moment of insanity—saying the same thing repeatedly while expecting a different result—that while

I may not have held a deep feeling of indignity around sugaring, I didn't trust that a biased culture would be good to me. And so, I became a liar.

I lied to protect myself from the judgment I'd experienced when I came out as a dancer at nineteen. An age when I was unprepared and too fragile and unsure of myself to hold it. I lied about my return to dancing, and then I lied about sugaring. I lied about Wes, and I lied to myself every day the two years I sold my body to John.

It wasn't just the work I had to conceal. During those years, I had hidden my queerness. Afraid that if John knew, it would threaten the arrangement, and I'd lose the job. So I played the role, keeping parts of myself locked away, living in fragments of truth. But now, standing at the precipice of something new, I could feel the weight of it lifting. I was ready to return to myself—to step back into all my identities fully.

After the first exercise of the retreat, Annie and I reunited puffy eyed outside the auditorium. While I still had some courage from my earlier confessions, I admitted that I hadn't been truthful with her earlier. "I told you that I was in between work, but that isn't true," I said quickly. Rushing my words before I could chicken out. "I'm a sex worker. I'm quitting, but I've been a sugar baby for a few years."

I felt another knot in my stomach come loose. Annie was the second person I was confessing my secret to, but she was the first person I faced my dishonesty with. I had no time to worry about her response, because as soon as I'd said the words, Annie wrapped her arm over my shoulders and said, "Thanks for telling me." She was as unaffected as my exercise partner.

"You don't think that makes me a bad person?" I asked, testing the ice.

"Not at all," she said. "Sex work is not inherently bad. Surely you know that? You can trust yourself, ya know." We carried on, quietly, in the dark. Wind rustling through the trees. I could tell that Annie *really* wanted this to sink in, which it sort of did, until a raccoon dashed across the paved walkway, scaring both of us.

"There's something about Northern California that makes me skittish," I told Annie as we watched the critter climb halfway up a Douglas fir. Its beady eyes translucent in the dark. "My dad says this is where Bigfoot lives."

Annie laughed, but then stopped and said, "Hey, don't change the subject."

"Okay. Well, what about the fact that I lied to you? Do you think that makes me a bad person?"

"You really think you're the first person to lie for self-preservation?" she said.

I smiled. "Guess not."

We walked on.

It was confusing. The acceptance I'd felt from Annie and my exercise partner that night made me wonder if I'd been wrong to keep sugaring a secret. Had I accidentally caused myself enormous injury by being so self-protective?

"Give yourself some credit," Annie said. "You probably intuited that keeping this secret was the best option for you. Also, we're at a self-help retreat. Everyone here is a stranger, working on acceptance. They don't know you, and they don't have preconceived notions of you, so the stakes are lower. *But* if this is something you want to share in your real life, I hope this experience can give you courage."

We were far enough away from any light pollution that we could see complete constellations. Annie knew a few. "That's Scorpio," she said, pointing to a cluster of stars. "Do you see its tail?"

When I tried to follow her finger, little flashes started up in my vision. "Oh, no," I said. "I'm having a migraine." I told Annie that this had been happening more and more frequently. That a twinkling light would develop in my vision and, within seconds, become a mammoth kaleidoscope—pink and yellow and green—spinning hastily in my mind's eye. She asked me questions: When had these migraines started? (Early on in my arrangement.) What was often happening before they came on? (Different things. My mom telling me about her lack of retirement plan. John telling me he was moving to DC. My dad packing his father's grave. And right now, moments after I'd confessed to Annie.) Always meaningful timings, we both acknowledged.

"It sounds like your migraines are connected to stress," Annie said. "The accumulation of stress and the release of it."

This made perfect sense to me, but how did I make them stop? I closed my eyes and saw the aura brighter now amidst the dark. Annie kneeled to the ground, fumbled around a bit, and plucked a mint leaf. "This stuff grows everywhere," she said. "Chew on it. It'll help." She reached out and touched my forehead, then my cheeks. "Did you know that you're fevered?"

I lifted my hand and felt heat radiating from my skin. I should've suspected a fever. I'd noticed my back and limbs aching during the "I am" exercise. I figured my body was having a visceral response to my confessions. This sometimes happened. A few years earlier, I'd spent the night at a friend's house so chock-full of negativity that I woke up to a sty on my eyelid, which the internet confirmed could be a physical manifestation of toxic energy. I knew it wasn't just a coincidence, because it'd happened to me twice, months apart, in the same house.

When I told Annie this, she pulled up a website on her phone and read a series of questions: *Did I oftentimes find myself overwhelmed by sensory inputs? As a child was I very shy? Did loud noises overwhelm me?* My answers were all yeses.

"And you startle very easily," Annie said, regarding the racoon. "You're a highly sensitive person, like me. *Like Alanis.*"

I smiled. Moved to be told I was akin to my idol. We kept walking. The stars above now invisible in contrast to the aura. The path harder to see. Annie led the way home.

★

Morning came and my body was stiff and sore. I was sweaty, fevered, and clogged. When I pushed my curtain aside, Annie saw me, nodded, and said, "I knew it. I could feel it from my pod. Your spirit is purging." Annie suggested that I let the sickness run its natural course, *for the spiritual lesson of suffering.* To her disapproval, I swallowed 1000 mg of Tylenol, relieved when my fever broke just before our morning workshop.

This session was an important one. Designed to help us explore our shadow sides, which, Alanis explained, was the part of ourselves that held our judgments. From the stage, she instructed the group to split into pairs where we would confess all our worst thoughts to one another. We were going to feel ashamed admitting our feelings out loud, Alanis said. Because our most critical thoughts reveal something we fear about ourselves.

My partner, Ruth, a woman I had not noticed the night before, was a pixie-cut brunette in her late thirties. She was very assertive when we discussed who should be the first speaker (me), and the listener (she). "I'm your ear," Ruth told me, touching one gentle finger to her breastbone. "You're safe to unleash your most critical thoughts with me."

"Thank you," I said, feverless but still faint. I closed my eyes, hoping to see a collage of my most negative feelings. But there was only John's face, which appeared as a bald, shiny, floating head.

"I have a sugar daddy," I told Ruth, "and I can be very judgmental of him. I judge him for lying. I judge that he is obsessed with money. I judge him for buying sex. For buying sex from *me.* I judge him most, I think, because John confuses wanting sex for wanting to be loved. But he doesn't understand the value of authentic intimacy. It's why he thinks he can just buy it. He's confused money as the answer to everything."

During the instructions, Alanis suggested that the listener ask questions to assist the sharer in going deeper. Whenever she spoke into the microphone, I had to be sure to pay attention to what she was saying and not just be awed by hearing Alanis Morissette's voice. Ruth, thankfully, had been paying attention. "Where do you think that judgment stems from? Do you see yourself in John?"

I paused for a long beat to consider this. "Maybe. I obviously care about money too, but not in the same way. John comes from wealth. He wants to continue the status of it. My want for money feels different. I just want to live with my head above water."

"Keep digging," Ruth said.

I took a deep breath. "I also judge John for feeling like he never has enough. Which is something my dad said about *me*. And I'm struggling to bite the bullet and walk away. I want to leave sugaring, but I'm scared," I told her. "I still feel like I *need more*. A wider safety net, so I could really help my family out." I paused. "It's interesting. Whenever I think about my desire for more money, I find some upstanding way of defending myself for it."

"Can you say more about that?" Ruth asked. "Is that something you're doing now?

I looked intently at Ruth, who appeared as though she truly wasn't judging me. "Can I tell you something really terrible?" I said.

"Of course," she said, smiling. "I'm *your ear*."

"I considered blackmailing John a few weeks ago. I found out that he's married. And my professor had me convinced I should use this information to ask for $100,000." I told Ruth everything. The long and short of it. She frowned.

"Hey," I said, pressing my cardigan sleeve into the corner of my eyes.

"No judgment," she said, flashing her palms. "I just feel stumped. Like, *was* blackmail the right thing to do for you and your family? Or is blackmail inherently wrong? Would I have done it myself?"

We sat there together, contemplating this. "I don't think I'm supposed to be asking those kinds of questions anyway," Ruth said.

Damn, I thought, because there was something I still wasn't getting from this exercise. It would've been the perfect time for Alanis to come over and check in, but she was on stage, engaged in her own shadow dialogue.

"Oh gosh," I said. "I just remembered something."

Ruth nodded. "Tell me."

"I once asked John what he thought would be worse, his whole family knowing he were involved in a scandal or dying, and he said scandal. But I just realized that I've never asked myself that same question," I said. Then I began to laugh at my own hypocrisy.

"My whole life feels like a lie right now," I told Ruth. "And it's because I've been so afraid of what people might think if they knew I was a sex worker. I have locked myself away and killed off my social life. So, didn't I choose the same thing? A sort of death over scandal?" Without warning, my voice went hoarse, like this last sentence had scraped its way out. My fever broke through the Tylenol, and my whole body turned to gooseflesh. When Annie saw me in our dorm room later, she would rejoice, "You spoke your truth!"

Now Ruth smiled. Pleased by my realization.

I had a new question for both John and me. What's worse, dying or our arrangement being revealed in my writing?" Because my Patricia—the monumental secret I had been keeping from John—was that I had written everything down. The night we dined at Morton's Steakhouse and John tipped the valet extra. Our first kiss at the Cheesecake Factory. I had penned, in gruesome detail, my dread of the sex. The way John looked when I turned his sixth proposal down.

I understood that if I dedicated the next few years in school to chronicling the story of John and our arrangement, I would have to confront myself fully. I would have to introduce myself to my peers as a sex worker and expose, word by word, the lies I'd told everyone around me over the past few years. It was terrifying to think about, but the one thing I wanted above all else—even more than continuing my life, secret tucked away in my bones—was to free myself of this double life, this shadow self, this big, abysmal lie. Writing it down was the only way I could bear to tell the truth.

Back to my question: Would John rather die or read about our arrangement in my work, face the truth, and give himself the chance, like I was going to give myself the chance, to be loved despite it?

Alanis was back on the mic. Thanking us for our vulnerability. I was shivering with fever. Eager for my bunk. Ruth looked me in the eye and said, "Good work."

★

The only proper way to tell a story is from out the other side of it.

Time, then, to end things with John.

It must be said that even in the face of all the concession—my body, my sanity, my honesty, my joy—it was an insufferable feat to leave behind a life of ease. A life of financial security. The hope for my whole family. In that decision, there was so much at stake. Best not to give myself a moment of pause then. No need to second-guess myself. No *What if I just waited until July?* No *What if I just made $20,000 more?* I knew there would never be a good point of exit. It was purely a matter of when I had the will. I had it now. I had to act.

I knew for a clean break I needed to be direct and simple and ask for nothing.

I know that you're married, I texted John. *The arrangement is over. Please don't try and convince me otherwise.*

As I anxiously waited for his response, I thought about our car ride to the airport last month. How I'd made it ceremonious for myself because I'd hoped that I'd have the strength to leave sugaring behind. I was counting on never seeing John again.

Through the window of his Lexus, I said farewell to the landmarks. My favorite supermarket, the cobalt blue door on a particularly handsome brownstone, an oak tree beyond Exit 131. Soon, the first airport sign appeared before us. Abruptly sentimental—*this was my last ever car ride with John, the end of our arrangement, an era*—I reached toward John and touched his arm, his cheek, the back of his head. When we veered toward departures, I stretched myself across the console and pressed my forehead into his shoulder. I took it as a sign of finality that John was wearing the same leather jacket as the first night we met.

The blinker clacked away as John parked outside of the Southwest doors. I wanted to take his face in my palms and thank him for changing my life. But the moment slipped away when John, unaware of the significance, opened his door, lifted my suitcase from the trunk to the sidewalk, and walked toward me with open arms. I folded into him. I was a bag of bones that day. Ravished by the experience itself. "I love you, John," I said, in a small voice. It was cruel, knowing full well that I was not giving him a proper conversation, a chance for closure, a goodbye. I knew John wanted this "love" to mean something more. But I cared about him. I think I just wanted him to know that.

With little drama, I spun, grasped the handle of my suitcase, and hastily headed for the parted doors of the terminal. John called at the back of my frame, "I love you too, Michelley." I did not turn around to face him. I couldn't bear my own behavior. Instead, I lifted my hand, feet still moving forward, and, without the kindness of turning around to face him, waved goodbye.

John responded quickly. Admitting guilt without hesitation. He was, in fact, married. He wrote over and over again that he was sorry. *I didn't mean to hurt you*, he said, as if I were heartbroken. I felt bad about that.

I also felt bad that I immediately missed the money. In one split second my bank account was no longer a replenishing pot, but a stack I would draw from, draw on. I remembered the envelope John handed me after our first kiss. The original installment of $1,200. The way I'd felt the whole world open up. I knew that night, when I leaned toward him, that I was saying yes to something bigger than selling my body. I knew a new life awaited on the other side. When I first touched John's lips, I was eager to be spit out at the finish line. And here I was. In that moment. Shaking like a doe, glistening with a symbolic sickness of being reborn, wondering how I would steady my legs without the arrangement supporting me.

But I had made it out.

I had chosen the truth. Now, I would find a way to live in it.

The retreat did, in fact, end with a group photo with Alanis Morissette.

After our last exercise on Sunday morning, I, along with Annie and the other attendees, was shuffled on stage. I tried to slink as close as possible to Alanis, which ended up being about five women away. I could see the crown of her head. Under the yellow glow of stage lights, it was easy to imagine a halo. The photo itself was quick. Taken first on a cell phone, then on a real camera. Alanis would eventually post it to her Instagram, and I'd scan the photo, concentrating on the place where my face should've been, but instead only saw the top of someone else's hat. *I was there*, I would say to myself. At the end of it all, *I was right there*.

When I left the retreat, I was a cup turned upside down, emptied out, then turned right side up again. Ready for life to replenish me. The sun was bright and high when I stepped into it, raising my face, squinting my brow. Sunlight, if I remembered correctly, was a gift from the future. "Whatever is going to happen," a friend told me long ago, "is already on its way."

If I could've peered into my future, I would come to a moment in five years' time: my whole family gathered in my living room. In an apartment that I shared with my girlfriend, Daisy. This evening would be a prequel to a reading Daisy and I would host in Denver, where I planned to read an excerpt from my manuscript—a book about John, about my years underwater with him, detailing everything I thought was unlovable about myself, a book Daisy would have read ten times over. She would read it with such care that I would appoint her my stay-at-home editor, and she would kiss me after each chapter, sometimes in tears, sometimes not, and tell me she loved me. Something my character on the page felt would never be possible. My family would be mentioned in the excerpt I'd chosen to read, and I'd want them to hear it first, in case it was upsetting or, more likely, embarrassing.

They'd make a big show of it, Daisy, my mom, sister, dad, and nephew. They'd bring snacks to share. My mom would present a fruit tray for health-conscious me, lush with strawberries and pineapple chunks. My sister would bring cream cheese and chocolate dipping sauces to accompany it, saying, "Chuy and I don't like eating that shit plain." My nephew would laugh, feeling seen, and then he'd hold up a big bag of Tostitos and the queso dipping sauce he and Daisy liked most.

Everyone would settle in on the couch, glistening bright and excited like a row of Peeps, and over the chorus of their chewing, I would read. To them, about them, and they would smile. Laugh at my jokes. Laugh at their own expense.

Eventually I'd come to a line, *My dad lifted his spork at me and said,* "*With all the classes they offer at school, how come they don't have one for common sense?*"

"You can't use that one," my dad would say, interrupting. "It's a Gabriel Iglesias joke."

I'd take out my pen and cross it out. "Imagine if the best thing I ever write is plagiarized."

"You should probably run all my lines by me first," my dad said. "I can tell you if they're my originals or not."

"Classic," my mom would tease. "Caught cheating!"

When I'd arrive at the end of the chapter, my nephew would lead the way for a sitting ovation.

"If you get rich off this, I finally want some mini goats," my dad said.

And then all four voices would stack on top of one another, each complementing the other's pitch, as they sang that familiar tune: "I want a new mattress!" "NBA tickets!" "A trip to Dollywood!" "A whale-watching boat ride!" "iPhone 14!" "McDonald's gift card!" "A new snowmobile!"

"Sure," I'd say, with a laugh. If I ever get rich.

Acknowledgments

Wow, they weren't kidding when they said it takes a village to write and publish a book! I have so many people that I'm indebted to.

First and foremost, my earliest readers, my generous friends, my mentors: April Jordan, Jess Woolfson, Nini Berndt, Marisa Tirado, Alex Cuff, Mark Sundeen, Andrew Bourelle, Nik Rodriguez, Julia Brennan, April French, Jecca Bowen (my first editor!), Celia Laskey, Clare Haley, Kani Aniegboka, Zak Muñoz, Melissa Coss-Aquino, Dan Mueller, Lisa Chavez, Cyrus Dunham, Greg Martin, and my sister.

To the University of New Mexico MFA where this book all began and all the talented friends I made along the way: Ari McGuirk, Mitch Marty, Emily Murphy, Evelyn Olmos, Victoriano Cárdenas, Finn Shepard, and Jennifer Tubbs.

Especially, Jane Kalu, thank you for your sharp eye and unrelenting support.

And Amarlie Foster, who allowed me to borrow her faith when I had none.

My marvelous and dedicated agent, Hannah Strouth, and the Sanford J. Greenburger Associates team. Thank you for taking a chance on me and this book. We did it!

To Kathy Schneider and the Jane Rotrosen Agency team. Kathy, I am forever grateful for the faith you had in this project. The book is changed for the better thanks to your keen eye and edits.

I'm eternally grateful for my editor, Allison Woodnutt, for shepherding this book into the world and pushing me deeper into the story. Thank you to the entire Unnamed Press crew, especially Chris Heiser, Cassidy Kuhle, and Jaya Nicely for the stunning cover.

A special thank you to Cassie Mannes Murray at Pine State Publicity for your creative genius.

To the publishers and editors who released early versions of various chapters at *Alien Magazine*, *Pangyrus*, *Homology Lit*, *StoryQuarterly*, and *Joyland Magazine*. A special thank you to the readers and editors that selected the excerpt "Exit Route" to pass along to their 2021 contest judge, T Kira Māhealani Madden, whose support I've sincerely valued. I'm pretty sure that essay and that sequence of events are how Hannah found me and, in part, how I've wound up here. Thank you.

To a few crucially supportive friends (forgive me if I'm missed you): Jacque Fitzpatrick, Sabina Karlsson, Malin Karlsson, Megan Faulkner, Juliet Kinkade-Black, Sofie Hecht, the Atterburys, Chyanne Corry, Megan Harvey, Nikki Williamson, Chase Locke, and to "John."

Thank you, thank you, thank you to my family. Who love me so dearly. Who laugh at the jokes. Who let me share their stories too.

And at last, my sweetheart, my wife, my at-home editor, Daisy Atterbury. Thank you for seeing me as I am in this story. For all the love and support I have spent my life searching for.